Recent Advances in Nanomagnetism

Editor

Davis S. Schmool

MDPI • Basel • Beijing • Wuhan • Barcelona • Belgrade • Manchester • Tokyo • Cluj • Tianjin

Editor
Davis S. Schmool
Université Paris-Saclay, UVSQ,
CNRS, GEMaC
France

Editorial Office
MDPI
St. Alban-Anlage 66
4052 Basel, Switzerland

This is a reprint of articles from the Special Issue published online in the open access journal *Magnetochemistry* (ISSN 2312-7481) (available at: https://www.mdpi.com/journal/magnetochemistry/special_issues/nanomagnetism).

For citation purposes, cite each article independently as indicated on the article page online and as indicated below:

LastName, A.A.; LastName, B.B.; LastName, C.C. Article Title. *Journal Name* **Year**, *Volume Number*, Page Range.

ISBN 978-3-0365-5773-1 (Hbk)
ISBN 978-3-0365-5774-8 (PDF)

Cover image courtesy of Riccardo Hertel

© 2022 by the authors. Articles in this book are Open Access and distributed under the Creative Commons Attribution (CC BY) license, which allows users to download, copy and build upon published articles, as long as the author and publisher are properly credited, which ensures maximum dissemination and a wider impact of our publications.
The book as a whole is distributed by MDPI under the terms and conditions of the Creative Commons license CC BY-NC-ND.

Contents

About the Editor vii

Preface to "Recent Advances in Nanomagnetism" ix

David S. Schmool
Recent Advances in Nanomagnetism
Reprinted from: *Magnetochemistry* **2022**, *8*, 110, doi:10.3390/magnetochemistry8090110 1

David S. Schmool, Daniel Markó, Ko-Wei Lin, Aurelio Hierro-Rodríguez, Carlos Quirós, Javier Díaz, Luis Manuel Álvarez-Prado, and Jong-Ching Wu
Ferromagnetic Resonance Studies in Magnetic Nanosystems
Reprinted from: *Magnetochemistry* **2021**, *7*, 126, doi:10.3390/magnetochemistry7090126 5

Luis M. Álvarez-Prado
Control of Dynamics in Weak PMA Magnets
Reprinted from: *Magnetochemistry* **2021**, *7*, 43, doi:10.3390/magnetochemistry7030043 23

Roshni Yadav, Chun-Hsien Wu, I-Fen Huang, Xu Li, Te-Ho Wu and Ko-Wei Lin
Effects of Perpendicular Magnetic Field Annealing on the Structural and Magnetic Properties of [Co/Ni]$_2$/PtMn Thin Films
Reprinted from: *Magnetochemistry* **2021**, *7*, 38, doi:10.3390/magnetochemistry7030038 37

Hamza Cansever and Jürgen Lindner
Microresonators and Microantennas—Tools to Explore Magnetization Dynamics in Single Nanostructures
Reprinted from: *Magnetochemistry* **2021**, *7*, 28, doi:10.3390/magnetochemistry7020028 47

Swapneel Amit Pathak and Riccardo Hertel
Geometrically Constrained Skyrmions
Reprinted from: *Magnetochemistry* **2021**, *7*, 26, doi:10.3390/magnetochemistry7020026 59

Panagiotis Ziogas, Athanasios B. Bourlinos, Jiri Tucek, Ondrej Malina and Alexios P. Douvalis
Novel Magnetic Nanohybrids: From Iron Oxide to Iron Carbide Nanoparticles Grown on Nanodiamonds
Reprinted from: *Magnetochemistry* **2020**, *6*, 73, doi:10.3390/magnetochemistry6040073 71

About the Editor

David S. Schmool

David Schmool is professor of physics at the Université Paris-Saclay/UVSQ and a researcher and previous director of the GEMaC laboratory of the Université Paris-Saclay/UVSQ, CNRS in Versailles, France. He has held previous teaching posts at the University of Perpignan (professor) and researcher at PROMES, CNRS and the University of Porto (assistant professor), where he was also researcher and deputy director of the IFIMUP laboratory. He has held a number of research posts at the University of Exeter, UK; the University of Versailles/Saint-Quentin en Yvelines, France; the University of the Basque Country in Bilbao, Spain; Istituto MASPEC (IMEM), CNR, Parma, Italy and the University of Liverpool, UK. He completed his doctoral studies in Physics at the University of York, UK. He has further been visiting fellow/researcher at the following institutions: the University of Glasgow, UK; the University of Versailles/Saint-Quentin en Yvelines, France; the University of Duisburg - Essen, Germany and Simon Fraser University, Canada. His research interests include nanomagnetism, magnetisation dynamics, magnetic thin films and multilayers, magnetic nanoparticles and magneto-plasmonics. He has written books on Nanotechnologies: the Physics of Nanomaterials (two-volume set) and Solid State Physics. He has published over 100 research articles, chapters and reviews.

Preface to "Recent Advances in Nanomagnetism"

Nanomagnetism has emerged as an area of fundamental research in magnetic materials and as a broad subject in the domain of nanotechnology. Indeed its importance can be noted by the large proportion of magnetics research, which is related to the low dimensionality of the system studied, whether that be as an experimental study or as a piece of theoretical work, including simulations of magnetic behaviour in nanostructure systems. This current edition, or Special Issue, collects a number of studies that are concerned with various aspects of magnetic behaviour in low dimensional systems, such as thin films, multilayers, nanoparticles and periodic arrays of nanostructures. This work is principally aimed at researchers and postgraduate students in magnetism and related subjects. Moreover, given the high number of applications of magnetic materials and magnetic nanostructures, this work could also be of interest for research scientists engaged in technological and industrial applications. I would like to thank the editorial staff at MDPI for their assistance in the preparation of this Special Issue on Recent Advances in Nanomagnetism. I am particularly indebted to Jamie Yang who has been directly involved in much of this preparation.

Davis S. Schmool
Editor

Editorial

Recent Advances in Nanomagnetism

David S. Schmool

GEMaC, CNRS, UVSQ, Université Paris-Saclay, 78000 Versailles, France; david.schmool@uvsq.fr

Citation: Schmool, D.S. Recent Advances in Nanomagnetism. *Magnetochemistry* **2022**, *8*, 110. https://doi.org/10.3390/magnetochemistry8090110

Received: 13 September 2022
Accepted: 14 September 2022
Published: 19 September 2022

Publisher's Note: MDPI stays neutral with regard to jurisdictional claims in published maps and institutional affiliations.

Copyright: © 2022 by the author. Licensee MDPI, Basel, Switzerland. This article is an open access article distributed under the terms and conditions of the Creative Commons Attribution (CC BY) license (https://creativecommons.org/licenses/by/4.0/).

Nanomagnetism covers a broad range of research in magnetism and magnetic properties of low-dimensional systems, including both experimental methods in sample fabrication and characterization, as well as theoretical modeling and simulations. Size limitations in one, two, and three dimensions have led to a number of technologically important developments, having an extensive range of applications in sensors and activators, notably in the magnetic recording industry and spintronic devices and more recently in biomedical applications. Magnetic systems can have a variety of symmetries, from thin film geometries to wires and dots, as well as a number of nanoparticle structures, which can also have core-shell substructures. The magnetic state of nanometric magnetic structures results from the equilibrium between competing magnetic anisotropies, interactions, and the applied magnetic field. This can produce a number of phenomena, such as exchange bias effects, skyrmions, as well as magnetic instabilities, which can lead to superparamagnetic effects in magnetic nanoparticles and nanostructures. The physical dimensions and shape of a magnetic structure, as well as its intrinsic magnetic anisotropies, will determine whether it is a single domain or has a more complex magnetic domain structure. Traditionally patterned nanostructures have been arrays of nanomagnets, though recent trends have shown how this can be extended to three-dimensional structures where more complex magnetic configurations are possible and give rise to unprecedented magnetic properties.

This special issue on *Recent Advances in Nanomagnetism* includes six contributions covering a broad spectrum of interests in the topics from magnetic nanoparticles to perpendicular magnetic anisotropies, and from magnetization textures to magnetizations dynamics in magnetic nanostructures. This special issue should contain subjects of interest for researchers in nanomagnetism and current developments in magnetism.

The first contribution is by *P. Ziogas* and *A. B. Bourlinos* from the University of Ioannina (Greece), *J. Tucek* from the University of Pardubice (Czech Republic), *O. Malina* from Palacky University Olomouc and *A. P. Douvalis* from the University Research Center of Ioannina (Greece), ref. [1], presents a study of the synthesis and characterization of novel magnetic properties of iron-based magnetic nanoparticles, which are composed of spinel type iron oxides to iron carbide nanoparticles. These are prepared by thermal processing in vacuum at varying annealing temperatures, whereby fine maghemite (γ-Fe_2O_3) nanoparticle seeds are deposited on the surface of nanodiamond nanotemplates. The resulting nanoparticles vary from fine dispersed spinel-type non-stoichiometric 5 nm magnetite ($Fe_{3-x}O_4$) nanoparticles at low annealing temperatures, to 10 nm single-phase cementite (Fe_3C) iron-carbide structures for intermediate annealing temperatures. Larger Fe_3C and Fe_5C_2 iron-carbides are produces for higher annealing temperatures. The magnetic properties of the nanoparticles have been characterized using magnetometry and thermomagnetic measurements as well as Mössbauer spectroscopy, with properties ranging from superparamagnetic to soft and hard ferromagnetic behavior.

The contribution by *S. A. Pathak* and *R. Hertel* from the University of Strasbourg (France), ref. [2], concerns a theoretical study of various aspects of geometrically constrained skyrmions, which are magnetization textures formed by a swirling of the magnetization and typically have nanometric dimensions. The geometric contraint in this study is introduced via a thickness modulation of a thin film host material, FeGe. Dot-like pockets are introduced, forming preferential sites for the skyrmion formation and act as pinning centers. Such skyrmionic structures could have important applications for data storage in racetrack-like shift register devices.

H. Cansever and *J. Lindner* from the Institute of Ion Beam Physics and Materials Research in Dresden (Germany), ref. [3], consider the use of microresonators and microantennas as a tool for the study of magnetization dynamics in single magnetic nanostructures. The study of single element nanostructures is a complex problem due to the reduced magnetic signals that are available. To enhance the detection of single magnetic elements, the authors have used a microcavity and microresonator planar structures to detect the ferromagnetic resonance (FMR) signals of these elements. Fixed frequency cavities and broadband measurements of permalloy ($Ni_{80}Fe_{20}$) and $Fe_{60}Al_{40}$ microstrips demonstrate the excellent signal-to-noise obtained using these methods.

The contribution by *R. Yadav, C.-H. Wu, I-Fen Huang and K.-W. Lin* from the National Chung Hsing University (Taiwan), *X. Li* from Xiamen University (China) and *T.-H Wu* from the National Yunlin University of Science and Technology (Taiwan), ref. [4], describe the effects of a perpendicular magnetic field annealing on the structural and magnetic properties of $[Co/Ni]_2$/PtMn thin films. In this study the authors use a post-deposition perpendicular magnetic field annealing process which induces interlayer diffusion at both the Co and Ni interfaces as well as that with the PtMn layer. Structural and magnetic characterization were studied using TEM, XPS and VSM techniques.

The study of the control of spin dynamics in weak perpendicular magnetic anisotropy (PMA) systems is the subject of the contribution by *L. M. Álvarez-Prado* from the Center of Research on Nanomaterials and Nanotechnology and the University of Oviedo (Spain), ref. [5]. In this work, the formation of weak magnetic stripe domains is achieved due to the PMA of a $NdCo_5$ layer coupled to a soft permalloy film via an intervening Al spacer. By varying the thickness of this spacer layer it is possible to control the coupling and hence the overall properties of the composite magnetic structure. The resulting imprinting of the stripe domain structure has been simulated along with the FMR properties of these hybrid systems, which show a non-reciprocal response with respect to the stripe domain regions and the applied magnetic field. The study further considers the nature of the reconfigurability of these magnetic structures.

The final contribution to this special issue considers aspects of ferromagnetic resonance in the study of magnetic nanosystems by *D. S. Schmool* and *D. Markó* from the University Paris-Saclay/University of Versailles Saint-Quentin-en-Yvelines (France), *K.-W. Lin* from the National Chung Hsing University (Taiwan), *A. Hierro-Rodríguez, C. Quirós, J. Díaz* and *L. M. Álvarez-Prado* from the Center of Research on Nanomaterials and Nanotechnology and the University of Oviedo (Spain) and *J.-C . Wu* from the National Changhua University of Education (Taiwan), ref. [6]. In this paper the authors present the broadband VNA-FMR technique which has been applied to the study of periodic Co/Ag bilayer nanostructures as well as to the multilayer system comprised of NdCo/Al/permalloy films. In the former system the modification of the FMR spectra of the nanodot structures with respect to continuous layers is illustrated, showing the variation of pinning parameters and the emergence of a localized resonance. In the latter system, the low-field/low-frequency response of the FMR is studied in detail, illustration the effect of domain structures and the hysteresis in the dynamic measurements, which can be correlated to static hysteresis in these layers. The switch between acoustic and optical excitation allows the evaluation of the periodicity of the domain structures to be performed and shows excellent agreement with static measurements.

I hope that this Special Issue on *Recent Advances in Nanomagnetism* will provide some useful insights into this rapidly developing area of current research in to magnetism and magnetic materials. I would like to thank all the authors who contributed to this Special Issue for their work and the high standard of their contributions. I finally wish to acknowledge the assistance and dedication of the editorial staff of *Magnetochemistry*, who have greatly assisted me in the preparation of this Special Issue.

Funding: This research received no external funding.

Conflicts of Interest: The authors declare no conflict of interest.

Abbreviations

The following abbreviations are used in this manuscript:

FMR	Ferromagnetic resonance
PMA	Perpendicular magnetic anisotropy
TEM	Transmission electron microscopy
VNA	Vector network analyzer
VSM	Vibrating sample magnetometry
XPS	X-ray photoelectron spectroscopy

References

1. Ziogas, P.; Bourlinos, A.B.; Tucek, J.; Malina, O.; Douvalis, A.P. Novel Magnetic Nanohybrids: From Iron Oxide to Iron Carbide Nanoparticles Grown on Nanodiamonds. *Magnetochemistry* **2020**, *6*, 73. [CrossRef]
2. Pathak, S.A.; Hertel, R. Geometrically Constrained Skyrmions. *Magnetochemistry* **2021**, *7*, 26. [CrossRef]
3. Cansever, H.; Lindner, J. Microresonators and Microantennas - Tools to Explore Magnetization Dynamics in Single Nanostructures. *Magnetochemistry* **2021**, *7*, 28. [CrossRef]
4. Yadav, R.; Wu, C.-H.; Huang, I.-F.; Li, X.; Wu, T.-H.; Lin, K.-W. Effects of Perpendicular Magnetic Field Annealing on the Structural and Magnetic Properties of [Co/Ni]2/PtMn Thin Films. *Magnetochemistry* **2021**, *7*, 38. [CrossRef]
5. Álvarez-Prado, L.M. Control of Dynamics in Weak PMA Magnets. *Magnetochemistry* **2021**, *7*, 43. [CrossRef]
6. Schmool, D.S.; Markó, D., Lin, K.-W.; Hierro-Rodríguez, A.; Quirós, C.; Díaz, J.; Álvarez-Prado, L.M.; Wu, J.-C; Ferromagnetic Resonance Studies in Magnetic Nanosystems. *Magnetochemistry* **2021**, *7*, 126. [CrossRef]

Article

Ferromagnetic Resonance Studies in Magnetic Nanosystems

David S. Schmool [1,*,†], Daniel Markó [1,†], Ko-Wei Lin [2], Aurelio Hierro-Rodríguez [3,4], Carlos Quirós [3,4], Javier Díaz [3,4] and Luis Manuel Álvarez-Prado [3,4] and Jong-Ching Wu [5]

[1] GEMaC, CNRS, UVSQ, Université Paris-Saclay, 78035 Versailles, France; daniel.marko@uvsq.fr
[2] Department of Materials Science and Engineering, National Chung Hsing University, Taichung 402, Taiwan; kwlin@dragon.nchu.edu.tw
[3] Departamento de Física, Facultad de Ciencias, Universidad de Oviedo, 33007 Oviedo, Spain; hierroaurelio@uniovi.es (A.H.-R.); quiroscarlos@uniovi.es (C.Q.); jidiaz@uniovi.es (J.D.); lmap@uniovi.es (L.M.Á.-P.)
[4] Centro de Investigación en Nanomateriales y Nanotecnología (CINN), CSIC-Universidad de Oviedo, 33940 El Entrego, Spain
[5] Department of Physics, National Changhua University of Education, Changhua 500, Taiwan; phjcwu@cc.ncue.edu.tw
* Correspondence: david.schmool@uvsq.fr
† These authors contributed equally to this work.

Abstract: Ferromagnetic resonance is a powerful method for the study of all classes of magnetic materials. The experimental technique has been used for many decades and is based on the excitation of a magnetic spin system via a microwave (or rf) field. While earlier methods were based on the use of a microwave spectrometer, more recent developments have seen the widespread use of the vector network analyzer (VNA), which provides a more versatile measurement system at almost comparable sensitivity. While the former is based on a fixed frequency of excitation, the VNA enables frequency-dependent measurements, allowing more in-depth analysis. We have applied this technique to the study of nanostructured thin films or nanodots and coupled magnetic layer systems comprised of exchange-coupled ferromagnetic layers with in-plane and perpendicular magnetic anisotropies. In the first system, we have investigated the magnetization dynamics in Co/Ag bilayers and nanodots. In the second system, we have studied Permalloy ($Ni_{80}Fe_{20}$, hereafter Py) thin films coupled via an intervening Al layer of varying thickness to a NdCo film which has perpendicular magnetic anisotropy.

Keywords: ferromagnetic resonance; magnetization dynamics; magnetic nanodots; coupled magnetic thin films; perpendicular magnetic anisotropy

1. Introduction

Ferromagnetic nanosystems cover a broad range of materials and geometries, which are designed to exploit the intrinsic properties of magnetic materials as well as modify them via structuring, coupling magnetic components (exchange, dipolar, etc.), or a combination of the two [1]. This allows the tailoring of magnetic properties and behavior, which can then be exploited in specific applications, such as magnetic read-heads, data storage systems, or other spintronic devices [2,3]. Research in the area of magnetic materials is wide-ranging and covers extensive areas of materials, experimental methods, theory, and simulations [4–6]. In this paper, we will discuss some of the issues concerning nanodot arrays and coupled magnetic layer systems with specific emphasis on the use of magnetization dynamics.

The study of spin dynamics in magnetic systems allows a detailed analysis of the intrinsic and extrinsic properties of magnetic systems [7]. In the former, we include the magnetic properties, such as the magnetization, magnetocrystalline anisotropies, and g-factors of the materials in question. Extrinsic properties arise from the nanostructuring of magnetic film structures as well as from the magnetic interactions between magnetic components of the system in question. For example, the magnetic exchange coupling between ferromagnetic layers will give rise to a modified dynamic response, which depends on the nature and strength of the coupling. Furthermore, reducing the physical dimensions of a magnetic body can cause a number of effects due to magnetic confinement [8–10], which can alter the magnetic anisotropy (surface anisotropy) of the material and in certain cases can be manifested as the excitation of standing spin-wave modes, which give rise to multi-peaked FMR spectra.

In this paper, we will present the methodology for the vector network analyzer method for performing ferromagnetic resonance measurements [11]. This technique has been applied to the study of various nanometric systems, such as for nanostructured dot arrays of Co capped with Ag and magnetic layered structures of Py and NdCo separated by a non-magnetic layer of Al. In the latter, the composition of the NdCo has been varied as well as the thickness of the Al layer, which controls the magnetic coupling between the Py and NdCo films.

2. Vector Network Analyzer Ferromagnetic Resonance

In recent years, a number of alternative FMR methods [11,12] have been developed, which have adapted the basic principles of the FMR experiment, making it more suitable for the measurement of nanostructured materials and nanoparticles. Of the methods available, the use of micro-resonators and stripline technologies in tandem with the vector network analyzer (VNA) is extremely promising and has now developed into a well-established method of performing ferromagnetic resonance (VNA-FMR) on thin films and low-dimensional structures. In this technique, the VNA acts as both source and detector, in which the two-port VNA device is connected, via high-frequency cables, to a coplanar waveguide (CPW) or stripline. The use of a planar micro-resonator (PMR) [13] can also increase sensitivity of the measurement, though limits measurements to a fixed frequency, as we will discuss shortly. For the coplanar stripline, there is no resonant cavity, which means that measurements can be made over a broad range of frequencies (commonly referred to as a broadband FMR measurement). In this case, measurements can be made continuously up to tens of gigahertz. The two-port VNA is connected via high-frequency cables to the CPW through which a high-frequency electrical signal is passed from the VNA. The detection is made by measuring the four scattering or S-parameters; these consist of the two transmitted signals (port 1 → port 2, S_{21} and port 2 → port 1, S_{12}) and the two reflected signals (port 1 ↔ port 1, S_{11} and port 2 ↔ port 2, S_{22}). These four parameters make up the elements of the S-matrix. Since the CPW is impedance-matched (50 Ω) to the VNA output, this will maximize the transmitted signal, which makes the technique very sensitive to changes in the line impedance. The method requires a full two-port calibration to be implemented to remove background reflections from the cable/waveguide system.

The formal description of the signal obtained by the VNA-FMR method is based on the transmission and reflection coefficients, which are given in the form of the scattering or S-parameters and take into account the line impedance including the sample. These are expressed as lumped elements with the effective inductance (L), series resistance (R), shunt conductance (G), and capacitance (C), and can be expressed as [12,14]:

$$S_{11} = \frac{i\omega L + R + Z_0/[1 + Z_0(G + i\omega C)] - Z_0}{i\omega L + R + Z_0/[1 + Z_0(G + i\omega C)] + Z_0} \quad (1)$$

and

$$S_{21} = \frac{2Z_0/[1 + Z_0(G + i\omega C)]}{i\omega L + R + Z_0/[1 + Z_0(G + i\omega C)] + Z_0} \quad (2)$$

where Z_0 is the characteristic impedance of the stripline and ω is the microwave angular frequency. For a symmetric setup, we would expect $S_{11} = S_{22}$ and $S_{21} = S_{12}$. In terms of the complex reflection coefficient, we can write:

$$\Gamma = \frac{Z - Z_0}{Z + Z_0} \qquad (3)$$

or alternatively we can write:

$$\frac{Z}{Z_0} = \frac{1 + \Gamma}{1 - \Gamma} \qquad (4)$$

where Z is the impedance of the (sample) loaded stripline.

It should be noted that the sensitivity of this method can be limited by the quality of the cables and connectors. Often poor-quality components will introduce further reflections, thus limiting the transmission characteristics of the high-frequency signals. This is particularly true of measurements made at the high-frequency end and above around 40 GHz in general. The magnetic sample, usually in thin-film form, is placed (face-down) on top of the waveguide and located inside the poles of an electromagnet whose field direction should be ideally parallel to the stripline. Placing the sample on the stripline changes the characteristic impedance of the waveguide.

The signal-to-noise ratio is improved by covering as much of the stripline as possible. This can be important for broadband measurements where there is no signal amplification due to Q-factors. The measurement of the FMR spectrum can then proceed in one of two methods: (i) field sweep at a fixed frequency or (ii) frequency sweep with a fixed static magnetic field, H_{dc}. The VNA provides a measurement of the line impedance via transmission and reflection coefficients, which are related to the various S parameters. It should be noted that the electrical signal which passes through the CPW will produce a small oscillating magnetic field, h_{rf}, around the CPW. It is this high-frequency magnetic field that is the driving field for the resonance measurement. As the field or frequency is swept through the resonance of the ferromagnetic sample placed on the CPW, the line impedance will change, hence altering the S-parameters, providing the measurement of the resonance itself. Figure 1 shows a schematic representation of a VNA-FMR setup.

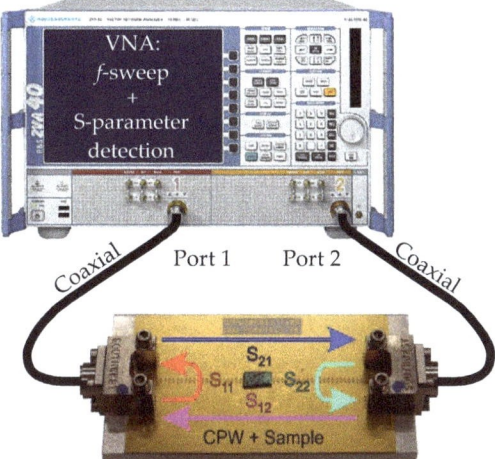

Figure 1. Components of a typical VNA-FMR spectrometer: A two-port VNA is connected to a CPW using coaxial cables and end launch connectors. The sample lies in the x–y plane face-down on top of the CPW with the x-axis along the CPW. An electromagnet (not shown) generates a static bias field H_{dc}, whereas the microwave current flowing through the CPW generates a weak oscillating field h_{rf} along the y-axis. The four S-parameters that can be detected with such a two-port setup are schematically shown as well.

A limitation of the traditional FMR experiment resides in the fact that it must be, by its very nature, a fixed-frequency measurement. The VNA-FMR technique, however, overcomes this problem since it does not require a cavity, and broadband measurements are possible. This, therefore, allows for direct measurement of the frequency–field dispersion relation for a magnetic sample. Excellent agreement with theory is found using this technique, as illustrated in the example of the dispersion relation for a thin Py film, shown in Figure 2.

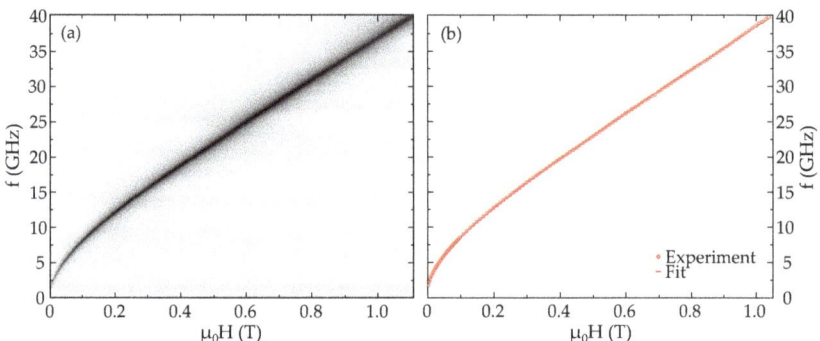

Figure 2. (**a**) In-plane VNA-FMR data for a 50 nm thick Py film [15] showing the frequency–field characteristics. The color variation shows the absorption intensity. (**b**) Extracted experimental data (points) from (**a**) and corresponding fit (line).

3. Fundamental Theory of Spin Wave Dispersion in Ferromagnetic Structures

The theory of FMR and more generally spin-wave excitations in ferromagnetic structures has a long history, with major development commencing in the 1950s, with the work of Kittel, Suhl, and co-workers, which in large part derived from the work of Landau and Lifshitz [16] and later Gilbert [17]. In this section, we will provide a summarized introduction to the principal considerations required for the understanding of spin dynamics in low-dimensional structures (thin films and nanostructures). The motion of the magnetization vector can be expressed in a phenomenological form and is frequently given by the Landau–Lifschitz equation, with Gilbert damping also referred to as the LLG equation, and is written as:

$$\frac{1}{\gamma}\frac{\partial \mathbf{M}}{\partial t} = -(\mathbf{M} \times \mathbf{H}_{\text{eff}}) + \frac{\alpha}{\gamma M_s}\left(\mathbf{M} \times \frac{\partial \mathbf{M}}{\partial t}\right) \quad (5)$$

Here $\mathbf{M}$ and $\mathbf{H}_{\text{eff}}$ represent the magnetization and effective magnetic field vectors and $\gamma = |e|g/2m$ is the magneto-gyric ratio, in which g is the g-factor. The first term on the right-hand side of Equation (5) can be viewed as the precessional motion of the magnetization vector about the effective magnetic field. The second term concerns the relaxation of this motion and is characterized by the value of α, the Gilbert damping parameter. The combination of the two terms gives rise to a damped precessional motion of $\mathbf{M}$.

The magnetization is comprised of a static and dynamic component; $\mathbf{M}(t) = \mathbf{M}_0 + \mathbf{m}(t)$, with the latter arising from the addition of a microwave component, $\mathbf{h}_{\text{rf}}$, to the applied magnetic field, $\mathbf{H}_{\text{dc}}$. The total (effective) magnetic field, $\mathbf{H}_{\text{eff}}$, has several components, which we can express as: $\mathbf{H}_{\text{eff}} = \mathbf{H}_{\text{dc}} + \mathbf{h}_{\text{rf}} + \mathbf{H}_{\text{in}}$. For ferromagnetic materials, we need to consider not only the static magnetic field, $\mathbf{H}_{\text{dc}}$, and dynamic field, $\mathbf{h}_{\text{rf}}$, but also the internal magnetic field, $\mathbf{H}_{\text{in}}$, which has a very important role to play in FMR. It will be this internal field component which will provide all the angular dependences due to the various magnetic anisotropies which may exist in the sample; magneto-crystalline anisotropy, shape anisotropy, and surface and interface anisotropy. In a standard FMR experiment, we can make the assumption that the dynamic component of the magnetization is much smaller than the static component; $|\mathbf{M}_0| \gg |\mathbf{m}|$, such that we can neglect second-order effects. This is a valid assumption when the microwave power used is low as in the case of standard microwave spectrometers and vector network analyzers.

Manipulation of the LLG equation via the substitution of the various components of $\mathbf{M}$ and $\mathbf{H}$ and the expansion of the equilibrium conditions for small-angle deviations, leads to the so-called Smit–Beljers (SB, also known as Smit–Suhl) equation [18,19]:

$$\left(\frac{\omega}{\gamma}\right)^2 = \frac{1}{M^2 \sin^2 \theta} \left\{ \left(\frac{\partial^2 E}{\partial \theta^2}\right) \left(\frac{\partial^2 E}{\partial \phi^2}\right) - \left(\frac{\partial^2 E}{\partial \theta \partial \phi}\right)^2 \right\} \quad (6)$$

where $\omega = 2\pi f$ is the angular frequency. This equation neglects damping effects, which will add a small correction to the resonance frequency. Equation (6) uses the second derivatives of the free energy, E, with respect to the polar and azimuthal angles, θ and ϕ, in conjunction with the equilibrium conditions which are defined by the first derivatives of the free energy with respect to the polar and azimuthal angles:

$$\frac{\partial E}{\partial \theta} = 0 \quad \text{and} \quad \frac{\partial E}{\partial \phi} = 0 \quad (7)$$

These equilibrium conditions define the direction of the magnetization vector under the specific conditions of the free energy density, including all magnetic anisotropies and applied external magnetic fields. The equilibrium (orientation) angles are often designated as θ_{eq} and ϕ_{eq} and the resonance condition will then be evaluated at this orientation. Contributions to the free energy will depend on the magnetic sample under consideration and will in effect be the same contributions that are considered in the effective magnetic field, where we have simply transferred from considering the effective field to considering the total energy of the system. In FMR, the Zeeman energy will always be a principal component due to static and dynamic (microwave) magnetic fields that are required. Additional contributions will also be required and are typically due to magnetostatic (or shape) energy and magneto-crystalline anisotropies. Further manipulation of the LLG Equation (5) [20–22] allows for the exchange effects to be considered. This leads to a quadratic equation in (Dk^2) of the form:

$$\left(\frac{\omega}{\gamma}\right)^2 = (Dk^2)^2 + \left\{ \frac{1}{M} \frac{\partial^2 E}{\partial \theta^2} + \frac{1}{M \sin^2 \theta} \frac{\partial^2 E}{\partial \phi^2} \right\} Dk^2 + \frac{1}{M^2 \sin^2 \theta} \left\{ \left(\frac{\partial^2 E}{\partial \theta^2}\right) \left(\frac{\partial^2 E}{\partial \phi^2}\right) - \left(\frac{\partial^2 E}{\partial \theta \partial \phi}\right)^2 \right\} \quad (8)$$

where $D = 2A_{ex}/M_s$ and k represents the wave vector of the standing spin-wave mode whose allowed values are determined by the boundary (or pinning) conditions, where we have neglected the small correction due to the damping. Evidently for FMR, we can set $k = 0$, whereby Equation (8) reduces to Equation (6) for the uniform FMR mode. The extent to which spin-wave terms are important can be principally defined by the exchange stiffness constant, A_{ex}, the boundary conditions [20], and the size of the magnetic entity. In many nanosystems, the size constriction is such that volume modes will not be excited, though arguments for surface modes can be made depending on the boundary conditions permitting surface freedom [23]. We will return to this question at a later stage.

The LLG equation is an intrinsically non-linear expression since the effective field is dependent on the magnetization. In the approximation that we consider under normal experimental conditions, where the dynamic component of the magnetization is small with respect to the static component, we can make an expansion of the variable magnetization in the form of a plane wave, with wave vector (k), such that:

$$\mathbf{m}(\mathbf{r}, t) = \sum_k \mathbf{m}_k(t) e^{i \mathbf{k} \cdot \mathbf{r}} \quad (9)$$

Using the contribution of the spatial variation of the magnetization to the time derivative of the magnetization $\partial \mathbf{M}/\partial t$, the dipole-exchange spin-wave dispersion relation for an infinite ferromagnetic medium can be written in the general form as [24]:

$$\left(\frac{\omega}{\gamma}\right)^2 = \mu_0^2 (H + Dk^2)(H + Dk^2 + M\sin^2\theta_k) \tag{10}$$

where θ_k defines the angle between the directions of the wave vector and the static magnetization.

For the case, where the film is in the x–y plane and the field applied along the x-axis, the resonance equation can be expressed in the form [25]:

$$\left(\frac{\omega}{\gamma}\right)^2 = \mu_0^2 (H + Dk^2)[H + Dk^2 + MF_{qq}(k_\parallel L)] \tag{11}$$

Here, $F_{qq}(k_\parallel L)$ is the matrix element of the magnetic dipole interaction and L denotes the film thickness. In the case of free and perfect pinning, the wave vectors can be expressed in the form:

$$k^2 = k_x^2 + k_y^2 + \left(\frac{p\pi}{L}\right)^2 = k_\parallel^2 + \left(\frac{p\pi}{L}\right)^2 \tag{12}$$

The quantization for the spin waves has the same general pattern of modal number separated by 1 for the two cases. However, for an arbitrary angle between $k_\parallel$ and M, the matrix elements of the dipole interaction are expressed in a modified form as [25]:

$$F_{qq}(k_x, k_y) = 1 + P_{qq}(k)[1 - P_{qq}(k)]\left(\frac{\mu_0 M}{H + Dk^2}\right)\left(\frac{k_y^2}{k^2}\right) - P_{qq}(k)\left(\frac{k_x^2}{k^2}\right) \tag{13}$$

If the spin wave propagates in the plane of the film, but perpendicular to the external magnetic field ($k_z = 0, k_y = k_\parallel$), the expression for $F_{qq}(k_\parallel L)$ takes the form:

$$F_{qq} = 1 + P_{qq}(k)[1 - P_{qq}(k)]\left(\frac{\mu_0 M}{H + Dk^2}\right) \tag{14}$$

For the lowest value mode, $q = 0$, the function $P_{qq}(k)$ takes the form:

$$P_{00}(k) = 1 + \frac{1 - e^{-k_\parallel L}}{k_\parallel L} \tag{15}$$

More complex function forms of $P_{qq}(k)$ exist for higher mode numbers. If we neglect the exchange, the dispersion relation for the lowest modes results in the so-called Damon–Eshbach (DE) surface magnetostatic modes, expressed in the form:

$$\left(\frac{\omega_{DE}}{\gamma}\right)^2 = \mu_0^2 [H(H + M) + M^2(1 - e^{-2k_\parallel L})/4] \tag{16}$$

When the film is magnetized in the plane with $k_\parallel \perp M$, spin-wave modes can be divided into dipole dominated modes ($k = 0$), with frequencies expressed in Equation (16), and exchange dominated modes ($k > 0$), with frequencies given by the perpendicular standing spin-wave (PSSW) modes:

$$\left(\frac{\omega}{\gamma}\right)^2 = \mu_0^2 \left\{H + D\left[k_\parallel^2 + k_\perp^2\right]\right\}\left\{H + \left[D + H\left(\frac{M/H}{p\pi/L}\right)\right]k_\parallel^2 + Dk_\perp^2 + M\right\} \tag{17}$$

For the uniform FMR mode in thin films, the resonance condition can be expressed in the simple Kittel form [26] as:

$$\left(\frac{\omega}{\gamma}\right)^2 = \mu_0^2 [H\cos(\theta - \Theta_H) + M\cos^2\theta][H\cos(\theta - \Theta_H) + M\cos 2\theta] \qquad (18)$$

From this, the resonance field is obtained, and therefore Equation (18) can be used to fit angle-dependent FMR measurements, once the equilibrium conditions of the magnetization have been determined from the free energy of the system.

In the simple case of a single magnetic thin film, we can consider the allowed wave vectors for the standing spin wave modes via a simple model, where we reduce the wave vector to the direction (1D) perpendicular to the film plane. For the cases of perfect pinning and free pinning conditions, the wave vectors are generated for the pth mode as:

$$k^{(\text{pp})} = p\frac{\pi}{L} \qquad (19)$$

and

$$k^{(\text{fp})} = (p-1)\frac{\pi}{L} \qquad (20)$$

Intermediate or partial pinning is more complex since the surface spins have a freedom which differs from zero (perfect pinning) and bulk freedom (free pinning). We can introduce a pinning factor, δ, which allows us to vary the pinning, such that:

$$k^{(\text{part})} = (p-\delta)\frac{\pi}{L} \qquad (21)$$

From Equation (21) we can see that the two limiting cases of perfect pinning and freedom can be obtained for values of $\delta = 0$ and $\delta = 1$, respectively. Thus we can write that for intermediate pinning $0 < \delta < 1$. The case of asymmetric pinning can also be considered. In this case, we can write:

$$k^{(\text{asym})} = \left[p - \frac{1}{2}(\delta_1 + \delta_2)\right]\frac{\pi}{L} \qquad (22)$$

The values of δ_1 and δ_2 conform to the limits of δ given above. This general case is seen to be coherent with the general representation, so for the case of symmetric pinning; $\delta_1 = \delta_2 = \delta$ and Equation (21) is re-established. For the case of surface localized modes, where the surface freedom exceeds the bulk value, the wave vector becomes imaginary, $k \to i\tau$, where τ is a real number, and the mode profile will be such that the surface spins precess with a greater amplitude than bulk spins.

The existence of spin-wave modes in the resonance spectra is manifested by multiple absorption peaks in the FMR spectrum. The uniform or FMR mode will be shifted from its normal value, to a lower field, and the higher-order spin-wave modes are located at fields below that of the uniform mode. For the case of localized or surface modes, the resonance lines are shifted to higher field values with respect to the lowest spin-wave mode. A comprehensive account of higher-order spin-wave modes has been treated in [23].

4. Results and Discussion
4.1. Co/Ag Bilayers and Nanodots

Samples of 50 nm thick Co thin films were deposited on thermally oxidized silicon wafer substrates by Ion Beam Assisted Deposition (IBAD) [27]. During deposition, a Kaufmann ion source operating at 800 V and 7.5 mA was used to sputter the Co target. The base vacuum and deposition pressure were 6.7×10^{-5} Pa and 4×10^{-3} Pa, respectively. After the Co deposition, a 30 nm thick Ag capping layer was subsequently deposited without breaking the vacuum. A combination of electron beam lithography and ion milling was then used to pattern the Co/Ag thin film into a 0.5×0.5 mm^2 nanodot array with an individual dot diameter of about 200 nm and a pitch of 400 nm. In Figure 3, we show scanning electron micrographs of a typical nanodot array at three different magnifications.

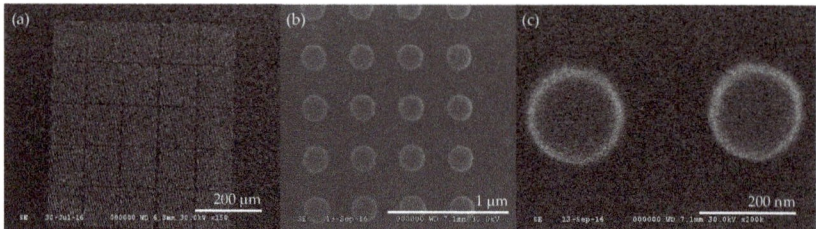

Figure 3. Planar view SEM images of a Co/Ag nanodot array at (**a**) 150×, (**b**) 50,000×, and (**c**) 200,000× magnification.

To better understand the nature of the VNA-FMR data, we use a continuous thin film with the same thickness profiles as for the nanodot structures. This serves as a reference from which we can compare the resonance spectra to determine the effect of nanostructuring. In Figure 4, VNA-FMR spectra for both the Co(50 nm)/Ag(30 nm) bilayer and nanostructured dots are shown. We will analyze the bilayer sample first and then consider the nanodot sample.

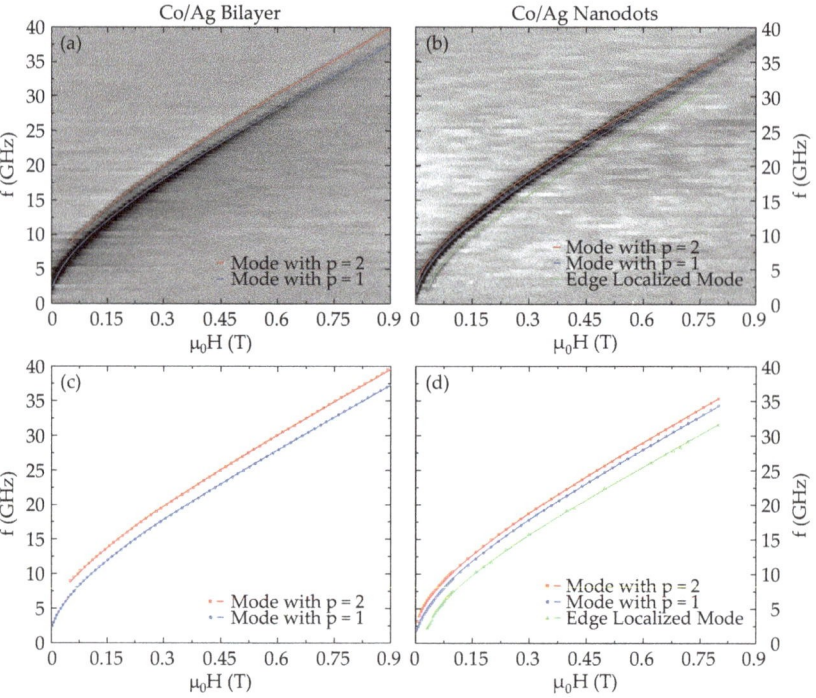

Figure 4. VNA-FMR spectra for the Co(50 nm)/Ag(30 nm) samples. Raw data for (**a**) the bilayer sample and (**b**) the nanostructured dots, extracted data and fits for (**c**) the bilayer sample and (**d**) the nanostructured dots. The solid lines are the fits obtained from Equation (23), using the wave vector profiles given in Equation (21).

For the bilayer system, we observe two clear resonance lines, which we interpret as arising from the first two perpendicular standing spin-wave (PSSW) modes, with $p = 1$

and $p = 2$. The frequency–field characteristic and extracted data for the continuous thin film are illustrated in Figure 4a,c, respectively. The fits to the data are performed using Equation (10), which for our purposes takes the form:

$$\left(\frac{\omega}{\gamma}\right)^2 = (\mu_0 H + \mu_0 M_s + Dk^2)(\mu_0 H + Dk^2) \quad (23)$$

We then use Equation (21) in the fitting process to determine the relevant wave vectors and hence pinning parameter, δ. For this we have assumed a symmetric pinning, with $\delta_1 = \delta_2 = \delta$. For the data shown in Figure 4c we obtain $\delta = 1.1$ for $p = 1$ and $\delta = 1.4$ for $p = 2$. The fitting procedure also used the following parameters: $M_s = 1.08$ T, a g-factor of $g = 2.04$ and an exchange stiffness constant of $A_{ex} = 1.0 \times 10^{-11}$ J·m^{-1} [28], which is reasonable for a 50 nm thick Co film. The fits shown in Figure 4c are in good agreement with the data and the physical parameters are consistent with the Co film studied. With regards to the pinning conditions, we note that the value for δ is close to unity and is consistent with the almost perfect pinning condition.

We now turn our attention to the results for the nanodot structures. These are shown in Figure 4b,d for the raw and extracted data, respectively. The two resonance lines observed in the continuous thin film also appear to be present in the nanodot sample, though with modified wave vectors, these are shown in blue and red in Figure 4c,d. In addition to these modes, there is a further resonance mode in the nanostructured sample, as seen in the spectra and illustrated by the line in green in Figure 4d. This mode has a significantly weaker absorption, but is more clearly observed in the low frequency and low field range. The shift of resonance fields can be clearly attributed to the effect of nanostructuring. The first line that we can consider is the blue line, which appears to be very close to the corresponding blue line in the continuous film data for the $p = 1$ mode. The red line is somewhat shifted to smaller resonance frequencies with respect to the continuous film ($p = 2$ mode), but otherwise appears to be the same mode, which can be accounted for by a modified wave vector for this mode. Fitting these two lines can be based on the same principles as that for the thin film sample. In the latter, we considered that for a thin film the in-plane wave vectors should be zero since the film is effectively infinite in the film plane: $k_{x,y} = (p_{x,y} - \delta_{x,y})\pi^2/L_{x,y}^2 = 0$ since $L_{x,y} \to \infty$ and thus $k_\parallel = 0$, see Equation (12). For the case of our circular nanodots, the lateral dimensions, corresponding to the 200 nm diameter, can give rise to pinning conditions at the dot edges and thus we should consider the three-dimensional aspect of magnetic confinement. Using Equation (12), we can take into account the dot geometry and the edge pinning conditions, which we can express in a similar manner to the thin film case, from which we can write:

$$k^2 = k_x^2 + k_y^2 + \left(\frac{p'\pi}{L}\right)^2 = [(p - \delta_d)^2 + (q - \delta_d)^2]\left(\frac{\pi}{d}\right)^2 + (r - \delta_L)^2\left(\frac{\pi}{L}\right)^2 = k_{pqr}^2 \quad (24)$$

where δ_d denotes the edge pinning conditions and δ_L those of the upper and lower interfaces, d is the dot diameter, L the films thickness. In considering the three-dimensional case, we need to account for the mode numbers in three directions, as represented by the integers p, q, and r. We note that Equation (24) considers that the pinning is equivalent in both lateral directions and is symmetric. This is justified for the current geometry, since there is no reason to suppose that there should be any variation of the pinning at the edges of the dot structure. In our calculations, we consider that the in-plane anisotropy is weak and that inter-dot (dipole–dipole) interactions are sufficiently weak that we can neglect their effect.

In the case of the first two bulk (PSSW) modes (i.e., the blue and red lines in Figure 4d), the resonance lines are slightly shifted towards a bulk-like uniform mode, since the origin of this curve is shifted to zero. The principal resonance line (denoted in blue) is very similar to that of the continuous film and can be expected to derive from similar boundary conditions as that of the $p = 1$ mode in the continuous thin film. The red line is much closer to the principal resonance (blue line) than that for the continuous film, which must be due to the modified boundary conditions for the nanodot structures. Since the lateral dimensions are almost four times greater than the perpendicular (thickness) dimension, we can expect the second term, in general, to dominate for the wave vector, Equation (24). This will not be the case, however, for edge localized modes, since the degree of localization can be such that the in-plane wave vectors can rapidly increase for strong localization. We will discuss this issue shortly. We can express the resonance modes in terms of the quantization numbers p, q, and r, from which we can write the lowest order modes as $k_{111}, k_{211}, k_{121}, k_{221}$, etc. As previously, the quantization numbers are integer and commence at 1. We note that due to the circular symmetry, certain modes will be degenerated; $k_{121} = k_{211}$, $k_{122} = k_{212}$ etc., but $k_{211} = k_{121} \neq k_{112}$. By analyzing the lowest modes, we can assess which are the ones most likely to correspond to the modes observed in the FMR spectra. Setting $n_1 = \pi^2/d^2$ and $n_2 = \pi^2/L^2$, from Equation (24) we can write:

$$k_{111}^2 = 2(1-\delta_d)^2 n_1 + (1-\delta_L)^2 n_2 \qquad (25)$$

$$k_{121}^2 = k_{211}^2 = [(2-\delta_d)^2 + (1-\delta_d)^2] n_1 + (1-\delta_L)^2 n_2 \qquad (26)$$

$$k_{112}^2 = 2(1-\delta_d)^2 n_1 + (2-\delta_L)^2 n_2 \qquad (27)$$

$$k_{221}^2 = 2(2-\delta_d)^2 n_1 + (1-\delta_L)^2 n_2 \qquad (28)$$

$$k_{122}^2 = k_{212}^2 = [(2-\delta_d)^2 + (1-\delta_d)^2] n_1 + (2-\delta_L)^2 n_2 \qquad (29)$$

Before we analyze in more detail the mode ordering, we should note that since the principal resonance line in the nanodot system (blue) can be assumed to derive from the first resonance ($p = 1$) mode in the continuous film, the additional resonance in the nanodots (indicated in green in Figure 4d) must therefore arise from a localized resonance mode. We conclude this from the fact that this resonance is situated at a higher magnetic field with respect to the principal resonance. This means that the wave vector is imaginary and pushes the resonance field to higher values since $Dk^2 = D(i\tau)^2 = -D\tau^2$. Inserting this into the resonance equation, Equation (23), means that the resonance field is shifted up in value (or alternatively, the resonance frequencies shift down), while normal bulk or PSSW modes are situated at lower fields or higher frequencies. This can be seen from the resonance lines shown in Figure 4. This conclusion is supported by the fact that the mode intensity is significantly weaker than the principal mode, which is to be expected since the modal intensity is proportional to the transversal dynamic magnetization. Using Equation (23), we find a good fit to this (green) resonance for which $\tau = 2.85 \times 10^7$ m^{-1}, see Figure 4d.

To analyze the mode ordering, we first note that $n_1 \simeq 2.47 \times 10^{14}$ m^{-2} and $n_2 \simeq 3.95 \times 10^{15}$ m^{-2}, where we have used d = 200 nm and L = 50 nm, respectively. We therefore see that $n_2 > n_1$ and can make the second terms in Equation (24) dominate the wave vector. Since we can assume that the upper and lower pinning conditions should be close to those of the thin film, i.e., $\delta_L \sim 1$, we can further simplify the analysis. In effect, this means the second terms for the modes with $r = 1$ will effectively vanish, for example in Equations (25), (26) and (28), etc. We can reasonably assign mode numbers corresponding to the wave vectors k_{111} and k_{211} or k_{121} to the first two PSSW modes, i.e., the blue and red lines shown in Figure 4d. This is coherent with the decreased mode separations, with respect to the continuous thin film since this will depend on the first terms in the wave vectors and hence the lateral dimensions of the nanodot. Based on this analysis, we can provide excellent fits to the experimental data, as illustrated in Figure 4d. For the fits we have used the following fit parameters: M_s = 1.09 T, a g-factor of g = 2.04, and an exchange stiffness constant of $A_{ex} = 1.0 \times 10^{-11}$ J·m^{-1}, which are in agreement with the parameters used in the fits for the continuous thin films. We note that the edge localized mode required a reduced value of the magnetization, M_s = 0.82 T. This parameter is important for setting the slope of the linear portion of the curve and may be interpreted as being due to a reduced magnetization at the edges of the nanodots.

4.2. NdCo/Al/Py Layered Structures

Trilayer samples consisting of a 64 nm thick amorphous NdCo$_x$ film with PMA and a 10 nm thick polycrystalline Py film with IMA, which are coupled through a nonmagnetic Al spacer, have been deposited via the magnetron sputtering technique. The trilayer structure itself is sandwiched between Al seed and capping layers, all of which have been grown on Si/SiO$_2$ substrates. The magnetic properties of the coupled thin films can be controlled by two independent parameters. On the one hand, varying the Co concentration (x = 5, 7.5, and 9) in the NdCo$_x$ film allows the modification of the strength of its PMA. A maximum has been found for x = 5, whereas higher or lower Co concentrations lead to a gradually weaker PMA, respectively [29,30]. On the other hand, by adjusting the Al spacer thickness (t = 0 nm, 2.5 nm, 5 nm, and 10 nm), the type of coupling between the two magnetic layers can be set to either direct exchange coupling ($t \leq 1.5$ nm) or stray field coupling ($t \geq 2.5$ nm). In addition to the coupled bi- and trilayers, a series of reference samples, consisting of a single 10 nm thick Py film as well as single 64 nm thick NdCo$_x$ films with varying Co concentrations x, has also been prepared. For the remainder of this paper, the coupled trilayers will be named according to their Co concentration and Al spacer thickness as, e.g., X5T10 for a sample based on a NdCo$_5$ film and a 10 nm thick Al spacer.

The magnetic properties of the samples have been studied using magnetometry (AGM), MOKE, and FMR. In a previous work, we have analyzed the VNA-FMR data of these samples both as a function of the composition and as a function of the Al spacer thickness [31]. Further characterization has been performed using magnetic force microscopy (MFM). Indeed, these measurements show that the remnant state of the sample has a marked stripe domain pattern, with a periodicity of around 140 nm. This stripe domain pattern has been shown to originate in the NdCo layer and is replicated in the coupled Py film. In our previous study, we presented data for the in-plane FMR with the external magnetic field $\mathbf{H}_{dc}$ applied along the in-plane hard axis of the samples. We now present the comparison of the in-plane easy and hard axis measurements for samples with a composition value of $x = 7.5$. The experimental FMR data are displayed in Figure 5.

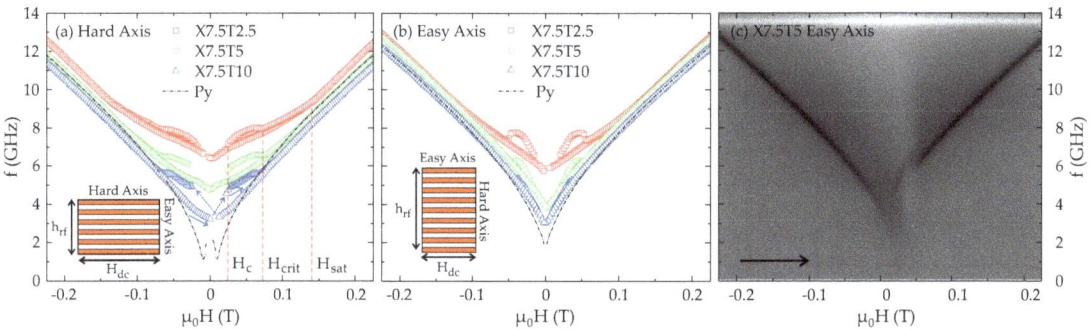

Figure 5. In-plane frequency–field characteristics for VNA-FMR measurements of samples with composition $x = 7.5$. The f–H characteristics are shown for the hard (**a**) and easy (**b**) axis of the sample. The corresponding insets illustrate the field configurations with respect to the in-plane hard and easy axis along with the virgin-state stripe domain pattern, after initial saturation at $\mathbf{H}_{dc} = +0.9$ T along the in-plane hard or easy axis. (**c**) Raw VNA-FMR data for the easy axis of sample X7.5T5 for the up-swept field, showing the absorption line discontinuity passing through zero-field.

In this study, we note that the FMR signal comes solely from the Py layer and no explicit resonance is observed for the NdCo film. The FMR measurements were performed in a specific manner to enable us to correctly interpret and reproduce data. Prior to the FMR measurements, the samples were saturated with a static in-plane magnetic field of $\mathbf{H}_{dc} = +0.9$ T along their easy or hard axis, respectively, i.e., along the direction of the actual measurement. We then perform a full hysteresis cycle from $+0.3$ T to -0.3 T and then back to $+0.3$ T in steps of 2.5 mT. Since the spectra only show the Py FMR, we also show the FMR line for a single uncoupled Py film of the same thickness, as shown by the dash-dotted line in Figure 5a,b. This is useful since it also gives a reference line for comparison with the FMR of the coupled Py layers. We note that the single Py film has a small in-plane anisotropy, which we estimate from the graph to give an anisotropy field of around $H_k = 2K_u/\mu_0 M_s = 9$ mT. We also note that the initial domain pattern after saturation are stripe domains, which are oriented in a direction parallel to $\mathbf{H}_{dc}$. Indeed, it is due to this characteristic that the sample system exhibits a reconfigurable anisotropy. We use the Py FMR as a method to probe the properties and the effect of the NdCo layer due to the magnetic coupling between the two ferromagnetic materials.

There are a number of important observations that we can make before considering a more detailed analysis. Firstly, we note that for the sample series under consideration, the non-magnetic Al spacer thickness allows us to vary the strength or the magnetic coupling between the $NdCo_{7.5}$ and Py layers. As the thickness increases, the coupling will reduce, and the Py layer characteristics will be expected to approach those of the isolated film (dashed line). This is roughly what can be observed in Figure 5 and is more clearly seen for the easy axis orientation Figure 5b. We have previously shown that the hysteretic behavior of the FMR line is strongly correlated to the hysteretic loop from magnetometry measurements. This allows us to find the coercive field, H_c, and the saturation field, H_{sat}, as indicated in Figure 5a, for the X7.5T2.5 sample. A further critical field, H_{crit}, is indicated, which refers to the field at which the two branches of the hysteresis loop meet [31]. The resonance line follows the arrows shown in Figure 5a, where we note that the dashed arrows indicate the transition through zero-field, where the two branches (up-sweep and down-sweep) of the characteristics cross. Figure 5c shows the corresponding raw FMR data for the X7.5T5 sample. In fact, we note that the transition through zero-field is a little more complex than the data points suggest. In the up-swept data shown, the resonance line appears to cross the zero-field and a jump in the resonance line occurs for small positive fields. This branch then increases and joins the uniform FMR line at the critical field. The down-swept line has lower values of resonance frequency than the up-swept branch in this field range. This then results in the hysteretic behavior of the resonance frequency. In this region, the resonance line appears to be rather weak. Above H_c, the resonance line is more pronounced and gradually joins the principal uniform resonance mode as the field reaches H_{sat}.

For the hard axis measurements, the critical field appears to be independent of the spacer layer thickness, though the hysteresis is strongly influenced by the strength of the magnetic coupling of the Py layer with the $NdCo_{7.5}$ underlayer. If we consider the evolution of the FMR f–H characteristics for the sample series, as t decreases and the magnetic coupling increases, the FMR branches generally shift to higher frequencies, the saturation fields increase and the hysteresis loops appears to be reduced. We also see from this that the zero-field values are strongly affected by the coupling, and increase significantly from the uncoupled Py data. In considering the free Py layer, we note that the coupled Py film in the trilayers have an induced stripe domain texture, which is responsible for these low field differences in the FMR behavior.

The easy axis data show that while the FMR shifts also follow similar trends to that observed along the hard axis, the shifts are generally smaller and the strength of the hysteresis is inverted with respect to the hard axis. Furthermore, the critical field values appear to decrease with increasing Al thickness. The easy axis data also shows that the FMR characteristics of the coupled Py layers approach those of the single Py film as the Al layer thickness increases and decoupling from the NdCo film increases.

In consideration of the FMR behavior in the regions below the coercive field, we note that FMR measurements are highly sensitive to the relative orientation of the stripe domains and the rf magnetic field. This can lead to acoustic and optical modes, due to in-phase and out-of-phase precession of the magnetization in adjacent stripe domains [32], see Figure 6. As simulated in [33] for a single 200 nm thick Py film, stripe domains and rf magnetic field $\mathbf{h}_{rf}$ (dc magnetic field $\mathbf{H}_{dc}$) are always perpendicular (parallel) during the entire hysteresis cycle and independent of the field sweep direction.

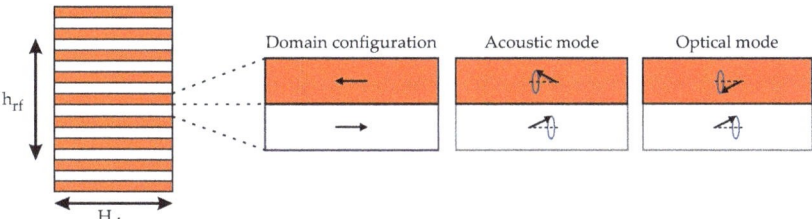

Figure 6. Schematic illustration of the stripe domain pattern for the coupled Py layer illustrating the precessional configurations for the acoustic and optical modes. Black arrows indicate the direction of the x-component of the in-plane magnetization m_x in the coupled Py layer inside the stripe domains shown in orange and white color.

Above saturation, the magnetization of the coupled Py layer will be homogeneous and only the uniform FMR mode is observed. However, for applied magnetic fields lower than the saturation fields, stripe domains can give rise to two FMR modes, an acoustic mode and an optical mode, with the latter having a higher resonance frequency at the same magnetic field. The frequency difference between these modes can be substantial, though manipulation of the films can lead to a significant reduction in the separation of modes [33,34]. However, it should be mentioned that in the coupled trilayers, always just one type of mode is observed when sweeping the bias field $\mathbf{H}_{dc}$ from positive to negative saturation and vice versa, with the mode order being always the following: uniform FMR mode → acoustic mode → optical mode → uniform FMR mode.

In order to understand the evolution of the resonance line, particularly in the region below saturation and between positive and negative coercive fields, we need to consider the orientation of the magnetization and the nature of the domain structure from the point of domain nucleation as the applied magnetic field $\mathbf{H}_{dc}$ reduces from saturation to field strengths below the coercive field. This is intimately connected to the magnetization loops of the Py film. In the saturated state, the magnetization is rigorously aligned to the external field, with $H > H_{sat}$. In this domain state, the FMR absorption will rigidly follow the normal uniform mode, as given by the Kittel equation, such as expressed by Equation (23). We know that below both the saturation field and the coercive field, the magnetization can relax from the applied field orientation. In the coupled trilayers, any deviation from the Kittel equation would be indicative of a relaxation of the Py magnetization from the applied field direction, though the Py layer remains in a stripe domain state. Only below the coercive field does domain nucleation occur and the sample enters a multidomain state. For a stripe domain system, such as observed in Py coupled to NdCo, the relative sizes of the oppositely aligned domains will vary, as illustrated schematically in Figure 7. These oppositely aligned domains will undergo FMR in either the acoustic or optical modes, as shown previously in Figure 6, which occur at different magnetic fields (or frequencies).

From the hard axis data, see Figure 5, we note that the resonance line continues without deviation, on passing through $-H_c$, suggesting that the acoustic mode is excited (see Figure 8a). The resonance line continues undeviated on passing through zero-field. However, once the positive coercive field is reached, $+H_c$, there is an abrupt jump in the resonance line, as indicated by the red arrow in Figure 8b. At this point in the field sweep, the sample is by definition in a state with equal volumes of the two magnetic domains. To understand the jump in the resonance line, we suggest that at this point the acoustic mode is suppressed and the optical mode becomes visible. For equal volumes of oppositely aligned domains, we expect the transverse magnetization to be zero, so at the exact value of $H = +H_c$, the absorbed intensity will be zero. However, any further increase in H will bring about an increase in the positive domains with respect to the negatively pointing domains, and the transverse magnetization will be non-zero and thus an optical mode can be observed (see Figure 8a). We can resume this scenario in Figure 9, in which we follow the FMR hysteresis from negative to positive fields.

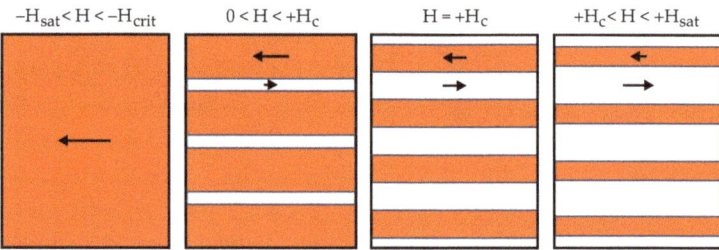

Figure 7. Schematic illustration of the stripe domain pattern of the coupled Py layer for increasing magnetic field, starting at negative saturation, $-H_{sat}$, and increasing in the positive direction up to $+H_c < H < +H_{sat}$. Black arrows indicate the direction of the x-component of the in-plane magnetization m_x in the coupled Py layer, whereas their length is proportional to the magnitude of m_x inside the stripe domains. The change of the width of the stripe domains in the direction perpendicular to $\mathbf{H}_{dc}$ is, however, largely exaggerated and in reality only very small.

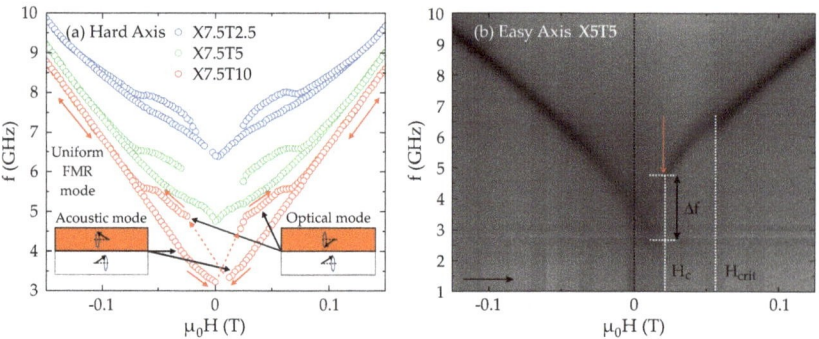

Figure 8. (a) Hard axis data of the X7.5 series. Red arrows indicate the field sweep directions with respect to the FMR line hysteresis around zero-field. The suggested modes corresponding to the different field regions of the f–H characteristic are also shown. (b) Easy axis frequency–field characteristic of the X5T5 sample for the up-sweep field direction. Critical and coercive fields are also indicated.

If we consider the resonance equation for the acoustic and optical excitations, we can adapt the FMR equation for the effective wave vectors associated with these modes. Since the in-phase, acoustic excitation follows from the uniform mode, we can consider a value of $k_{ac} = 0$, while the optical mode should have a k-vector given by $k_{opt} = 2\pi/\Lambda_D$, where Λ_D corresponds to the periodicity of the stripe domain texture. We can now consider the frequency shift at $H = H_c$ as deriving from the resonance equations for these two excitations. Thus we can write:

$$\Delta f = f_{opt} - f_{ac} = \frac{\mu_0 \gamma^2 (2H_c + M) D k_{opt}^2 + \gamma^2 (D k_{opt}^2)^2}{4\pi^2 (f_{opt} + f_{ac})}, \tag{30}$$

where f_{opt} and f_{ac} are defined in Figure 9. Given that the wave vector for the optical mode must physically correspond to a real value, we can express the optical mode wave vector from Equation (30) as:

$$k_{opt}^2 = \left(\frac{2\pi}{\Lambda_D}\right)^2 = \frac{\sqrt{\mu_0^2 (2H_c + M)^2 + 16\pi^2 \Delta f (f_{opt} + f_{ac})/\gamma^2} - \mu_0 (2H_c + M)}{2D} \tag{31}$$

This allows us to directly assess the domain structure periodicity (at $H = H_c$), and if we require, its evolution with increasing field up to the critical field, H_{crit}. Once this field is reached, the sample becomes a single domain, at which k must be zero, and $\Lambda_D \to \infty$. Any further increase of the applied field aligns the magnetization along this field direction. The saturation field will bring the system back to rigorous saturation and the uniform FMR mode is recovered. In fact, any difference between the uniform FMR frequency and the actual observed FMR frequency will be due to the misalignment of M and H.

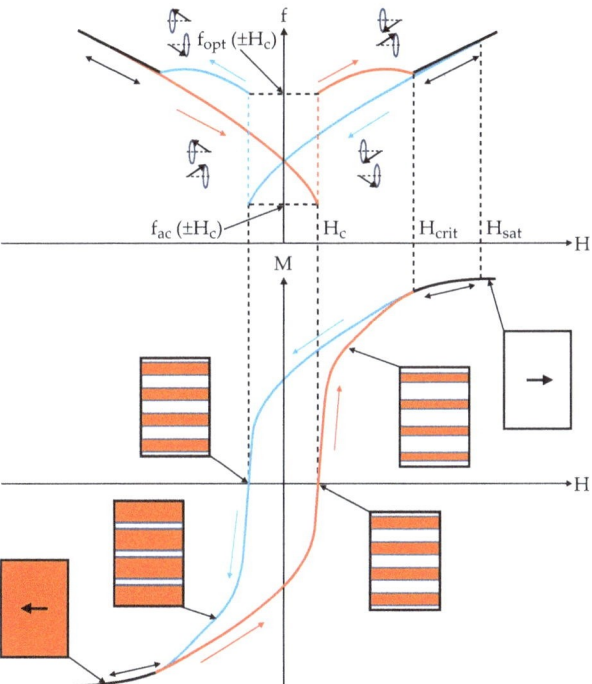

Figure 9. Schematic illustrations of the in-plane magnetization and in-plane FMR hysteresis loops. In the lower panel, for the M–H loop, we indicate the stripe domain patterns, which schematically show the relative sizes of the oppositely aligned magnetic stripe domain structure. The reversible portions (black), as well as the up-sweep (red) and down-sweep (blue) branches of the magnetization reversal loop, are also shown. The corresponding color scheme is also used in the upper panel for the FMR hysteresis. Indicatively shown are the expected acoustic and optical modes.

The proposed model, schematically illustrated in Figure 9, depicts the general form of both the magnetization and FMR hystereses. This is in agreement with previous findings [31] and with the data presented in this paper. At this point, we note that our proposed model is made under the assumption that the imprint of the magnetic stripe domain pattern from the NdCo film into the coupled Py layer is strong. However, the strength of interaction between those two magnetic layers varies according to the thickness of the Al spacer. Synchrotron-based experiments are in progress to understand this issue in more detail.

From the fact that the second term in the square root of Equation (31) is much larger than the first, we can simplify the expression and obtain an approximate relation between the stripe domain periodicity and the difference in frequency, $\Delta f = f_{opt} - f_{ac}$, such that:

$$\Lambda_D \simeq \frac{(2\pi\gamma D)^{0.5}}{[(f_{opt} + f_{ac})\Delta f]^{0.25}} \tag{32}$$

The exchange stiffness constant for Py is of the order of $A_{ex} = 1.3 \times 10^{-11}$ J·m^{-1} [35], which allows us to evaluate the spin wave constant $D = 2A_{ex}/M_s$. Using a value of $M_s = 0.7$ T (from fits of the in-plane VNA-FMR data of the 10 nm thick Py reference sample), we obtain $D = 4.309 \times 10^{-17}$ T·m^2. Furthermore, we use $\gamma = g\mu_B/\hbar = 165.33$ GHz/T. From the values of $f_{opt} = 4.6$ GHz and $f_{ac} = 3.7$ GHz for the hard axis measurement of sample X7.5T10, we calculate the stripe domain periodicity to be $\Lambda_D \simeq 135$ nm. This is in excellent agreement with MFM images for this sample, where the periodicity was found to be around 140 nm.

There is a further element that requires explanation, which concerns the deviation of the FMR line from the uniform FMR line between the saturation and critical fields, as illustrated in Figure 5. Indeed, this deviation is significant for samples with strong coupling between the ferromagnetic layers, i.e., with low Al interlayer thicknesses. This is particularly noticeable in the hard axis measurements, where the deviations are more significant. For the thinnest Al interlayer of $t_{Al} = 2.5$ nm, there is a very large increase. From the increase of the zero-field frequency for the free Py layer, we can estimate an increase of the resonance frequency in the region of 4.2–4.5 GHz for this sample. For the sample with $t_{Al} = 10$ nm, this value drops to around 1.0–1.5 GHz. The value of this deviation of the resonance frequency, δf, should be related to the ferromagnetic coupling strength between the NdCo and Py layers. We can convert these frequencies into effective fields using a simple relation: $H_{eff} = \delta\omega/\gamma = 2\pi\delta f/\gamma$. Using the zero-field values for the frequencies, we estimate that the effective coupling field, H_{eff}, between the NdCo and Py layers drops from about 0.4 T to about 0.1 T as the Al interlayer thickness increases from 2.5 nm to 10 nm. This represents a significant ferromagnetic coupling between the layers.

5. Conclusions

Ferromagnetic resonance is an extremely sensitive tool for probing the dynamic magnetic behavior in ferromagnetic nanostructures and allows us to analyze in detail the properties of various types of nanometric systems. This will include a consideration of the dynamic magnetic properties of the system as well as boundary and magnetic coupling effects.

In this paper, we have shown two examples of the application of the VNA method for performing FMR experiments in magnetic nanostructures. In the first case, we use this technique to study the effect of nanostructuring on the dynamic magnetic properties of Co films and in particular the modification of the FMR spectra due to size reduction and edge effects. We show that the FMR for a continuous thin film can be interpreted from the excitation of PSSW modes, from which we can assess the pinning conditions arising at the magnetic boundaries of the upper and lower surface of the magnetic thin film. The effect of nanostructuring is seen to modify the wave vector of the PSSW modes and shifts the resonances accordingly. This arises from a consideration of the lateral confinement effect in the nanodot structure and can be taken into account in the expression of the three-dimensional wave vector. Furthermore, we note that an additional resonance is also observed and can be attributed to the existence of an edge localized resonance, which is due to the edges of the dot itself. The fit to the experimental values requires a small modification of the magnetization, which could also indicate that the edges of the ferromagnetic dots are reduced with respect to the bulk of the dot structure.

The second magnetic system that we have considered here are layered structures consisting of a hard magnetic NdCo film with perpendicular anisotropy coupled to a soft magnetic Py film, which naturally has an in-plane anisotropy. The coupling between the layers is controlled by the thickness of a non-magnetic Al spacer layer. Our FMR data were performed by making both up and down field sweeps from saturation and allowed us to highlight the hysteretic properties of the dynamic response. We have been able to explain the existence of this hysteresis by accounting for the switching of the modes between acoustic and optical resonances that naturally occur in unsaturated systems with different magnetic domains. Since the NdCo layer induces a regular magnetic stripe domain structure in the Py film, we have been able to further interpret the data using a simple model to explain the frequency shift between the modes. This has ultimately been supported by the relation between the frequency shift and the stripe domain periodicity. The calculation of this periodicity gives a value of $\Lambda_D \simeq 135$ nm and is in excellent agreement with MFM domain images, where a periodicity of 140 nm was observed.

Author Contributions: Conceptualization, D.S.S., D.M., K.-W.L. and L.M.Á.-P.; methodology, D.S.S., D.M. and L.M.Á.-P.; formal analysis, D.S.S. and D.M.; investigation, D.S.S., D.M., K.-W.L., A.H.-R., C.Q., J.D. and L.M.Á.-P.; resources, D.S.S., K.-W.L., L.M.Á.-P. and J.-C.W.; data curation, D.M., K.-W.L. and L.M.Á.-P.; writing—original draft preparation, D.S.S.; writing—review and editing, D.S.S., D.M., K.-W.L., L.M.Á.-P. and J.-C.W.; visualization, D.S.S. and D.M.; supervision, D.S.S., K.-W.L. and L.M.Á.-P.; project administration, D.S.S., K.-W.L. and L.M.Á.-P.; funding acquisition, D.S.S., K.-W.L. and L.M.Á.-P. All authors have read and agreed to the published version of the manuscript.

Funding: D.S.S., D.M. and L.M.Á.-P. acknowledge financial support from the Institut de Physique of CNRS for experimental equipment, a post doc position, and guest researcher stays, respectively. A.H.-R. acknowledges European Union's Horizon 2020 framework program for research and innovation under the Marie Skłodowska-Curie Action No. H2020-MSCA-IF-2016-746958. A.H.-R., C.Q., J.D. and L.M.Á.-P. would like to thank the Spanish Ministerio de Ciencia e Innovación (MCI) for financial support under Project PID2019-104604RB/AEI/10.13039/501100011033. The contributions of F. Valdés-Bango in the initial stage of the NdCo/Py/Al research project are acknowledged.

Institutional Review Board Statement: Not Applicable.

Informed Consent Statement: Not Applicable.

Data Availability Statement: The data presented in this study are available on request from the corresponding author.

Conflicts of Interest: The authors declare no conflict of interest.

Abbreviations

The following abbreviations are used in this manuscript:

AGM	Alternating gradient magnetometry
CPW	Coplanar waveguide
dc	Direct current
DE	Damon–Eschbach
FMR	Ferromagnetic resonance
IMA	In-plane magnetic anisotropy
LLG	Landau–Lifshitz–Gilbert
MFM	Magnetic force microscopy
MOKE	Magneto-optical Kerr effect
PMA	Perpendicular magnetic anisotropy
PSSW	Perpendicular standing spin wave
Py	Permalloy
rf	Radio frequency
SWR	Spin-wave resonance
VNA	Vector network analyzer

References

1. Bland, J.; Heinrich, B. (Eds.) *Ultrathin Magnetic Structures III: Fundamentals of Nanomagnetism*; Springer: Berlin/Heidelberg, Germany, 2005.
2. Heinrich, B.; Bland, J. (Eds.) *Ultrathin Magnetic Structures IV: Applications of Nanomagnetism*; Springer: Berlin/Heidelberg, Germany, 2005.
3. Hirohata, A.; Yamada, K.; Nakatani, Y.; Prejbeanu, I.L.; Diény, B.; Pirro, P.; Hillebrands, B. Review on spintronics: Principles and device applications. *J. Magn. Magn. Mater.* **2020**, *509*, 166711. [CrossRef]
4. Heinrich, B.; Bland, J. (Eds.) *Ultrathin Magnetic Structures II: Measurement Techniques and Novel Magnetic Properties*; Springer: Berlin/Heidelberg, Germany, 1994.

5. Schmool, D.S.; Kachkachi, H. Chapter Four–Single-Particle Phenomena in Magnetic Nanostructures. In *Solid State Physics*; Academic Press: Waltham, MA, USA, 2015; Volume 66, pp. 301–423. [CrossRef]
6. Schmool, D.; Kachkachi, H. Chapter One–Collective Effects in Assemblies of Magnetic Nanoparticles. In *Solid State Physics*; Academic Press: Cambridge, MA, USA, 2016; Volume 67, pp. 1–101. [CrossRef]
7. Bland, J.; Heinrich, B. (Eds.) *Ultrathin Magnetic Structures I: An Introduction to the Electronic, Magnetic and Structural Properties*; Springer: Berlin/Heidelberg, Germany, 1994.
8. Hillebrands, B.; Ounadjela, K. (Eds.) *Spin Dynamics in Confined Magnetic Structures I*; Springer: Berlin/Heidelberg, Germany, 2002. [CrossRef]
9. Hillebrands, B.; Ounadjela, K. (Eds.) *Spin Dynamics in Confined Magnetic Structures II*; Springer: Berlin/Heidelberg, Germany, 2003. [CrossRef]
10. Hillebrands, B.; Thiaville, A. (Eds.) *Spin Dynamics in Confined Magnetic Structures III*; Springer: Berlin/Heidelberg, Germany, 2006. [CrossRef]
11. Kalarickal, S.S.; Krivosik, P.; Wu, M.; Patton, C.E.; Schneider, M.L.; Kabos, P.; Silva, T.J.; Nibarger, J.P. Ferromagnetic resonance linewidth in metallic thin films: Comparison of measurement methods. *J. Appl. Phys.* **2006**, *99*, 093909. [CrossRef]
12. Maksymov, I.S.; Kostylev, M. Broadband stripline ferromagnetic resonance spectroscopy of ferromagnetic films, multilayers and nanostructures. *Phys. E Low-Dimens. Syst. Nanostruct.* **2015**, *69*, 253–293. [CrossRef]
13. Cansever, H.; Lindner, J. Microresonators and Microantennas—Tools to Explore Magnetization Dynamics in Single Nanostructures. *Magnetochemistry* **2021**, *7*, 28. [CrossRef]
14. Ding, Y.; Klemmer, T.J.; Crawford, T.M. A coplanar waveguide permeameter for studying high-frequency properties of soft magnetic materials. *J. Appl. Phys.* **2004**, *96*, 2969–2972. [CrossRef]
15. Markó, D.; Schmool, D.S. Université Paris-Saclay, UVSQ, CNRS, GEMaC, Versailles, France. Unpublished work, 2019.
16. Landau, L.D.; Lifshitz, E. On the theory of the dispersion of magnetic permeability in ferromagnetic bodies. *Phys. Z. Sowjet.* **1935**, *8*, 153.
17. Gilbert, T. A Lagrangian formulation of the gyromagnetic equation of the magnetic field. *Phys. Rev.* **1955**, *100*, 1243.
18. Smit, J.; Beljers, H.G. Ferromagnetic Resonance Absorption in $BaFe_{12}O_{19}$, a Highly Anisotropic Crystal. *Philips Res. Rep.* **1955**, *10*, 113–130.
19. Vonsovskii, S.V. (Ed.) Ferromagnetic Resonance: The Phenomenon of Resonant Absorption of a High-Frequency Magnetic Field in Ferromagnetic Substances. Pergamon. 1966. Available online: https://www.sciencedirect.com/book/9780080110271/ferromagnetic-resonance (accessed on 19 August 2021).
20. Rado, G.; Weertman, J. Spin-wave resonance in a ferromagnetic metal. *J. Phys. Chem. Solids* **1959**, *11*, 315–333. [CrossRef]
21. Maksymowicz, A. Spin-wave spectra of insulating films: Comparison of exact calculations and a single-wave-vector model. *Phys. Rev. B* **1986**, *33*, 6045–6053. [CrossRef] [PubMed]
22. Schmool, D.S.; Barandiarán, J.M. Ferromagnetic resonance and spin wave resonance in multiphase materials: Theoretical considerations. *J. Phys. Condens. Matter* **1998**, *10*, 10679–10700. [CrossRef]
23. Puszkarski, H. Theory of surface states in spin wave resonance. *Prog. Surf. Sci.* **1979**, *9*, 191–247. [CrossRef]
24. Herring, C.; Kittel, C. On the Theory of Spin Waves in Ferromagnetic Media. *Phys. Rev.* **1951**, *81*, 869–880. [CrossRef]
25. Kalinikos, B.A.; Slavin, A.N. Theory of dipole-exchange spin wave spectrum for ferromagnetic films with mixed exchange boundary conditions. *J. Phys. C Solid State Phys.* **1986**, *19*, 7013–7033. [CrossRef]
26. Farle, M. Ferromagnetic resonance of ultrathin metallic layers. *Rep. Prog. Phys.* **1998**, *61*, 755–826. [CrossRef]
27. Li, X.; Alkadour, B.; Chuang, W.C.; Marko, D.; Schmool, D.; Wu, J.C.; Manna, P.K.; Lin, K.W.; van Lierop, J. Temperature evolution of the magnetic properties of Ag/Fe nanodot arrays. *Appl. Surf. Sci.* **2020**, *513*, 145578. [CrossRef]
28. Eyrich, C. Exchange Stiffness in Thin-Film Cobalt Alloys. Master's Thesis, Simon Fraser University, Burnaby, BC, Canada, 2012.
29. Mergel, D.; Heitmann, H.; Hansen, P. Pseudocrystalline model of the magnetic anisotropy in amorphous rare-earth–transition-metal thin films. *Phys. Rev. B* **1993**, *47*, 882–891. [CrossRef] [PubMed]
30. Cid, R.; Alameda, J.M.; Valvidares, S.M.; Cezar, J.C.; Bencok, P.; Brookes, N.B.; Díaz, J. Perpendicular magnetic anisotropy in amorphous Nd_xCo_{1-x} thin films studied by x-ray magnetic circular dichroism. *Phys. Rev. B* **2017**, *95*, 224402. [CrossRef]
31. Markó, D.; Valdés-Bango, F.; Quirós, C.; Hierro-Rodríguez, A.; Vélez, M.; Martín, J.I.; Alameda, J.M.; Schmool, D.S.; Álvarez-Prado, L.M. Tunable ferromagnetic resonance in coupled trilayers with crossed in-plane and perpendicular magnetic anisotropies. *Appl. Phys. Lett.* **2019**, *115*, 082401. [CrossRef]
32. Ebels, U.; Buda, L.; Ounadjela, K.; Wigen, P.E. Ferromagnetic resonance excitation of two-dimensional wall structures in magnetic stripe domains. *Phys. Rev. B* **2001**, *63*, 174437. [CrossRef]
33. Cao, D.; Song, C.; Feng, H.; Song, Y.; Zhong, L.; Pan, L.; Zhao, C.; Li, Q.; Xu, J.; Li, S.; et al. Microwave excitations and magnetization dynamics of stripe domain films. *arXiv* **2019**, arXiv:1903.00656.
34. Cao, D.; Pan, L.; Song, Y.; Cheng, X.; Feng, H.; Zhao, C.; Li, Q.; Xu, J.; Li, S.; Liu, Q.; et al. Influence of the Phase Structure on the Acoustic and Optical Mode Ferromagnetic Resonance of FeNi Stripe Domain Films. In Proceedings of the 2018 IEEE International Magnetics Conference (INTERMAG), Singapore, 23–27 April 2018. [CrossRef]
35. Shull, R.; Kabanov, Y.; Gornakov, V.; Chen, P.; Nikitenko, V. Shape critical properties of patterned Permalloy thin films. *J. Magn. Magn. Mater.* **2016**, *400*, 191–199. [CrossRef] [PubMed]

Article
Control of Dynamics in Weak PMA Magnets

Luis M. Álvarez-Prado [1,2]

1 Department of Physics, University of Oviedo, 33007 Oviedo, Spain; lmap@uniovi.es; Tel.: +34-985103307
2 Center of Research on Nanomaterials and Nanotechnology, CINN (CSIC-Universidad de Oviedo), 33940 El Entrego, Spain

Abstract: We have recently shown that a hybrid magnetic thin film with orthogonal anisotropies presenting weak stripe domains can achieve a high degree of controllability of its ferromagnetic resonance. This work explores the origin of the reconfigurability through micromagnetic simulations. The static domain structures which control the thin film resonance can be found under a deterministic applied field protocol. In contrast to similar systems reported, our effect can be obtained under low magnetic fields. We have also found through simulations that the spin wave propagation in the hybrid is nonreciprocal: two adjacent regions emit antiparallel spin waves along the stripe domains. Both properties convert the hybrid in a candidate for future magnonic devices at the nanoscale.

Keywords: nanomagnetism; magnetic multilayers; micromagnetism; magnetization dynamics

1. Introduction

In the late 1900s of the last century, there has been a turning point in magnetic materials research from the in-plane magnetized materials to materials having out-of-plane components due to its perpendicular magnetic anisotropy (PMA). A gaining in recording density was behind this transition [1]. The preferential research has commonly involved hard magnets where the PMA is so strong that it overcomes the demagnetizing energy due to charges. Typical examples are Pt, Pd alloys with Co or Fe [2] or multilayers formed by a sequential arrangement of magnetic and non-magnetic materials [3]. However, these materials need costly growth procedures and post-growth processes and the PMA involves using high magnetic fields for its control. In this context, the use of materials with low PMA is beneficial. A plethora of low PMA materials can be found: the former materials [2,3] with different growth conditions and/or that are subjected to another post-treatments, GdFe [4], Permalloy ($Ni_{80}Fe_{20}$) [5], CoSiB [6], CoFeZr [7], FeGa [8], TbFeGa [9], FeN [10], c-Co [11] and some slight variants of them. Besides these materials, our group has also used $NdCo_x$ [12] and $FeSi_x$, [13] and YCo_5 [14].

The dynamical properties of magnets have been long used as a method to obtain the magnetic fundamental parameters of the materials [15,16] and/or to aid in the designing of devices [17]. However, compared to studies at high magnetic fields, the analysis of dynamic properties under saturation is comparatively scarce in the literature. Some exceptions can be found in references [11,18–20]. This could mainly be due to its intrinsic complexity and the lack of appropriate tools for analysis. In the last few years, some groups have been promoting a more careful study of the physics in the low-field range due to the possibilities that the developed domains are carrying with [21–25].

Nowadays, there is a need for obtaining magnet-based logic and filtering operations of signal carriers with processing units holding some degree of versatility at the nanoscale scale. Obtaining reconfigurable magnetic systems is one of the milestones needed for improving the versatility and efficiency of such gigahertz devices. This work will focus on a material which presents some of the above-mentioned peculiarities. Micromagnetic simulations will help us in understanding the origin of some of the interesting dynamical properties that weak PMA $NdCo_x$ alloys coupled to a 10 nm thick Permalloy film present.

As low thickness Permalloy holds in-plane magnetic anisotropy (IMA), we will deal with a hybrid magnet distinguished by its coupled regions with orthogonal anisotropies. In particular, we will treat the capability of this system for tuning its ferromagnetic resonance (FMR). There is a field range where the system can resonate at will at two different values under the same applied magnetic field. Although other proposals of reconfigurable systems can be found in the recent literature, they are helped by costly nanoscale shaping [26] and mainly use only IMA materials (resulting in a lower domain density as mentioned above) [27]. Simulations will also show that these hybrids have another useful property in the GHz regime. At remanence, they present the possibility of using their stripe domains as nonreciprocal spin-wave nanochannels. Both properties, reconfigurability and nonreciprocity, can be used in the improvement of logical devices and interconnections for beyond-CMOS architectures [28].

We will start with a brief discussion about the nanodomain sizes which can be obtained using low PMA $NdCo_x$ alloys. We will focus here on the most common cobalt ratio: x_{Co} = 5 (Section 2.1). After, we will present the peculiar static magnetic distribution of $NdCo_x$ and Permalloy when they are placed in proximity, separated just by a thin non-magnetic material (Section 2.2). To continue, we will describe how this static magnetization modulates the dynamic behavior of the whole system resulting in reconfigurability (Section 2.3.1) and nonreciprocity (Section 2.3.2). Finally, some possible improvements are listed and the conclusions will be given.

2. Results and Discussion

2.1. Nanodomain Size

One of the main issues that the low PMA thin films present in order to host domains at the nanoscale is that to develop a domain structure with out-of-plane components (called weak stripe domains), the sample must be thicker than the so-called critical thickness: t_c [29]. If the film is not thick enough, the samples prefer to rest in the monodomain state (or at list in-plane magnetized state due to the shape anisotropy). t_c is dependent on the PMA/demagnetizing energy ratio (the so-called quality factor Q) and the exchange constant. The onset of weak stripe domains can be viewed as a phase transition. Its treatment leads to some analytical expressions [30] and algebraic equations [31] which can be used to obtain t_c. The repeated domain structures of these weak PMA materials can be characterized by a critical spatial wavelength (λ_c) when the film thickness is close to the critical one (t_c). So, there is a minimal wavelength for stripe domains as the thickness is lowered (keeping the film magnetic parameters fixed).

From the theoretical point of view, λ can be found by numerical means [32] or by using some simplifying assumptions on the spatial evolution of magnetization inside the thin film [33]. As a general rule, it can be said that as PMA gets bigger, both t_c and λ decrease. Two origins are behind this effect: (i) a thinner film is needed to develop stripe domains and, (ii) λ is a decreasing function of thickness (while the film is not too thin: see next paragraph and [30]).

Even if the modern trends followed by the magnetism community are to increase the miniaturization of devices until the nanoscale, unfortunately the low PMA thin films just form domains ranging from a few tens of nanometers to a few hundreds. On the contrary, domains in high PMA materials can have out-of-plane magnetization components even in few-nm-thick materials. But the price to pay in these ultrathin materials is that the exchange energy has an increased weight in the total energy of the samples. This fact widens the stripe domains, and the domain size/thickness ratio becomes much greater than one [34]. As we will see shortly, this ratio can be close to 1.5 in low PMA materials. Among the low PMA materials used in our laboratory, the harder one is $NdCo_5$. Under the common sputtering parameters used for its growing we have observed a stripe domain structure even in a 29 nm thick film. The FFT of the corresponding MFM image results in 45 nm wide domains (implying λ to be 90 nm). We will begin by characterizing the domains of the $NdCo_5$ composition at the remanent state.

We have selected two thicknesses close to the experimental one above-mentioned to illustrate the behavior close to criticality: 35 nm and 45 nm. The free GPU-based MuMax3 micromagnetic simulator was used for the simulations [35]. Among the MuMax3 outputs, the total energy density and its components can be found. Figure 1a displays the calculated total energy density weak stripe domain structure as a function of its wavelength λ. Blue and red arrows indicate the wavelength of the minimal total energy density, λ^*, for the 35 nm thick and the 45 nm thick nm at a given exchange constant (A = 7 × 10^{-12} J/m). When the simulated film thickness approaches the nominal one growth, 29 nm, we can see that the predicted λ^*, which gets closer to the one measured. In particular, the 35 nm thick (45 nm thick) film presents a λ^* equal to 105 nm (127 nm). As thinner films are modelled, the experimental domain width/thickness ratio (1.55) is approached (from below). Figure 1a also reflects that for changing, λ^* is more effective of a thickness variation than an exchange constant variation. This conclusion can be extracted from the comparison between i) the red (A = 5 × 10^{-12} J/m) and black curves (A = 7 × 10^{-12} J/m), having equal thickness and ii) the blue (t = 35nm) and black curves (t = 45nm), both being calculated with A = 5 × 10^{-12} J/m. For similar relative changes of both A and t (~25%), the relative change of λ^* is around four times lower in the first case (~5/127 = 4%).

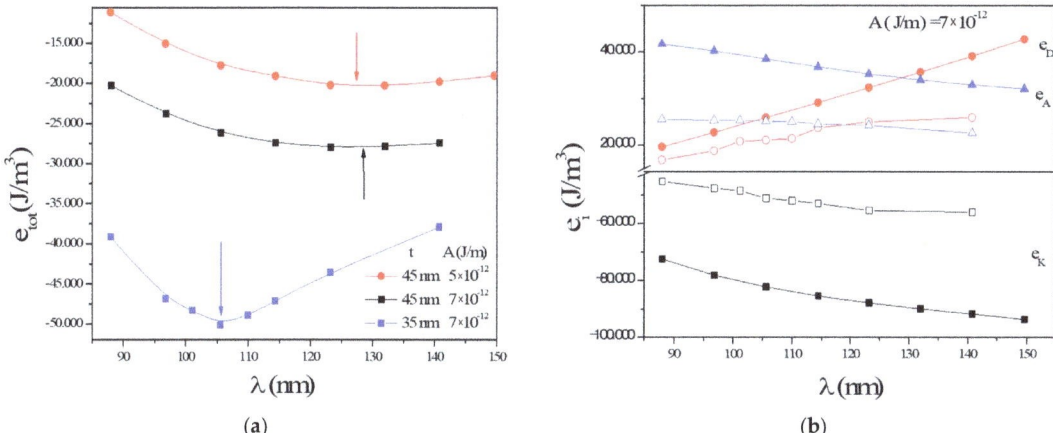

Figure 1. (a) Variation of the total energy density as a function of the stripe domain wavelength for a 45 nm thick (red and black) and 35 nm thick (blue) NdCo$_5$; (b) energy density contributions for 45 nm thick (full dots) and 35 nm thick (empty squares) NdCo$_5$ films. The exchange is kept constant for (b). No external magnetic field is considered.

On the other hand, Figure 1b reports the behavior of the three individual terms, summing up in e$_{tot}$ versus λ − e$_{tot}$ has contributions from PMA (e$_K$/black), the demagnetizing energy (e$_D$/blue) and the exchange energy (e$_A$/red). Empty symbols belong to the 45 nm thick film and the empty ones to the 35 nm thick film [35]. In Figure 1b, the exchange constant, A, was kept fixed to 7 × 10^{-12} J/m. The saturation magnetization and perpendicular anisotropy used can be found in the methods section. As shown in Figure 1b, the exchange interaction favors bigger λ while the demagnetizing term promotes smaller ones. The anisotropy energy density is more sensitive to λ variations in the low λ range: here, regions of the material with magnetization not aligned to the easy axis represent a meaningful contribution to the total volume and increase the energy density. Another conclusion extracted from Figure 1b is that thinner NdCo$_5$ films result in greater absolute values of the energies involved. At the same time, the second derivate of the total energy density grows until the film becomes completely in-plane magnetized at t$_c$. We did not continue to further the analysis of the thickness impact due to non-negligible mistakes for the predicted t$_c$.

2.2. Static Properties of Stripe Domains

The energetics found in the previous subsection come from the inner distribution of NdCo$_5$ magnetization. This distribution is visualized in Figure 2 where the three magnetization components of a 65 nm thick NdCo$_5$ layer in the (0YZ) plane transverse to the stripe direction (0X) are shown. Only one full wavelength of the stripe domains, λ^*, is considered at the remanent (MFM measurements reveal a stripes wavelength ~140 nm [36]). Figure 2a shows the cartesian axes used through this work and the direction used for the saturating external field. The out-of-plane component of the magnetization (m_z) can be observed in Figure 2b. A big part of the stray field that the Permalloy feels (placed on top of the Al/NdCo$_x$ bilayer) is due to that component. Figure 2c shows the in-plane magnetization component perpendicular to the stripes main direction (m_y). Its value lies in the lowering of the demagnetizing energy that it affords. The triangular domains inside Figure 2c are commonly denoted as closure domains (due to its flux closing properties) or Néel caps (due to the nature of its domains walls) [11]. Finally, Figure 2d shows the domain magnetization along the stripes (m_x). The main difference between weak PMA and hard PMA materials is that in the latter case, only the magnetization component of Figure 2b is markedly different from zero.

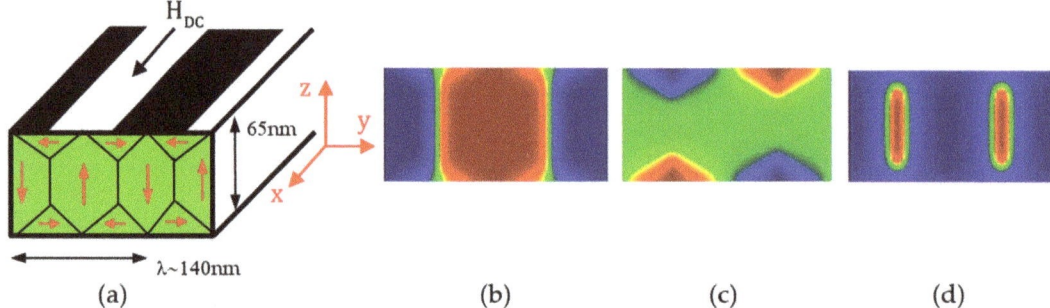

Figure 2. Sixty-five nm thick NdCo$_5$ remanent state: (**a**) reference axes, applied field direction and sketch of the stripe domain structure; (**b**) out-of-plane magnetization, in-plane components of the sample: (**c**) perpendicular; (**d**) parallel to the applied field H$_{DC}$.

The main topic of this work is the using of magnetic materials presenting weak stripe domain structures in the fabrication of devices working in the GHz range [37]. However, NdCo$_x$ alloys (due to its rare-earth content) have a very broad resonance which prevents its use as a good material for dynamics. We have recently shown how the growing of hybrid systems can help in surpassing this difficulty [36]. If another material with the appropriate dynamic properties (Permalloy in our case) is grown on top of NdCo$_x$, the stripe domain structure of the latter is, at least partially, imprinted on Permalloy. In this way, Permalloy achieves the nice properties of stripe domains. We will consider a 10 nm thick Permalloy through this work. Notice that the interaction between the top and bottom layers must not be through direct contact: in this case there would be a tight movement of Permalloy and NdCo$_x$ which affects Permalloy dynamics. The exchange interaction between the two materials results in a globally poor dynamic performance. Due to this feature, we have used a few-nm-thick sputtered Al film as a separator. Al thickness also serves to control the NdCo$_x$ stripe domains imprinting on Permalloy: a thicker Al lowers the NdCo$_x$ stray field on Permalloy.

Figure 3 summarizes the magnetization state of the hybrid when a 10 nm thick Permalloy is coupled to a 65 nm thick NdCo$_5$ film through a 2.5 nm thick Al separator. We have selected this Al thickness among the experimental ones used [36] because here, the effects of the NdCo$_5$ stray field on Permalloy are the biggest ones. Before being plugged to NdCo$_x$, Permalloy is magnetized completely in-plane (due to its IMA). Once placed in close proximity to NdCo$_x$, the average in-plane Permalloy magnetization is parallel to the stripe domains' direction set in by H$_{DC}$ (shown in Figure 2a). This characteristic is observed regardless of the IMA Permalloy easy axis direction and it is due to the so-called rotatable anisotropy of stripe domains [13]. On the other hand, Permalloy also takes part in some sense in the uppermost closure domains of the whole sample (Figure 3b).

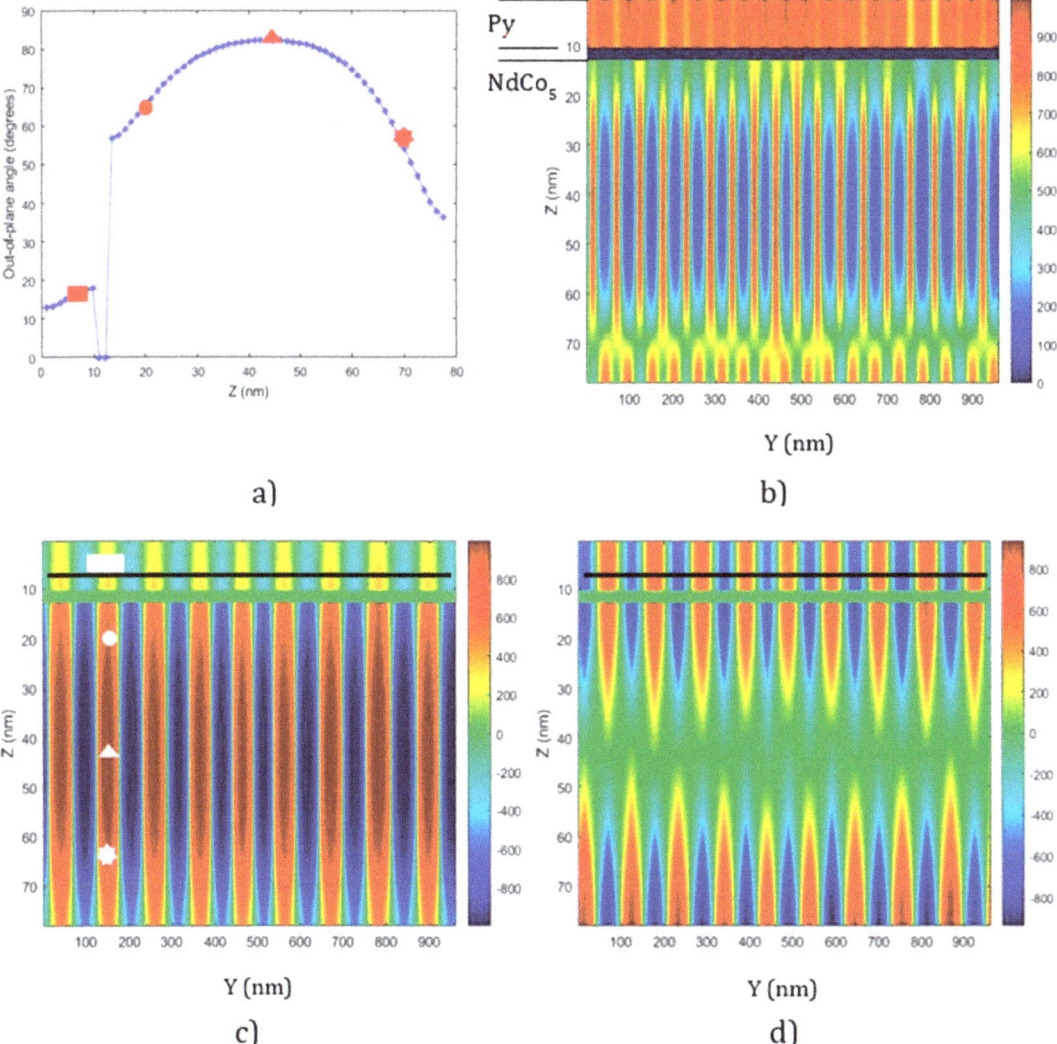

Figure 3. Remanent state of the NdCo$_5$-(2.5 nm-Al)-Py film; (**a**) 1-D profile of the out-of-plane angle through the thickness along an upwardly magnetized domain; (**b,d**) in-plane magnetization components: parallel, perpendicular to the previously applied H$_{DC}$; (**c**) out-of-plane magnetization. Red symbols of (**a**) are in correspondence with the white ones of (**c**). The magnetization units are KA/m. Black dashed lines in (**c,d**) indicate the place where the 1-D cuts in Figure 6b,c are obtained.

It means that the weak stripe domain distribution is imprinted partially in Permalloy and, due to its low anisotropy, Permalloy develops a 1-D periodic structure of magnetization. In addition to the non-zero M$_y$ inside the closure domains, an out-of-plane M$_z$ is developed (Figure 3c) and M_x becomes lower than M_S (Figure 3b). In Figure 3a we can see the 1-D variation of the angle between the magnetization and the film plane along the normal of the film. The variation is shown only for one of the domains with its magnetization pointing up (red domains in Figure 3c). Observe first that the out-of-plane angle does not cancel inside the closure domains (red circle and red star). These non-zero values imply that the magnetization at these places also contribute to the stray field in Permalloy. Secondly, the middle of the sample (red triangle) has a similar configuration to the one exhibited by hard PMA materials: the magnetization here is almost completely out-of-plane (in fact, the out-of-plane magnetic distribution of $NdCo_5$ in the trilayer is similar to its distribution as a single layer). Finally, the red rectangle indicates that the average Permalloy magnetization is rotated 15° from the film plane. This angle is mainly the result of the balance of the action on Permalloy magnetization of both the $NdCo_5$ stray field and the Permalloy demagnetizing field. Figure 3c contains white symbols signaling the positions where the red symbols of Figure 3a are placed. To complete this picture, we show in Figure 4a the full 3-D view of the whole structure and in Figure 4b, a zoom of the Permalloy and the $NdCo_5$ top part with unitary vectors [38].

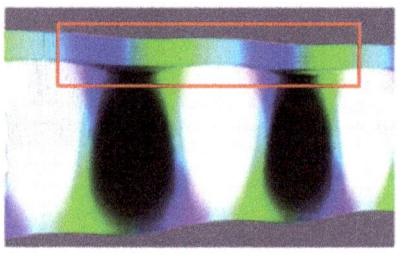 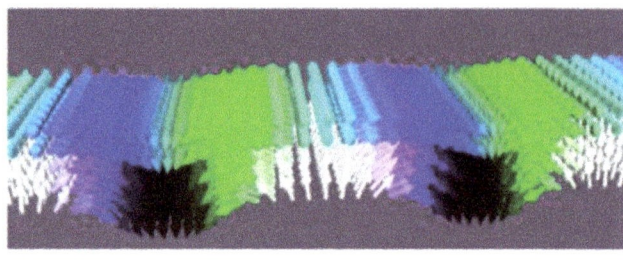

(a) (b)

Figure 4. Remanent state of the $NdCo_5$-(2.5 nm-Al)-Py; (**a**) global image of stripe domain structure; (**b**) zoom of the previous image (red triangle in (**a**)) containing unitary vectors [38].

2.3. Dynamics of Stripe Domain Dynamics

Once the static magnetic structure is characterized, one can go ahead with studying the dynamic properties of the stripe domains. The study is done by using the following transversal configuration where there are two applied magnetic fields: (i) a static one along a particular direction (the above mentioned H_{DC}) and (ii) a small time-varying field applied crossed to the former (h_{pulse}). Both are applied in-plane.

We will only focus on the case where H_{DC} is applied along the $NdCo_x$ in-plane hard axis: experimentally, the biggest effects have been found for this particular case [36]. Following the procedure reported in the methods section, we keep the magnetic system under linear response by applying a low amplitude h_{pulse}: 1mT. The h_{pulse} temporal variation follows a decreasing exponential to sample a broad frequency range with a unique numerical experiment (see Figure 5a). The temporal magnetic response (m_z) is followed for 15 ns. In Figure 5b we can see $m_z(t)$ for three H_{DC} values of decreasing amplitude. The obtained $m_z(t)$ is interpolated to values at regularly spaced times with Matlab© (this step must be done due to the fact that MuMax3 uses a variable time step procedure for the integration of the magnetization equations of motion). The interpolated $m_z(t)$ is then Fourier transformed to find the amplitudes in Fourier space. Figure 5c presents the corresponding amplitudes of Permalloy (red) and $NdCo_5$ (blue), normalized to the spectral for the amplitude of h_{pulse}, for the H_{DC} = 50nm case.

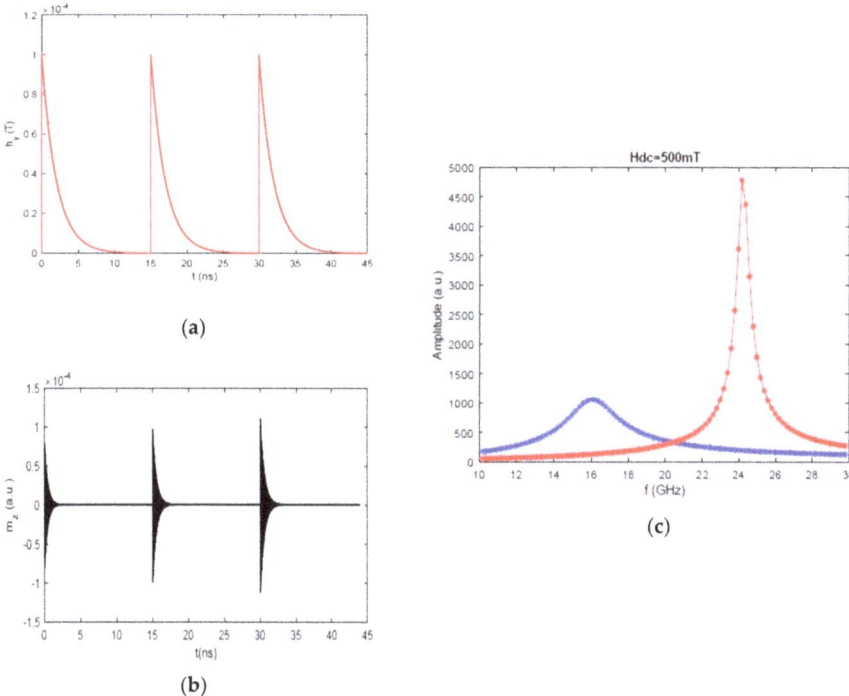

Figure 5. NdCo$_5$-(2.5 nm-Al)-Py; (**a**) temporal evolution of h$_{pulse}$ applied to the hybrid structure; (**b**) out-of-plane, m$_z$, dynamic Py response for H$_{DC}$ = 80, 60 and 50 mT (from left to right); (**c**) amplitude of the FT response of NdCo$_5$ (blue) and Permalloy (red) under 50 mT.

2.3.1. Reconfigurability

When the FMR is tracked, as H$_{DC}$ is varied, the VNA-FMR (f$_{res}$ vs. H) has a hysteretic behavior in analogy to the vibrating sample magnetometer hysteresis curves (M vs. H) [36]. The results of our simulations on a Py-(10nm-Al)-NdCo$_x$ trilayer (see methods) also account for the hysteretic behavior. Figure 6a includes the low field view of the change of the trilayer FMR when H$_{DC}$ is reduced from H$_{MAX}$ to −H$_{MAX}$ (black curve) and H$_{DC}$ increases from −H$_{MAX}$ to H$_{MAX}$ (red curve). As the saturation field of the system is close to 150 mT, H$_{MAX}$ was set to 800 mT. Despite the low density of simulation points, we can see that there is a difference in resonances for the descending-H$_{DC}$ (black) and the ascending-H$_{DC}$ (red) branches. We find that if H$_{DC}$ is 50 mT, the resonances are ~5.7 GHz (~6.1 GHz) for the ascending-H$_{DC}$ (descending-H$_{DC}$) applied fields. This implies a relative change of 6.6%. Experiments reflect a greater frequency difference: it can reach up to 25% for the used thin film geometry [36]. This discrepancy suggests that further magnetic parameters fitting needs to be done in these simulations.

Despite these divergences between the simulations and experiments, some conclusions can be obtained. What is the origin of this FMR difference? An answer to this question is reached by observing the characteristics of the two states of Figure 6a surrounded by a green rectangle. Both states are under the same field H$_{DC}$ (50 mT) but they have a different magnetic history. Figure 6b,c show 1-D cuts of two Permalloy reduced magnetization components: m$_z$ and m$_y$. The black (red) color indicates the results for the descending-H$_{DC}$ (ascending-H$_{DC}$) branch. The values are taken from the black dashed lines in Figure 3c,d. The out-of-plane component, m$_z$, is the one which better characterizes the dipolar interaction of NdCo$_x$ and Permalloy through Al. On the other hand, m$_y$ gives a measure of the capability of NdCo$_x$ to avoid magnetic charges. As can be seen, the ascending-H$_{DC}$ branch exhibits greater m$_y$ and m$_z$ than the descending-H$_{DC}$ branch.

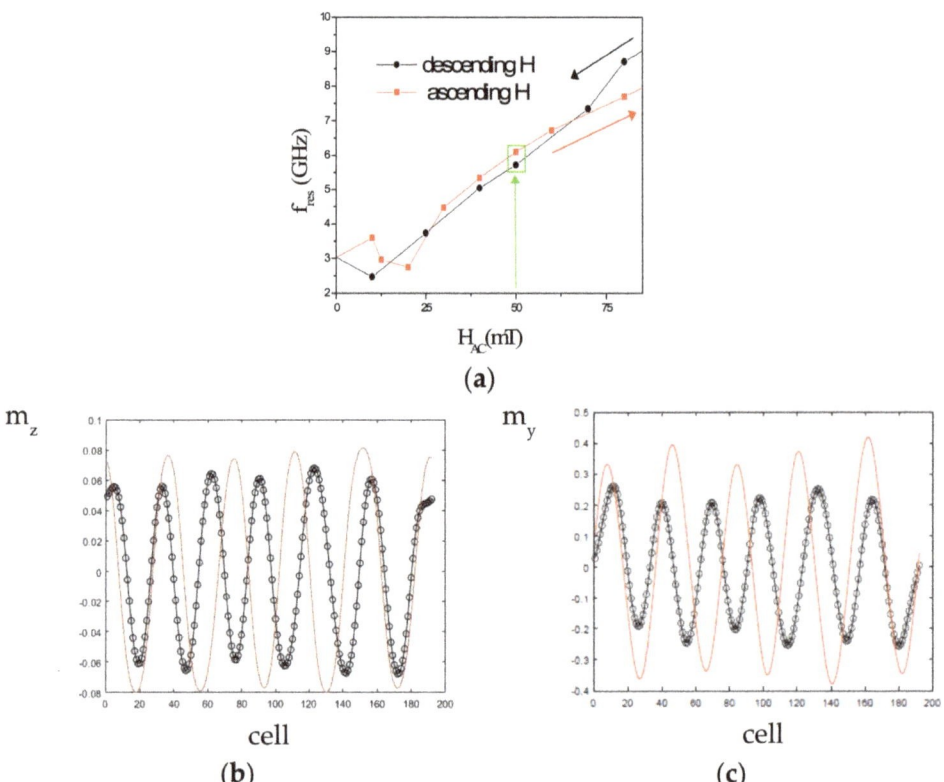

Figure 6. 65nm-NdCo$_x$-(10nm-Al)-Py: (**a**) Permalloy ferromagnetic resonance (FMR) evolution versus external field, 1-D profiles of reduced magnetization components under 50 mT; (**b**) m$_z$; (**c**) m$_y$ profiles are extracted from the black dashed lines at Figure 3c,d. In all Figures, black (red) colors belong to the descending-H$_{DC}$ (ascending-H$_{DC}$) magnetic field branch of (**a**).

It must be taken into account that the source of the periodical motion of magnetization around its equilibrium value is the so-called internal field [35]. Each energy term contributes to the total internal field with its own effective field. So, as a result of the difference in the static magnetization in the two states considered in Figure 6a, the internal field felt by Permalloy is different for the ascending-H$_{DC}$ and descending-H$_{DC}$ states. Roughly speaking, it can be said that the magnetization of the ascending-H$_{DC}$ state has an increased vortex character when compared to the magnetization of the descending branch. The greater vorticity of NdCo$_x$ magnetization implies a lowering in: (i) the NdCo$_x$ stray field on Permalloy; (ii) the Permalloy demagnetizing field (both resulting from the convolution of the corresponding magnetization and a geometrical tensor: $\overleftrightarrow{N}$); (iii) and the Permalloy exchange field (set by the second spatial derivate of Permalloy magnetization). On the other hand, there is an increase in the anisotropy field of Permalloy (proportional to m$_x^2$) [35]. All of these four fields act on the Permalloy magnetization. The fact that the FMR of the ascending-H$_{DC}$ state is the lowest means that the three former mentioned anisotropy fields cannot counterbalance the action of the anisotropy field in stablishing the Permalloy FMR.

We performed another kind of analysis of the hysteretic behavior of the f$_{res}$ vs. H$_{DC}$ curves. We excited the whole film with a sinusoidal h$_{AC}$ field of amplitude 1mT (Figure 7a).

The individual FMR of each state was accounted for in h_{AC}. Along Figure 7, the results marked with a green (blue) color belongs to the descending-H_{DC} (ascending-H_{DC}) state under H_{DC} = 50 mT. Even if the whole temporal evolution is saved (Figure 7b), we just analyzed the stationary range inside the colored rectangles (Figure 7c,d). The temporal evolution of the average Permalloy magnetization (red curves) along h_{AC} (black curves) for these two states results in two different elliptical motions of m_x at each FMR. The ellipses are the combined result of a sinusoidal $m_y(t)$ with a different amplitude and different phase relative to $h_{AC}(t)$. The ascending-H_{DC} state has an elliptical motion of lower amplitude and lower m_y-h_{AC} dephasing. These two facts confirm the interpretation given above: the ascending-H_{DC} state has the lowest internal field amplitude.

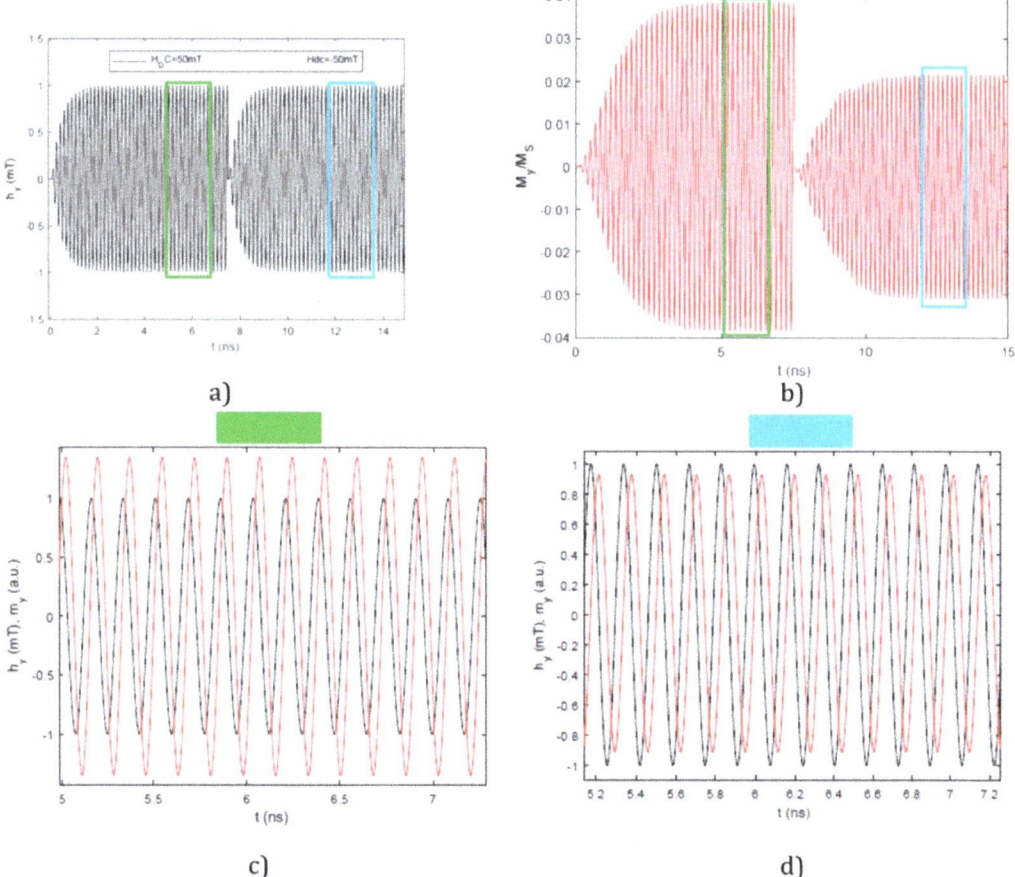

Figure 7. NdCo$_x$-(10nm-Al)-Py: (**a**) sinusoidal h_{ACx} temporal evolution for: descending-H_{DC} (0–7.5 ns)/ascending-H_{DC} (7.5 ns–15 ns); (**b**) corresponding average $m_y(t)$ in Permalloy, joint temporal stationary variation of average m_y in Permalloy and h_{AC}; (**c**) descending-H_{DC} (green); (**d**) ascending-H_{DC} (blue).

With this change in FMR, the hybrid trilayer can be used in future reconfigurable resonators (with performance at relatively low magnetic fields). Its working principle is as follows: once the system is set at one frequency under a given field strength (here called operation-field: ~40 mT [36]) reconfigurability is achieved due to a so-called erasing-field. The erasing-field must match two characteristics: (i) it may be strong enough to put the system in the reversible part of the hysteresis loop: ~75 mT [36]; (ii) it must be antiparallel to the actual average magnetization of the stripe domains: $\pm m_x$. Once the erasing-field is applied and the applied field returns to the operating-field value, the hybrid will work at the other available FMR.

2.3.2. Nonreciprocity

Finally, we want to point out another interesting characteristic of the hybrid material presented. As will shortly be proved, simulations show that our hybrid system offers nonreciprocity in the spin waves emitted from an exciting antenna. This property is useful in the building up of logic devices, switches and interconnects. Behind the motion of the whole magnetization (the FMR mode) a motion of the magnetization at selected parts inside the sample can be also achieved [39]. This motion is carried by spin waves. There is a recent interest in using the domain walls as channels of spin waves motion through field confinement [23]. Due to the especial geometry of the stripe domains (see Figure 2a), we have explored the capability of our weak stripe domains to channel spin waves.

The numerical experiment has been done again on the NdCo$_x$-(10nm-Al)-Py trilayer using only its remanent state. The spin wave motion has been performed by applying h_{AC} only locally (see Method section). Figure 8 shows the obtained results for a h_{AC} frequency equal to 2.5 GHz. A temporal snapshot of Δm_y is presented: the difference between the reduced magnetization parallel to h_{AC}, $m_y(\tau)$, and its equilibrium value $m_y(\tau = 0)$. Figure 8 give us two characteristics of the excited spin waves: (i) spin waves mainly propagate along one sense $\vec{k}$, for a given domain (along the other sense, $-\vec{k}$, spin waves are highly damped); (ii) the allowed $\vec{k}$ are antiparallel in two neighboring domains (when the blue curve represents the guided spin waves along $\vec{k}$, the red curve represents spin waves along $-\vec{k}$). When analyzing the distributions of m_x and Δm_x it can be stated that the allowed spin waves excited by the local h_{AC} at a given domain obey the following law: $\vec{k} = \vec{m} \times \vec{n}$ [40]. Here, $\vec{n}$ denotes the film normal and $\vec{m}$ the reduced magnetization of the Permalloy domains. The spin wavelength reported in Figure 8, λ_{SW}, is close to 122 nm for both Permalloy domains. The wavevector is parallel to the previously applied field H_{DC} (which at the same time sets the stripe domain/spin wave channel direction) and its module $\left|\vec{k}\right|$ is 51 rad$\times\mu$m^{-1}. The imaging of the spin waves at this spatial scale can be reached with X-ray techniques as recently demonstrated [41].

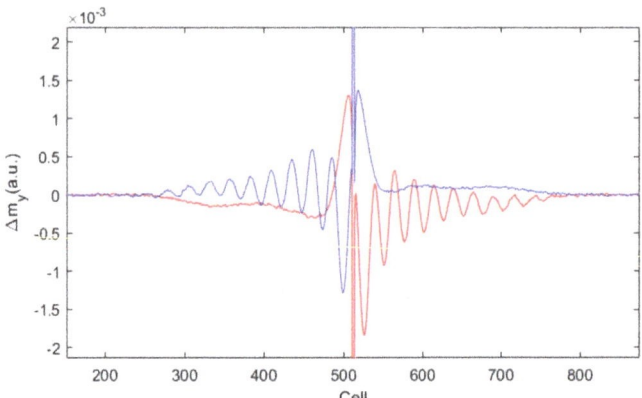

Figure 8. NdCo$_x$-(10nm-Al)-Py. Temporal snapshot of the deviation of the y-component of the Permalloy reduced magnetization from its equilibrium value. The exciting field frequency is 2.5GHz. H_{DC} = 0 mT.

Several origins have been found for explaining nonreciprocity in magnetic multilayers: interfacial-DMI exchange, spin pumping-based nonreciprocal damping, dipolar interactions or superficial anisotropies [42] and the nonreciprocal emission of waves by the antenna [43]. While the first two possibilities do not apply to our simulations (as they imply the existence of other kinds of materials) the three later ones are possible candidates. It is known that Ni-Al and Co-Al alloys form at room temperature, so the Al diffusion in Permalloy and NdCo$_x$ cannot be neglected [44,45]. Interdiffusion will decrease the actual magnetic volume of the layers and/or promote the creation of different magnetic parameters at interfaces. Our micromagnetic simulations assume that the Permalloy and NdCo$_x$ parameters are uniform so there is no room for special superficial parameters causing nonreciprocity (although they can be added to evaluate its influence and to better fit the experimental results). On the other hand, it must be considered that the NdCo$_x$ stray field is non-homogeneous along the film normal: its magnitude gets lower as we move away from the Permalloy-Al interface. The effect of this decay could be cast in terms of an effective superficial anisotropy or a graded material [46]. It is likely that the magnetization in Permalloy is parallel to the stray field of NdCo$_x$ (which sustains the interaction between Py and NdCo$_x$ in our system) and it makes the major contribution to the internal field felt by Permalloy. Further studies need to be taken to confirm this hypothesis and quantify the influence of each source.

For future research, several directions can be highlighted. The resonant frequency can be boosted by thin film patterning [47] or by using synthetic antiferromagnets (SAF) [48] and ferrimagnets [49] instead of Permalloy. Another promising area of research is the light control of magnetism which allows for reaching the faster terahertz range [50]. In this sense, stripe domains in high Q materials have been rotated by light pulses recently [51]. On the other hand, a higher miniaturization level could be achieved by an extension of spin waves to the pure exchange driven regime which results in lower wavelengths [52]. Finally, in order to build highly energy efficient spin-wave devices, voltage driven magnets should be fabricated [53,54].

3. Conclusions

In summary, we have shown how a hybrid magnetic material presenting weak stripe domains can exhibit the reconfigurability of certain functions in the GHz range. The system works thanks to the inherent crossed anisotropies of the system. These combined anisotropies allow the selection of different internal field strengths in the system through a proper magnetic history. We showed that reconfigurability is achieved under a magnetic field strength one order of magnitude lower than in previous systems [55]. The nonreciprocal emission of spin waves was also numerically shown, originated by interdiffusion effects at interfaces, inhomogeneity of stray field from the PMA material and/or the nonreciprocal emission of spin waves from the antennas. These two characteristics (reconfigurability and nonreciprocity) convert our hybrid system in a candidate for future magnonic devices.

4. Materials and Methods

Micromagnetic simulations were performed with the following magnetic parameters of our former work [36]: γ is 15.9×10^{10} radT^{-1}s^{-1}; for NdCo$_5$: $K_\perp = 16.2 \times 10^4$ J/m^3, $M_S = 1000$ KA/m, $A = 0.7 \times 10^{-11}$ J/m; for Py: $K_u = 423$ J/m^3, $M_S = 846$ KA/m, $A = 1.2 \times 10^{-11}$ J/m; for NdCo$_x$ we tentatively used $K_\perp = 5.4 \times 10^4$ J/m^3, $M_S = 390$ KA/m, $A = 0.35 \times 10^{-11}$ J/m. γ is the gyromagnetic ratio, $K_\perp$ the uniaxial PMA, M_S the saturation magnetization, A the exchange stiffness constant and K_u the uniaxial IMA. The trilayers were modelled by cells with a 5×5 nm^2 in-plane surface. Its height was 2.5 nm (2 nm) for an aluminum spacer thickness of 5 nm (10 nm). The surface of the working area is 0.48^2 (0.96^2) µm^2 for the NdCo$_5$ (Py/Al/NdCo$_x$) sample. Two-dimensional periodic boundary conditions are applied in the plane to approximate an infinite sample behavior. The visualization of Figures 2 and 3 was done with Matlab©. The visualization of Figure 4 was done with Muview [38].

The different dynamic responses were simulated as follows. The results in Figure 5 were obtained with the methodology already described in [36]. The results in Figures 7 and 8 were obtained by applying a sinusoidal source having a soft increasing envelope: (1-exp(-at)) sin(w×t), for t > 0. a = 0.5 ns^{-1} as in [36]. The damping parameter is reduced from α = 1 (used for static simulations) to a smaller value of 0.08 for NdCo$_x$ and 0.01 for Permalloy [36]. For Figure 8: (i) the surface of the working space was changed from squared (see above) to rectangular: 5.62 × 0.96 μm^2; (ii) the periodic boundary conditions were suppressed; (iii) an enveloping area with increased damping at the edges of the working area was used to simulate infinite extent samples (absorbing boundary conditions) [56]. The magnetic field was applied on a single row spin, transversal to the wavevector, $\vec{k}$ in order to take advantage of the absorbing boundary conditions (the cell 512th in Figure 8). We have checked that the width of the simulated antenna did not change the results presented up to a 0.8 μm wide antenna.

Funding: This work was funded by the Spanish Ministry of Science and Innovation (Project PID2019-104604RB/AEI/10.13039/501100011033).

Institutional Review Board Statement: Not applicable.

Informed Consent Statement: Not applicable.

Data Availability Statement: Mumax scripts are available from the authors upon request.

Acknowledgments: This work is dedicated to J. M. Alameda on his 71th birthday.

Conflicts of Interest: The author declares no conflict of interest.

Abbreviations

The following abbreviations are used in this manuscript:

1-D	Uni-Dimensional
3-D	Three-Dimensional
AC	Alternating Current
CMOS	Complementary Metal-Oxide-Semiconductor
DMI	Dzyaloshinksii-Moryia interaction
DC	Direct Current
FFT	Fourier Fast Transform
FMR	Ferromagnetic Resonance
GPU	Graphical Processing Unit
GHz	Gigahertz
IMA	In-plane Magnetic Anisotropy
PMA	Out-of-plane Magnetic Anisotropy
t_c	Critical Thickness

References

1. Iwasaki, S. Perpendicular magnetic recording-Its development and recent realization. *J. Magn. Magn. Mater.* **2012**, *324*, 244–247. [CrossRef]
2. Vavaro, G.; Laureti, S.; Fiorani, D. L1$_0$ FePt-based thin films for future perpendicular magnetic recording media. *J. Magn. Magn. Mater.* **2014**, *368*, 415–420. [CrossRef]
3. Spezzani, C.; Fortuna, F.; Delaunay, R.; Popescu, H.; Sacchi, M. X-Ray holographic imaging of magnetic order in patterned Co/Pd multilayers. *Phys. Rev. B* **2013**, *88*, 224420. [CrossRef]
4. Miguel, J.; Peters, J.F.; Toulemonde, O.M.; Dhesi, S.S.; Brookes, N.B.; Goedkoop, J.B. X-Ray resonant magnetic scattering study of magnetic stripe domains in a-GdFe thin films. *Phys. Rev. B* **2006**, *74*, 094437. [CrossRef]
5. Voltan, S.; Cirillo, C.; Snijder, H.J.; Lahabi, K.; García-Santiago, A.; Hernandez, J.M.; Atanasio, C.; Aarts, J. Emergence of the stripe domains in patterned permalloy films. *Phys. Rev. B* **2016**, *99*, 094406. [CrossRef]
6. Zhang, Y.; Wang, S.-S.; Li, F.; Jiang, W.; Zhang, Z.-L.; Chen, Z.-Y. Thickness and temperature dependent out-of-plane anisotropy of amorphous CoSiB thin films. *Phys. Stat. Sol. (B) Basic Solid State Phys.* **2018**, *255*, 1800041. [CrossRef]
7. Acher, O.; Boscher, C.; Brulé, B.; Perrin, G.; Vukadinovic, N.; Suran, G.; Joisten, H. Microwave permeability of ferromagnetic thin films with stripe domain structure. *J. Appl. Phys.* **1997**, *81*, 4057–4059. [CrossRef]

8. Song, N.; Lv, B.; Meng, J.; Gong, Z.; Zhang, X.; Zhang, Q. Tunable high-frequency properties of flexible FeGa films with rotatable stripe domain. *J. Magn. Magn. Mater.* **2020**, *519*, 167510. [CrossRef]
9. Bisero, D.; Fin, S.; Ranchal, R. Rotation of stripe domains in a sputter deposited Tb-Fe-Ga thin film. *Thin Solid Films* **2017**, *628*, 158–162. [CrossRef]
10. Tacchi, S.; Silvani, R.; Carlotti, G.; Marangolo, M.; Eddrief, M.; Rettori, A.; Pinni, M.G. Strongly hybridized dipole-exchange spin waves in thin Fe-N ferromagnetic films. *Phys. Rev. B* **2019**, *100*, 104406. [CrossRef]
11. Ebels, U.; Buda, L.; Ounadjela, K.; Wigen, P. Ferromagnetic resonance excitation of two-dimensional wall structure in magnetic stripe domains. *Phys. Rev. B* **2001**, *63*, 174437. [CrossRef]
12. Hierro-Rodríguez, A.; Cid, R.; Vélez, M.; Rodríguez-Rodríguez, G.; Martín, J.I.; Álvarez-Prado, L.M.; Alameda, J.M. Topological defects and misfit strain in magnetic stripe domains of lateral multilayers with perpendicular magnetic anisotropy. *Phys. Rev. Lett.* **2012**, *109*, 117202. [CrossRef]
13. Álvarez-Prado, L.-M.; Pérez, G.T.; Morales, R.; Salas, F.; Alameda, J.M. Perpendicular anisotropy detected by transversely biased initial susceptibility via the magneto-optic Kerr effect in Fe_xSi_{1-x} and FE_xSi_{1-x}/Si multilayers: Theory and experiment. *Phys. Rev. B* **1996**, *56*, 3306–3317. [CrossRef]
14. Álvarez-Prado, L.M.; Alameda, J.M. Micromagnetism of nanowires with low out-of-plane anisotropy. *Phys. B Condens. Matter.* **2004**, *343*, 241–246. [CrossRef]
15. Voltairas, P.A.; Fotiadis, D.I.; Massalas, C.V. Estimation of exchange constant A and g factor for Co_xNi_{1-x} microspheres from size-dependent ferromagnetic resonance modes. *J. Magn. Magn. Mater.* **2000**, *217*, L1–L4. [CrossRef]
16. Cao, D.; Cheng, X.; Pan, L.; Zhu, Z.; Feng, H.; Wang, Z.; Wang, J.; Liu, Q.; Han, G. Estimating the in.-plane anisotropy and saturation magnetization of magnetic films. *IEEE Trans. Mag.* **2017**, *52*, 2000706. [CrossRef]
17. Papp, A.; Csaba, G.; Dey, H.; Madami, M.; Porod, W.; Carlotti, G. Wavegiudes as sources of short-wavelength spin waves for low-energy ICT applications. *Eur. Phys. J. B* **2018**, *91*, 107. [CrossRef]
18. Salansky, N.M.; Khrustalev, B.P. Peculiarities of the resonance absorption in the magnetic films magnetized to non-saturated state. *Czech. J. Phys.* **1971**, *21*, 419–428. [CrossRef]
19. Trautvetter, C.-U. Spin-Wave spectra below saturation magnetization and at various orientations. *Phys. Stat. Sol. (B) Basic Solid State Phys.* **1974**, *65*, 671–676. [CrossRef]
20. Lee, S.J.; Tsai, C.C.; Cho, H.; Seo, M.; Eom, T.; Nam, W.; Lee, Y.P.; Ketterson, J.B. Hysteretic characteristics of low-field microwave absorption of a Co thin film. *J. Appl. Phys.* **2009**, *106*, 063922. [CrossRef]
21. García-Sanchez, F.; Borys, P.; Soucaille, R.; Adam, J.-P.; Stamps, R.L.; Kim, J.-V. Narrow Magnomic waveguides based on domain walls. *Phys. Rev. Lett.* **2015**, *114*, 247206. [CrossRef] [PubMed]
22. Wang, L.; Gao, L.; Jin, L.; Liai, Y.; Wen, T.; Tang, X.; Zheng, W.; Zhong, Z. Magnonic a waveguide based on exchange-spring magnetic structure. *AIP Adv.* **2018**, *8*, 055103. [CrossRef]
23. Grassi, M.; Geilen, M.; Louis, D.; Morteza, M.; Brächer, T.; Hehn, M.; Stoeffler, D.; Bailleul, M.; Pirro, P.; Henry, Y. Slow-Wave-Based Nanomagnonic Diode. *Phys. Rev. Appl.* **2020**, *14*, 024044. [CrossRef]
24. Park, H.-K.; Lee, J.-H.; Yang, J.; Kim, S.-K. Interaction of spin waves propagating along narrow domain walls with a magnetic vortex in a thin-film-nanostrip cross-structure. *J. Appl. Phys.* **2020**, *127*, 183906. [CrossRef]
25. Chang, L.-J.; Chen, J.; Qu, D.; Tsai, L.-Z.; Liu, Y.-F.; Kao, M.-Y.; Liang, J.-Z.; Wu, T.-S.; Chuang, T.-M.; Yu, H.; et al. Spin wave injection and propagation in a magnetic nanochannel from a vortex core. *Nanoletters* **2020**, *20*, 3140–3146. [CrossRef]
26. Haldar, A.; Kumar, D.; Adayeye, O.A. A reconfigurable waveguide for energy-efficient transmission and local manipulation of information in a nanomagnetic device. *Nat. Nanotech.* **2016**, *11*, 437–443. [CrossRef]
27. Wang, Q.; Pirro, P.; Verba, R.; Slavin, A.; Hillebrands, B.; Chumak, A.V. Reconfigurable nanoscale spin-wave directional coupler. *Sci. Adv.* **2018**, e1701517. [CrossRef]
28. Manipatruni, S.; Nikonov, D.E.; Young, I.A. Beyond CMOS computing with spin and polarization. *Nat. Phys.* **2018**, *14*, 338–343. [CrossRef]
29. Lehrer, S.S. Rotatable Anisotropy in negative magnetostriction Ni-Fe films. *J. Appl. Phys.* **1963**, *34*, 1207–1209. [CrossRef]
30. Murayama, Y. Micromagnetics on stripe domain films. I. Critical cases. *J. Phys. Soc. Jpn.* **1966**, *21*, 2253–2266. [CrossRef]
31. Gajdek, M.; Wasilewski, W. The description of the domain structure in thin ferromagnetic films with thickness near the critical value. *J. Magn. Magn. Mater.* **1983**, *37*, 246–252. [CrossRef]
32. Pant, B.B.; Matsuyama, K. Numerical investigation of stripe structures in ferromagnetic thin films with perpendicular anisotropy. *Jpn. J. Appl. Phys.* **1993**, *32*, 3817–3822. [CrossRef]
33. Marty, A.; Samson, Y.; Belakhovsky, M.; Dudzik, E.; Dürr, H.; Dhesi, S.S.; Van der Laan, G.; Goedkoop, J.B. Weak-stripe magnetic domain evolution with an in-plane field in epitaxial thin flms: Model versus experimental results. *J. Appl. Phys.* **2000**, *87*, 5472–5474. [CrossRef]
34. Sukstanskii, A.L.; Primak, K.I. Domain structure in an ultrathin ferromagnetic film. *J. Magn. Magn. Mater.* **1997**, *169*, 31–38. [CrossRef]
35. Leliaert, J.; Dvornik, M.; Mulkers, J.; De Clercq, J.; Milošević, M.V.; Van Waeyenberge, W. Fast micromagnetic simulations on GPU-recent advances made with mumax^3. *J. Phys D Appl. Phys.* **2018**, *51*, 123002. [CrossRef]

36. Markó, D.; Valdés-Bango, F.; Quirós, C.; Hierro-Rodríguez, A.; Vélez, M.; Martín, J.I.; Alameda, J.M.; Schmool, D.S.; Álvarez-Prado, L.M. Tunable ferromagnetic resonance in coupled trilayers with crossed in-plane and perpendicular magnetic anisotropy. *Appl. Phys. Lett.* **2019**, *115*, 082401. [CrossRef]
37. Gruszecki, P.; Banerjee, C.; Mruczkiewicz, M.; Hellwing, O.; Barman, A.; Krawczyk, M. The influence of the internal domain wall structure on spin wave band structure in periodic magnetic domain patterns. *Sol. Stat. Phys.* **2019**, *70*, 79–312.
38. Muview2 by Graham Rowlands. Available online: https://grahahamrow.github.io/Mumax2/ (accessed on 9 December 2020).
39. Camara, I.S.; Tacchi, S.; Garnier, L.-C.; Eddrief, M.; Fortuna, F.; Carlotti, C.; Marangolo, M. Magnetization dynamics of weak stripe domains in Fe-N thin films: A multi-technique complementary approach. *J. Phys. C Condens. Matter.* **2017**, *29*, 465803. [CrossRef] [PubMed]
40. Sekiguchi, K.; Yamada, K.; Seo, S.M.; Lee, K.J.; Chiba, D.; Kobayashi, K.; Ono, T. Nonreciprocal emission of spin-wave packet in NiFe film. *Appl. Phys. Lett.* **2010**, *97*, 022508. [CrossRef]
41. Träger, N.; Gruszecki, P.; Lisieki, F.; Groß, F.; Förster, J.; Weigand, M.; Głowiński, H.; Kuświk, P.; Dubowik, J.; Shütz, G.; et al. Real space observation of magnon interaction with driven space-time crystals. *Phys. Rev. Lett.* **2021**, *126*, 057201. [CrossRef]
42. Gladii, O.; Haidar, M.; Henry, Y.; Kostylev, M.P.; Bailleul, M. Frequency nonreciprocity of surface spin wave in permalloy thin films. *Phys. Rev. B* **2016**, *93*, 054430. [CrossRef]
43. Schneider, T.; Serga, A.A.; Neumann, T.; Hillebrands, B.; Kostylev, M.P. Phase reciprocity of spin-wave excitation by a microstrip antenna. *Phys. Rev. B* **2008**, *77*, 214411. [CrossRef]
44. Gallardo, R.A.; Alvarado-Seguel, P.; Schneider, T.; Gonzalez-Fuentes, C.; Roldán-Molina, A.; Lenz, K.; Lindler, J.; Landeros, P. Spin-wave non-reciprocity in magnetization-graded ferromagnetic films. *New J. Phys.* **2019**, *21*, 033026. [CrossRef]
45. Wang, Y.; Xing, Z.; Qiao, Y.; Jiang, H.; Yu, X.; Ye, F.; Li, Y.; Wang, L.; Liu, B. Asymmetric atomic diffusion and phase growth at the Al/Ni and Ni/Al interfaces in the Al-Ni multilayers obtained by magnetron deposition. *J. Alloys Comp.* **2019**, *789*, 887–893. [CrossRef]
46. Gas, P.; Bergman, C.; Lábár, J.L.; Barna, P.B.; d'Heurle, F.M. Formation of embedded Co nanoparticles by reaction in Al/Co multilayers and impact on phase sequence. *Appl. Phys. Lett.* **2008**, *84*, 2421. [CrossRef]
47. Talapatra, A.; Adayeye, O.A. Linear chains of nanomagnets: Engineering the effective magnetic anisotropy. *Nanoscale* **2020**, *12*, 20933–20944. [CrossRef]
48. Sud, A.; Zollitsch, C.W.; Kaminaki, A.; Dion, T.; Kahn, S.; Iihama, S.; Mikazumi, S.; Kurebayashi, H. Tunable magnon-magnon coupling mediated by dynamic dipolar interaction in synthetic antiferromagnets. *Phys. Rev. B* **2020**, *102*, 017203. [CrossRef]
49. Funada, S.; Nishimura, T.; Shiota, Y.; Kasukawa, S.; Ishibashi, M.; Moriyama, T.; Ono, T. Spin-wave propagation in ferrimagnetic Gd_xCo_{1-x}. *Jpn. J. Appl. Phys.* **2019**, *58*, 080909. [CrossRef]
50. Yoshimine, Y.; Tanaka, Y.Y.; Shimura, T.; Satoh, T. Unidirectional control of optically induced spin waves. *Eur. Phys. Lett.* **2017**, *117*, 67001–67004. [CrossRef]
51. López-Flores, V.; Mawass, M.-A.; Herrero-Albillos, J.; Uenal, A.-A.; Valencia, S.; Kronast, F.; Boeglin, C. A local view of the laser induced magnetization domain dynamics in CoPd stripe domains at the picosecond time scale. *J. Phys. C* **2020**, *32*, 465801.
52. Che, P.; Baumraertl, K.; Kúlolóvá, A.; Dubd, C.; Grundler, D. Efficient conversion od exchange magnons below 100 nm by magnetic coplanar waveguides. *Nat. Commun.* **2020**, *11*, 1145. [CrossRef] [PubMed]
53. Verba, R.; Carpentieri, M.; Finocchio, G.; Tiberkevich, V.; Slavin, A. Excitation of propagating spin waves in ferromagnetic nanowires my microwave voltage-controlled magnetic anisotropy. *Sci. Rep.* **2016**, *6*, 25018. [CrossRef] [PubMed]
54. Rana, B.; Otani, Y. Towards magnonic devices based on voltage-controlled anisotropy. *Comm. Phys.* **2019**, *2*, 90. [CrossRef]
55. Tang, M.; Zhao, B.; Zhu, W.; Zhu, Z.; Jin, Q.Y.; Zhang, Z. Controllable interfacial effects on the magnetic dynamic properties of perpendicular $[Co/Ni]_5/Cu/TbCo$ composite thin films. *ACS Appl. Mater. Interf.* **2018**, *10*, 5090–5098. [CrossRef]
56. Venkat, G.; Fanghor, H.; Prabhakar, A. Absorbing boundary layers for spin wave micromagnetics. *J. Magn. Magn. Mater.* **2018**, *450*, 34–39. [CrossRef]

Article

Effects of Perpendicular Magnetic Field Annealing on the Structural and Magnetic Properties of [Co/Ni]$_2$/PtMn Thin Films

Roshni Yadav [1], Chun-Hsien Wu [1], I-Fen Huang [1], Xu Li [2,*], Te-Ho Wu [3] and Ko-Wei Lin [1,*]

1. Department of Materials Science and Engineering, National Chung Hsing University, Taichung 402, Taiwan; roshniyadav05@gmail.com (R.Y.); sam_ntust@hotmail.com (C.-H.W.); 2305danny@gmail.com (I-F.H.)
2. Department of Physics, Xiamen University, Xiamen 361005, China
3. Graduate School of Materials Science, National Yunlin University of Science and Technology, Yunlin 640, Taiwan; wuth@yuntech.edu.tw
* Correspondence: xuliphys@xmu.edu.cn (X.L.); kwlin@dragon.nchu.edu.tw (K.-W.L.)

Abstract: In this study, [Co/Ni]$_2$/PtMn thin films with different PtMn thicknesses (2.7 to 32.4 nm) were prepared on Si/SiO$_2$ substrates. The post-deposition perpendicular magnetic field annealing (MFA) processes were carried out to modify the structures and magnetic properties. The MFA process also induced strong interlayer diffusion, rendering a less sharp interface between Co and Ni and PtMn layers. The transmission electron microscopy (TEM) lattice image analysis has shown that the films consisted of face-centered tetragonal (fct) PtMn (ordered by MFA), body-centered cubic (bcc) NiMn (due to intermixing), in addition to face-centered cubic (fcc) Co, Ni, and PtMn phases. The peak shift (2-theta from 39.9° to 40.3°) in X-ray diffraction spectra also confirmed the structural transition from fcc PtMn to fct PtMn after MFA, in agreement with those obtained by lattice images in TEM. The interdiffusion induced by MFA was also evidenced by the depth profile of X-ray photoelectron spectroscopy (XPS). Further, the magnetic properties measured by vibrating sample magnetometry (VSM) have shown an increased coercivity in MFA-treated samples. This is attributed to the presence of ordered fct PtMn, and NiMn phases exchange coupled to the ferromagnetic [Co/Ni]$_2$ layers. The vertical shift ($M_{shift} = -0.03$ memu) of the hysteresis loops is ascribed to the pinned spins resulting from perpendicular MFA processes.

Keywords: [Co/Ni]$_2$/PtMn multilayers; magnetic field annealing; hysteresis loop vertical shift; exchange coupling

1. Introduction

The discovery of magnetization switching by spin-orbit torques (SOT) has created new opportunities for digital and analog spintronic applications. The antiferromagnet/ferromagnet (AFM/FM) [1] systems engaging heavy metals are promising building blocks for SOT devices because of their enhanced control over the interface [2] and the effects like increased coercivity and shift in the hysteresis loops along the field axis, which was observed in the AFM/FM system [2,3]. The exchange bias field in such a system provides the required effective field for magnetization switching, enabling field-free SOT switching. Unravelling the magnetic properties of such a system is of vital importance for developing SOT devices. Fukami et al. showed the magnetization switching in the absence of applied field in the PtMn (AFM) and Co/Ni (FM) bilayer system with a perpendicular easy axis due to the exchange bias of the AFM [4]. Further, Van DerBrink et al. also reported the switching of the perpendicular magnetization by an in-plane current in the absence of magnetic field in the Pt/Co/IrMn structure [5]. The investigation on the local spin structure at the FM/AFM interface also helps to understand the correlation between the AFM crystalline structure and the amount of magnetization reversal. The coercivity (H_c, the reverse field required to reduce the magnetization to zero [6,7]) of AFM/FM system was reported to be strongly dependent on the layer structure. Hu et al. showed that the exchange coupling might cause reduced coercivity, depending on the interface coupling and AFM layer thickness. The strong exchange bias but weak coercivity can be obtained depending on the microstructural parameters in FM/AFM bilayer systems [8]. A study in bi-and tri-layered IrMn/NiFe further revealed that the H_c is not only dependent on the thickness of the AFM-layer but also on the alternative order of the layer deposition [9].

PtMn is one of the most extensively used CuAu-I ($L1_0$) type antiferromagnetic materials for the exchange biasing [10,11]. The as-deposited PtMn is non-magnetic with a face-centered cubic (fcc) structure. It transforms into antiferromagnetic with a face-centered tetragonal (fct) structure after annealing at elevated temperatures. The transition from fcc to chemically ordered fct phase after the annealing facilities strong exchange coupling field at the AFM/FM interface [12]. $(Co/Ni)_n$ was proposed to be a prototypical perpendicularly magnetized system [13]. Krishnaswamy et al. studied the structure and current-induced switching behavior of the magnetic domains in PtMn/[Co/Ni]$_{1.5}$ and PtMn/[Co/Ni]$_{2.5}$ clarifying the memristive behavior in AFM/FM structures and for further optimization of spin-orbit torque switching [14]. Hence, $(Co/Ni)_n$ multilayers with the heavy metal antiferromagnets have raised great interest because of their strong Dzyaloshinskii-Moriya Interaction (DMI), large SOT and SOT-induced magnetic switching in $(Co/Ni)_n$ [15–18].

In the previous research, the as-deposited PtMn/[Co/Ni]$_2$ multilayers typically possess in-plane magnetic anisotropy [1], which is not a favorable SOT application. MFA [19–21] is an effective methodology for modifying the magnetism of exchange-coupled films [22]. Li et al. reported that the annealed NiO/CoFe thin films show the morphological changes to nanocomposite single layers. The structural and compositional changes result in tailored magnetic properties, increased surface roughness and altered chemical composition, revealing that the MFA process at varied temperatures plays a pivotal role in the magnetism and film compositions [21]. While the SOT switching behavior in the annealed PtMn/[Co/Ni] multilayers was already reported [23], how the annealing process influenced the microstructure and magnetic properties of such a system remain unclear. Vergès et al. studied the spin-orbit torque (SOT) switching in as-deposited and annealed Pt/[Co/Ni]$_2$/PtMn samples. The as-deposited sample shows no exchange bias effect, and the SOT switching is observed under in-plane applied field. However, the annealed sample shows a moderate switching current in a zero magnetic field [24].

In this paper, we have studied the microstructure and magnetic properties of as-deposited and magnetic field annealed (MFA) Ag(8 nm)/[Co(2.5 nm)/Ni(2.3 nm)]$_2$/PtMn(t_{PtMn}) thin films. The correlation between the enhanced exchange coupling and the phase transition after magnetic field annealing provides a new understanding of the magnetism for multilayer PtMn-based ferromagnetic/antiferromagnetic film systems.

2. Results and Discussion

Figure 1a,b shows the 1×1 μm^2 surface morphology of as-deposited and magnetic field annealed Ag/[Co/Ni]$_2$/PtMn(t_{PtMn} = 32.4 nm) multilayers characterized by AFM. The film is uniform and possesses a smooth surface. As compared to the as-deposited thin film, the average roughness increases from 1.1 to 1.5 nm after the annealing process. This can be explained by the grain growth, which yields an increase in the surface roughness.

The crystalline structures of as-deposited and annealed Ag/[Co/Ni]$_2$/PtMn(t_{PtMn}) multilayers were characterized by X-ray diffraction (XRD), as shown in Figure 2a. The XRD characterization affirmed the polycrystalline structure of the thin films. Considerable changes were observed for the as-deposited and annealed thin films with the thickest PtMn (t_{PtMn} = 32.4 nm) layer. The diffraction peak at 39.9° (d = 2.25 Å) changed to 40.1° (d = 2.24 Å) after annealing, which corresponds to the phase transition from fcc PtMn (111) to fct PtMn (111). The d-spacing change from 2.25 Å to 2.24 Å verifies the phase transition after annealing [15]. The PtMn (fcc) is likewise seen at a diffraction pinnacle of 46.1° and 67.8°, which corresponds to the (200) and (220) planes. A small peak at 2θ = 44.2°

corresponds to the bcc NiMn (110) phase as shown in Figure 2a, in addition to Co (111) and Ni (111).

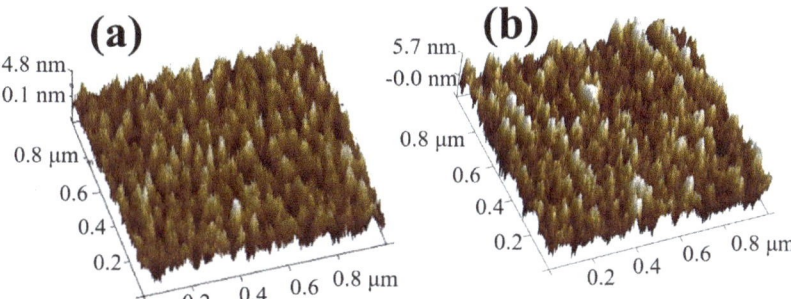

Figure 1. Antiferromagnet (AFM) images of (**a**) as-deposited and (**b**) magnetic field annealing (MFA) samples with a scan area of 1× 1 µm² Ag/[Co/Ni]$_2$/PtMn(32.4 nm) multilayers.

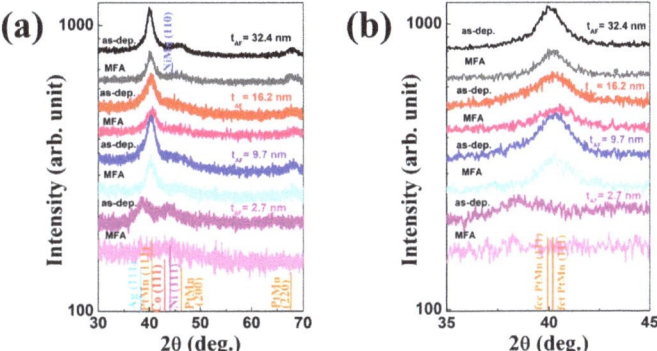

Figure 2. XRD spectra of the as dep. and MFA Ag/[Co/Ni]$_2$/PtMn(t_{PtMn}) multilayered thin films with 2θ from (**a**) 30 to 70 deg. and (**b**) 35 to 45 deg.

Compared with the as-deposited thin film, in the annealed thin film, the phase transformation in the PtMn (t_{PtMn} = 16.2 and 9.7 nm) from fcc (111) to fct (111) was observed where the PtMn (111) peak showed a slight shift of 0.3° from 40° to 40.3°. This shift is evidence of the phase transformation from fcc PtMn (111) to fct PtMn (111) [22]. The broad peak at 2θ = 40.5° (d = 2.22 Å) in samples with t_{PtMn} = 16.2 and 9.7 nm consist of both fcc PtMn (111) and fct PtMn (111) phases as shown in Figure 2b. The observed peak is a superposition of the two individual peaks, which cannot be resolved as they are too closely spaced [11]. During the phase transformation, the decrease in the PtMn (111) peak intensity and the shift to higher peak positions in [Co/Ni]$_2$/PtMn (t_{PtMn} = 16.2 and 9.7 nm) are observed as compared with the [Co/Ni]$_2$/PtMn (t_{PtMn} = 32.4 nm) film. In contrast, no phase transformation with decreasing PtMn thickness is present in the as-deposited samples. The change in intensity during annealing might be due to the fct particles' random orientation [25] or Mn deficiencies within the PtMn film [26]. A weak diffraction peak of fcc PtMn (200) and fct PtMn (220) was also observed. Similar changes were reported by Taras Pokhil et al., where the peak shift from 39.88° to 40.24° was observed, confirming the phase transformation after annealing [27]. In the as-deposited and annealed Ag/[Co/Ni]$_2$/PtMn (t_{PtMn} = 2.7 nm) samples, the thin PtMn layer's diffraction peaks were nearly undetectable possibly due to the small layer thickness.

Further, the elemental mapping along the cross-section of Ag/[Co/Ni]$_2$/PtMn (t_{PtMn} = 2.7 nm) by the Scanning Transmission Electron Microscopy (STEM) is shown in Figure 3. The as-deposited multilayers exhibited sharp contrast in atomic concentration in Figure 3a. In contrast, the annealed films show strong interdiffusion in Co and Ni interfaces, as evidenced by Co and Ni atoms' broad distribution in Figure 3b.

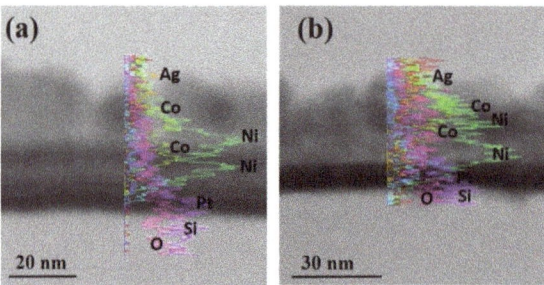

Figure 3. The STEM images and corresponding line scan profiles (a) as-deposited and (b) MFA Ag/[Co/Ni]$_2$/PtMn(2.7 nm) multilayers.

The high-resolution transmission electron microscopy (HRTEM) image of the annealed Ag/[Co/Ni]$_2$/PtMn multilayers (t_{PtMn} = 2.7 nm) is shown in Figure 4. While this sample exhibits poor XRD signal, the well-crystallized lattices can still be identified from the HRTEM image. A face-centered cubic (111) phase with an interplanar spacing of 0.227 nm was observed in the PtMn layer. The interplanar spacing of 0.222 nm and 0.204 nm were observed in the Ag layer, correlating to the fcc Ag (111) and Ag (200) phases. Similarly, Ni shows the interplanar spacing of 0.206 nm and 0.204 nm corresponding to the Ni (111), whereas the interplanar spacing of 0.204 nm was observed in the Co (111) phase.

Figure 4. The HRTEM image of Ag/[Co/Ni]$_2$/PtMn(2.7 nm) multilayers after MFA processes.

The annealed Ag/[Co/Ni]$_2$/PtMn multilayers also showed the polycrystalline structures with no sharp interfaces in the multilayer, pointing towards the inter-diffusion between the Ni with the Co and PtMn layers, respectively. The increased crystallinity in the films was observed in each layer after the magnetic field annealing. The lattice spacing of 0.227 nm and 0.224 nm was observed in the PtMn after the annealing, indicating the mixed phases of fcc PtMn (111) and fct PtMn (111) were present in the multilayer thin film consistent with the XRD results. The intermixed bcc NiMn (111) with the interplanar spacing of 0.204 nm was also observed in the Ni layer.

The XPS depth profile observed for as-deposited multilayer is consistent with those obtained by HRTEM, including Ag capping layer, Co, Ni, PtMn layers, and the SiO$_2$ substrate. The Mn is diffused into the [Co/Ni] layer giving rise to the alloyed NiMn phases. However, Pt remains unreacted with the top Ni (or Co) layers, as shown in Figure 5a. The composition gradient is likely to be present in the film, affecting the respected magnetic properties.

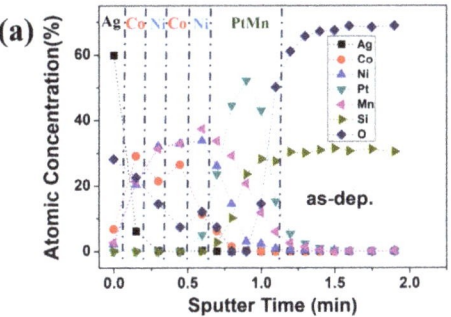

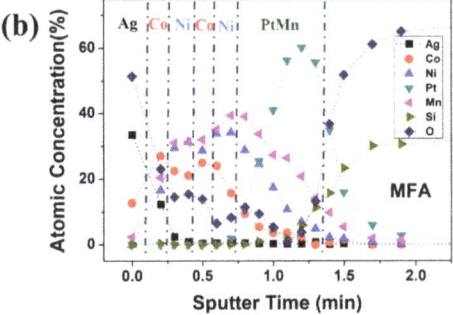

Figure 5. The XPS depth profile of (**a**) the as-deposited and (**b**) the MFA Ag/[Co/Ni]$_2$/PtMn (9.7 nm) multilayers.

Compared to the as-deposited multilayer, a similar layer sequence was observed after the MFA processes. Unlike the as-deposited multilayer, a surface oxide layer was observed by the increased oxygen content in Figure 5b. Diffusion of the Mn into Ni (or Co) layer is observed, indicating the reduction in magnetization contributed from ferromagnetic (FM) [Co/Ni]$_2$ layers.

The XPS spectra of Ag, Co, Ni, Pt, O, and Mn of as-deposited and MFA Ag/[Co/Ni]$_2$/PtMn (9.7 nm) multilayers were shown in Figure 6. The XPS spectra of Ag and O in the Ag capping layer is shown in Figure 6a,b. The binding energy of 367.8 and 373.3 eV in the as-deposited sample corresponds to the Ag 3d$_{5/2}$ and Ag 3d$_{3/2}$ (Figure 6a). However, after the MFA processes, the peak narrowing and shift towards higher binding energies of 368.2 eV (Ag 3d$_{5/2}$) and 374.2 eV (Ag 3d$_{3/2}$) indicate the surface oxidization to Ag$_2$O [28,29]. The Co 2p spectra (778.2 (Co 2P$_{3/2}$) and 793.4 eV (Co 2P$_{1/2}$)) [30] after the MFA processes (Figure 6c), exhibit a slight shift to higher energies due to the partially oxidized cobalt elements [30]. The O 1s spectra (532.2 eV) confirm the formation of Co-O bonds' in the Co layer (Figure 6d). The Ni 2p spectra (Figure 6e), (852.6 eV (Ni 2P$_{3/2}$), 858.6 eV (Ni 2P$_{3/2, sat.}$), and 870 eV (Ni 2P$_{1/2}$)) after the MFA processes exhibit a slight shift to higher energies. This indicates the formation of NiMn alloying phases. The O 1s spectra (529.6 eV), as shown in Figure 6f, indicate the formation of oxides such as Mn oxide due to the diffusion process (Figure 5). The Pt 4f spectra (71.2 eV (Pt 4f$_{7/2}$), 74.4 eV (Pt 4f$_{5/2}$)) as shown in Figure 6g indicate that Pt was in the metallic state [31,32]. The Mn 2p spectra (639.8 eV (2p$_{3/2}$), 650.9 eV (2p$_{1/2}$)), (Figure 6h) after MFA processes with a slight shift to higher energies, attribute to the alloy formation [32], i.e., PtMn/NiMn.

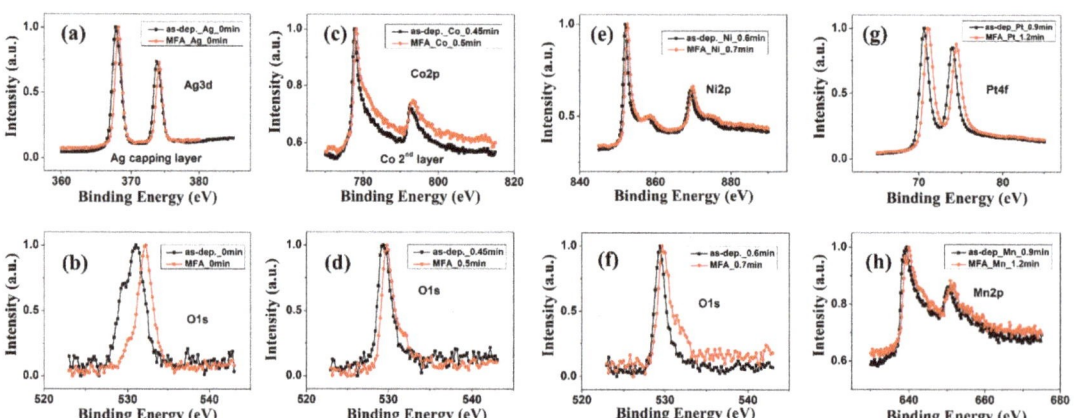

Figure 6. The XPS binding energy spectra of (**a**) Ag 3d, (**b**) O 1s (Ag layer), (**c**) Co 2p, (**d**) O 1s (Co layer), (**e**) Ni 2p, (**f**) O 1s (Ni layer), (**g**) Pt 4f, and (**h**) Mn 2p of the as-deposited and MFA Ag/[Co/Ni]$_2$/PtMn (9.7 nm) multilayers.

To identify the changes in magnetic properties induced by magnetic field annealing, the room temperature in-plane magnetic hysteresis loops of Ag/[Co/Ni]$_2$/PtMn multilayers were shown in Figure 7. As compared with the as-deposited sample, the reduction in the magnetization was seen as a result of the alloying effect between [Co/Ni]$_2$ and PtMn after annealing. The as-deposited and annealed samples of t_{PtMn} = 32.4 nm exhibit the same coercive field of H_c = 20 Oe (Figure 7a). Whereas, with the t_{PtMn} = 16.2 nm, the film shows the coercive field of H_c = 22 Oe in the as-deposited sample and coercive field of about H_c = 28 Oe in the annealed sample (Figure 7b). Similarly, the coercive field of H_c = 24 Oe was observed in the as-deposited sample and H_c = 28 Oe in the annealed sample for the t_{PtMn} = 9.7 nm (Figure 7c).

The vertical shift (m_{shift}) is observed in the annealed sample as compared to the as-deposited sample. The vertical shift along the M-axis is defined as $m_{shift} = \frac{1}{2}(M_{max} + M_{min})$ [33], where the m_{shift} of about −0.03 memu was observed in the sample with t_{PtMn} = 32.4 (Figure 7a). Similarly, m_{shift} of −0.03 memu was observed with the PtMn thickness of 16.2 nm (t_{PtMn}) (Figure 7b) and 9.7 nm (t_{PtMn}) (Figure 7c) respectively, indicating the exchange coupling between FM [Co/Ni]$_2$ and antiferromagnetic (AFM) PtMn layer due to the presence of pinned spins in the samples [33]. The vertical shift observed is due to the pinned moments that do not rotate with the applied field, which defines the bias direction [34].

With the increase in the PtMn thickness, the increased squareness is observed in the as-deposited and annealed samples, as shown in Figure 7d. The maximum squareness (M_r/M_s) observed after annealing is about 0.63, 0.50 and 0.33 with respect to t_{PtMn} = 32.4, 16.2, 9.7 nm as shown in Figure 7d. This can be attributed to the presence of AFM that plays a pivotal role in the enhancement of the M_r/M_s in FM/AFM [33]. With increasing PtMn thickness, the FM layer's magnetization reversal modes switch from domain rotation, pinned by the thin PtMn layer, to spin flipping, which is assisted by the exchange interaction from the thick PtMn layer [35]. The MFA results in higher squareness in samples with a thin PtMn layer, indicating that the MFA acts on the Co/Ni multilayer by repairing structural defects and enhancing magnetocrystalline anisotropy. The reduced squareness in annealed samples with thicker PtMn layer, on the other hand, is attributed to the accelerated interfacial diffusion, which promoted the domain pinning effect. The enhanced coercivity (H_c) of 28 Oe was observed for samples with t_{PtMn} of 9.7 nm and 16.2 nm after annealing because of the ordered fct PtMn during the magnetization reversal processes, as shown in

Figure 7e. As the PtMn layer thickness increases, the decrease in coercivity is observed, which can be explained by the fact that with the increase in PtMn thickness, the effective AFM anisotropy is also increased. The enhanced AFM spins eliminate the amount of reversible interfacial AFM spins, reducing the H_c [2].

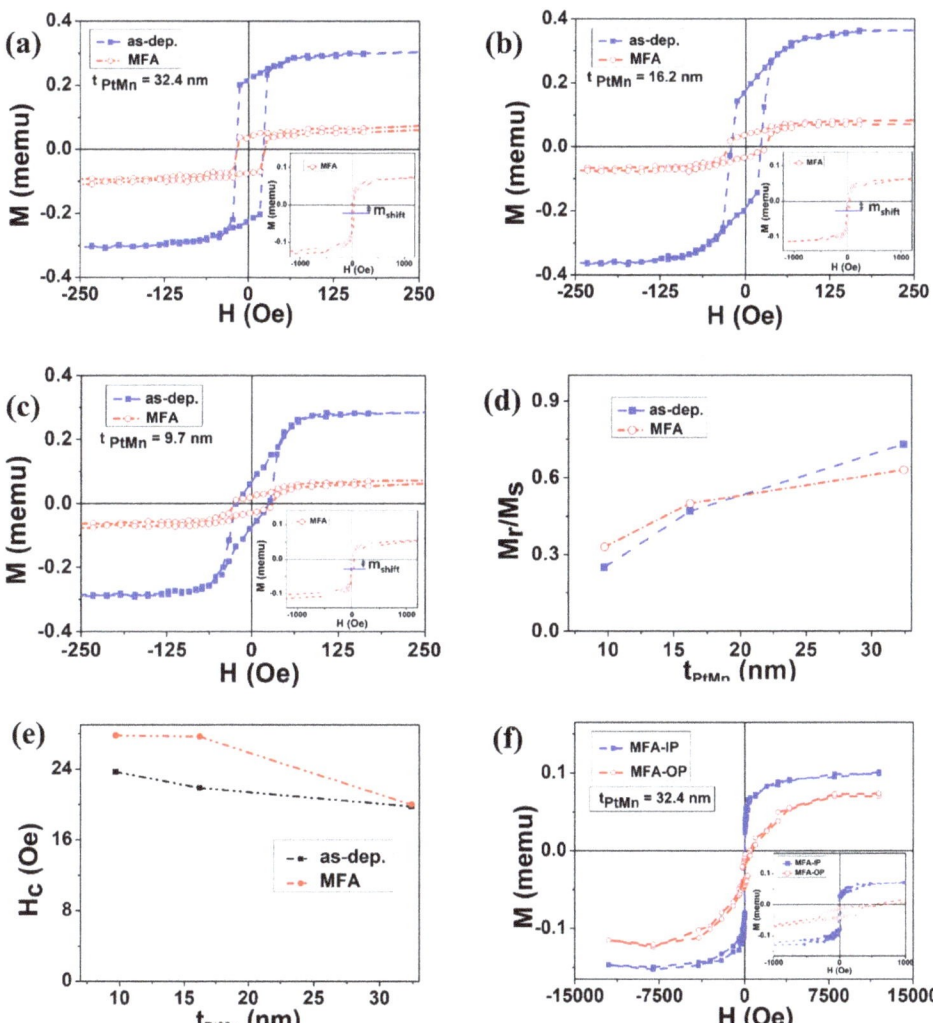

Figure 7. The room temperature in-plane magnetic hysteresis loops of as deposited and MFA Ag/[Co/Ni]$_2$/PtMn (t$_{PtMn}$) multilayers at (**a**) t$_{PtMn}$ = 32.4 nm, (**b**) t$_{PtMn}$ = 16.2 nm, (**c**) t$_{PtMn}$ = 9.7 nm. The squareness (M$_r$/M$_s$) and Coercivity vs. t$_{PtMn}$ is shown in (**d**,**e**), respectively. (**f**) The in-plane and out-of-plane hysteresis loops at t$_{PtMn}$ = 32.4 nm after MFA processes.

The in-plane and out-of-plane hysteresis loop of annealed Ag/[Co/Ni]$_2$/PtMn(32.4 nm) multilayers is shown in Figure 7f. The exchange bias of 2 Oe is observed for the thickest film with a PtMn layer of t$_{PtMn}$ = 32.4 nm. The OP magnetic hysteresis loop show notable hysteretic minor loop in the low field range (Figure 7f inset), indicating the existence of certain perpendicular magnetic anisotropy (PMA). However, this PMA is not strong enough to overcome the perpendicular demagnetization field. The magnetic anisotropy of the multilayer is thus dominated by the IP shape anisotropy, as indicated by the higher remnant magnetization in the in-plane direction. The out-of-plane and in-plane hysteresis loops are expected to have the same saturation magnetization under "absolute saturation" conditions. However, the measured saturation magnetization usually deviates from the absolute saturation magnetization due to the existence of magnetostriction effects and spin waves [36]. In many cases, the spin-wave spectra are different along different orientations [37]. As a result, the measured saturation magnetizations are not necessarily the same along all directions. In this study, the pinned spins in the in-plane and out-of-plane hysteresis loops (as indicated by the vertical shift in the magnetic hysteresis loops in Figure 7) contributed to the different saturation magnetization in the hysteresis loops. In the sample with PtMn thickness of 32.4 nm, the coercivity (20 Oe) observed is the same for as-deposited and MFA samples; this might be due to the alloyed NiMn dominant over fct PtMn as pinning sites to [Co/Ni]$_2$.

3. Materials and Methods

[Co(2.5 nm)/Ni(2.3 nm)]$_2$/PtMn(t_{PtMn}) multilayers [1] were prepared by Ion Beam Assisted Deposition (IBAD) technique [38,39]. Pt$_{69}$Mn$_{31}$ (at.%) [40] with different thicknesses (t_{PtMn}) of 32.4 nm, 16.2 nm, 9.7 nm, and 2.7 nm were deposited. A Kaufmann ion source operating at 800 V and 7.5 mA was used to subsequently sputter the PtMn, Ni, and Co targets with an argon flow of 3 sccm during the deposition process. The deposition rates for PtMn, Ni, and Co were 3.2, 2.3, and 2.5 nm/min, respectively. The magnetic field annealing (MFA) was conducted at 573 K in a vacuum for 1 h, and a magnetic field of 500 mT was applied perpendicularly to the thin film surface during annealing.

An End-Hall ion source with V_{EH} = 70 V, and I_{EH} = 500 mA was used for bombarding the PtMn layer for 1 min after its deposition. Further, an 8 nm thick Ag capping layer was deposited. The high-resolution lattice image and the line scan profile of the Ag/[Co/Ni]$_2$/PtMn thin films were obtained using a JEOL-JEM-2100F scanning transmission electron microscopy (STEM) working at 200 kV. The depth profile and binding energy of the Ag/[Co/Ni]$_2$/PtMn multilayers were characterized by a commercial ULVAC-PHI (PHI 5000 Versa Probe) x-ray photoelectron spectroscopy (XPS). A Veeco D3100 atomic force microscopy (AFM) was utilized to measure the thin multilayer film's surface roughness. The samples' magnetic hysteresis loops were measured by an ADE-DMS 1660 vibrating sample magnetometer (VSM) at room temperature. The saturation magnetization (M_s) is defined as the saturation value at which magnetization (M) becomes constant when a large magnetic field (H) is applied [41]. If the magnetic field (H) is reduced to zero after saturation in the positive direction, the magnetization in the hysteresis loop decreases from M_s to M_r, where M_r is defined as the remnant magnetization [6]. The squareness is defined as the ratio of the remnant magnetization (M_r) to the saturation magnetization (M_s).

4. Conclusions

The microstructure and magnetic properties of as-deposited and MFA Ag/[Co/Ni]$_2$/PtMn multilayers at different PtMn thickness were investigated. The Co and Ni layers have fcc structures with preferred (111) orientation. The fct PtMn (111) peak intensity increases with PtMn layer thickness in both the as-deposited and MFA samples. After annealing, the phase transformation from fcc (111) to fct (111) is observed in samples with thinner PtMn films (9.7 and 16.2 nm), as was confirmed by XRD and HRTEM. In the STEM, compared to the as-deposited sample, no distinct interface was observed between Co/Ni multilayers due to the inter-diffusion that occurred after the annealing process. The XPS depth profile in MFA Ag/[Co/Ni]$_2$/PtMn multilayers shows a similar layer sequence as those of the as-deposited sample except for the surface oxide layer. The NiMn alloyed phase formation was also confirmed by the XPS binding energy shift, which results in reduced magnetization.

Further, the magnetic properties measured by VSM show an increased coercivity in the MFA thin films. This is attributed to the presence of ordered fct PtMn, and NiMn phases exchange coupled to the ferromagnetic [Co/Ni]$_2$ layers. No exchange bias field was observed at room temperature. The vertical shift (M_{shift} = −0.03 memu) of the hysteresis loops is ascribed to the pinned spins resulting from perpendicular MFA processes. The squareness ratio (M_r/M_s) decreases with decreasing PtMn thickness. This work has revealed enhanced coercivity and perpendicular magnetic anisotropy in [Co/Ni]$_2$/PtMn multilayers. The results gain insight into developing perpendicularly magnetized spintronic devices through post-treatment techniques.

Author Contributions: Conceptualization, X.L. and K.-W.L.; data curation, K.-W.L.; formal analysis, R.Y., C.-H.W., I-F.H. and T.-H.W.; funding acquisition, X.L. and K.-W.L.; investigation, T.-H.W.; methodology, X.L. and K.-W.L.; supervision, K.-W.L.; writing—original draft, R.Y.; writing—review and editing, R.Y., X.L. and K.-W.L. All authors have read and agreed to the published version of the manuscript.

Funding: The research was supported by the MOST of Taiwan, the National Natural Science Foundation of China (No. 61804129), and the Science and Technology Project of Fujian Province of China (No. 2019H0002).

Conflicts of Interest: The authors declare no conflict of interest.

References

1. Li, X.; Wu, C.-H.; Lee, Y.-J.; Su, Y.-T.; Lin, K.-W.; Ruotolo, A.; Manna, P.K.; van Lierop, J. Correlating spin freezing and magnetic properties in [Co/Ni]$_n$/PtMn multilayers. *J. Magn. Magn. Mater.* **2020**, *508*, 166690. [CrossRef]
2. Nogués, J.; Schuller, I.K. Exchange bias. *J. Magn. Magn. Mater.* **1999**, *192*, 203. [CrossRef]
3. Meiklejohn, W.H.; Bean, C.P. New magnetic anisotropy. *Phys. Rev.* **1956**, *102*, 1413. [CrossRef]
4. Fukami, S.; Zhang, C.; Duttagupta, S.; Kurenkov, A.; Ohno, H. Magnetization switching by spin-orbit torque in an antiferromagnet-ferromagnet bilayer system. *Nat. Mater.* **2016**, *15*, 535. [CrossRef] [PubMed]
5. Van DenBrink, A.; Vermijs, G.; Solignac, A.; Koo, J.; Kohlhepp, J.T.; Swagten, H.J.M.; Koopmans, B. Field-free magnetization reversal by spin-Hall effect and exchange bias. *Nat. Commun.* **2016**, *7*, 10854. [CrossRef] [PubMed]
6. Spaldin, A.N. *Magnetic Materials: Fundamentals and Applications*, 2nd ed.; Cambridge University Press: New York, NY, USA, 2010; p. 19.
7. Tang, Y.J.; Roos, B.; Mewes, T.; Demokritov, S.O.; Hillebrands, B.; Wang, Y.J. Enhanced coercivity of exchange-bias Fe/MnPd bilayers. *Appl. Phys. Lett.* **1999**, *75*, 707. [CrossRef]
8. Hu, J.G.; Jin, G.J.; Ma, Y.Q. Thickness dependence of exchange bias and coercivity in a ferromagnetic layer coupled with an antiferromagnetic layer. *J. Appl. Phys.* **2003**, *94*, 2529. [CrossRef]
9. Gritsenko, C.; Dzhun, I.; Babaytsev, G.; Chechenin, N.; Rodionova, V. Exchange Bias and Coercivity Fields as a Function of the Antiferromagnetic Layer Thickness in bi- and tri-layered thin-films Based on IrMn and NiFe. *Phys. Procedia* **2016**, *82*, 51. [CrossRef]
10. Krén, E.; Kádár, G.; Pál, L.; Sólyom, J.; Szabó, P.; Tarnóczi, T. Magnetic structures and exchange interactions in the Mn-Pt system. *Phys. Rev.* **1968**, *171*, 574. [CrossRef]
11. Ladwig, P.F.; Chang, Y.A.; Linville, E.S.; Morrone, A.; Gao, J.; Pant, B.B.; Schlutz, A.E.; Mao, S. Paramagnetic to antiferromagnetic phase transformation in sputter-deposited Pt-Mn thin films. *J. Appl. Phys.* **2003**, *94*, 979. [CrossRef]
12. Lee, C.L.; Kools, J.; Devasahayam, A.J.; Mao, M.; Hu, C.C. Enhancement of exchange bias in thin PtMn antiferromagnets by Ru and Cr nano-lamination. *J. Magn. Magn. Mater.* **2005**, *286*, 200. [CrossRef]
13. He, X.D.; Zhang, L.L.; Wu, G.J.; Gao, J.W.; Ran, P.; Sajjad, M.; Zhou, X.W.; Cao, J.W.; Xi, L.; Zuo, Y.L.; et al. Controllable intrinsic Gilbert damping in Pt buffered [Co/Ni]$_n$ multilayers with enhanced perpendicular magnetic anisotropy. *J. Magn. Magn. Mater.* **2021**, *519*, 167429. [CrossRef]
14. Krishnaswamy, G.K.; Kurenkov, A.; Sala, G.; Baumgartner, M.; Krizakova, V.; Nistor, C.; MacCherozzi, F.; Dhesi, S.S.; Fukami, S.; Ohno, H.; et al. Multidomain Memristive Switching of Pt$_{38}$Mn$_{62}$/[Co/Ni]$_n$ Multilayers. *Phys. Rev. Appl.* **2020**, *14*, 044036. [CrossRef]
15. Duttagupta, S.; Kurenkov, A.; Tretiakov, O.A.; Krishnaswamy, G.; Sala, G.; Krizakova, V.; Maccherozzi, F.; Dhesi, S.S.; Gambardella, P.; Fukami, S.; et al. Spin-orbit torque switching of an antiferromagnetic metallic heterostructure. *Nat. Commun.* **2020**, *11*, 5715. [CrossRef] [PubMed]
16. DuttaGupta, S.; Kanemura, T.; Zhang, C.; Kurenkov, A.; Fukami, S.; Ohno, H. Spin-orbit torques and Dzyaloshinskii-Moriya interaction in PtMn/[Co/Ni] heterostructures. *Appl. Phys. Lett.* **2017**, *111*, 182412. [CrossRef]
17. Ma, X.; Yu, G.; Razavi, S.A.; Sasaki, S.S.; Li, X.; Hao, K.; Tolbert, S.H.; Wang, K.L.; Li, X. Dzyaloshinskii-Moriya Interaction across an Antiferromagnet-Ferromagnet Interface. *Phys. Rev. Lett.* **2017**, *119*, 027202. [CrossRef]
18. Itoh, R.; Takeuchi, Y.; Duttagupta, S.; Fukami, S.; Ohno, H. Stack structure and temperature dependence of spin-orbit torques in heterostructures with antiferromagnetic PtMn. *Appl. Phys. Lett.* **2019**, *115*, 242404. [CrossRef]
19. Svalov, A.V.; Savin, P.A.; Lepalovskij, V.N.; Larranaga, A.; Vaskovskiy, V.O.; Garcia Arribas, A.; Kurlyandskaya, G.V. Exchange biased FeNi/FeMn bilayers with coercivity and switching field enhanced by FeMn surface oxidation. *AIP Adv.* **2013**, *3*, 092104. [CrossRef]

20. Guo, J.Y.; Tzeng, Y.M.; van Lierop, J.; Chang, S.-Y.; Lin, K.-W. Thermal annealing effects on the structural, magnetic, and magnetotransport properties of NiFe/(Ni, Fe)O bilayers. *Jpn. J. Appl. Phys.* **2009**, *48*, 073003. [CrossRef]
21. Li, X.; Chang, Y.-C.; Chen, J.-Y.; Lin, K.-W.; Desautels, R.D.; van Lierop, J.; Pong, P.W.T. Annealing effect of NiO/Co$_{90}$Fe$_{10}$ thin films: From bilayer to nanocomposite. *Phys. Lett. A* **2018**, *382*, 2886. [CrossRef]
22. Xu, M.; Lu, Z.; Yang, T.; Liu, C.; Cui, S.; Mai, Z.; Lai, W. Relation between microstructures and magnetic properties upon annealing in Fe$_{50}$Mn$_{50}$/Ni$_{80}$Fe$_{20}$ films. *J. Appl. Phys.* **2002**, *92*, 2052. [CrossRef]
23. Kurenkov, A.; Zhang, C.; DuttaGupta, S.; Fukami, S.; Ohno, H. Device-size dependence of field-free spin-orbit torque induced magnetization switching in antiferromagnet/ferromagnet structures. *Appl. Phys. Lett.* **2017**, *110*, 092410. [CrossRef]
24. Vergès, M.; Kumar, V.; Lin, P.H.; Mangin, S.; Lai, C.H. Role of induced exchange bias in zero field spin-orbit torque magnetization switching in Pt/[Ni/Co]/PtMn. *AIP Adv.* **2020**, *10*, 085320. [CrossRef]
25. Soeya, S. Enhanced exchange anisotropy between antiferromagnetic PtMn and ferromagnetic Co system by AuCu underlayer. *Appl. Phys. Lett.* **2009**, *94*, 242507. [CrossRef]
26. An, Y.; Liu, J.; Ma, Y.; Wu, Z. Effect of grain size on the properties of NiFe/PtMn bilayers. *J. Phys. D Appl. Phys.* **2008**, *41*, 165003. [CrossRef]
27. Pokhil, T.; Linville, E.; Mao, S. Exchange anisotropy and micromagnetic properties of PtMn/NiFe bilayers. *J. Appl. Phys.* **2001**, *89*, 6588. [CrossRef]
28. Kaushik, V.K. XPS core level spectra and Auger parameters for some silver compounds. *J. Electron Spectros. Relat. Phenom.* **1991**, *56*, 273. [CrossRef]
29. Vasil'kov, A.Y.; Dovnar, R.I.; Smotryn, S.M.; Iaskevich, N.N.; Naumkin, A.V. Plasmon resonance of silver nanoparticles as a method of increasing their antibacterial action. *Antibiotics* **2018**, *7*, 80. [CrossRef]
30. Lin, K.W.; Lin, F.T.; Tzeng, Y.M. X-ray photoelectron spectroscopy and magnetic force microscopy studies of ion-beam deposited Ni$_{80}$Fe$_{20}$/Co-oxide bilayers. *IEEE Trans. Magn.* **2005**, *41*, 927. [CrossRef]
31. Shyu, J.Z.; Otto, K. Identification of platinum phases on γ-alumina by XPS. *Appl. Surf. Sci.* **1988**, *32*, 246. [CrossRef]
32. Hu, J.; Fang, C.; Jiang, X.; Zhang, D.; Cui, Z. PtMn/PtCo alloy nanofascicles: Robust electrocatalysts for electrocatalytic hydrogen evolution reaction under both acidic and alkaline conditions. *Inorg. Chem. Front.* **2020**, *7*, 4377. [CrossRef]
33. De La Venta, J.; Erekhinsky, M.; Wang, S.; West, K.G.; Morales, R.; Schuller, I.K. Exchange bias induced by the Fe$_3$O$_4$ Verwey transition. *Phys. Rev. B* **2012**, *85*, 13447. [CrossRef]
34. Ohldag, H.; Scholl, A.; Nolting, F.; Arenholz, E.; Maat, S.; Young, A.T.; Carey, M.; Stohr, J. Correlation between Exchange Bias and Pinned Interfacial Spins. *Phys. Rev. Lett.* **2003**, *91*, 017203. [CrossRef]
35. Sort, J.; Nogués, J.; Suriñach, S.; Muñoz, J.S.; Baró, M.D.; Chappel, E.; Dupont, F.; Chouteau, G. Coercivity and squareness enhancement in ball-milled hard magnetic-antiferromagnetic composites. *Appl. Phys. Lett.* **2001**, *79*, 1142. [CrossRef]
36. Kronmüller, H.; Grimm, H. High-field susceptibility and the spin-wave spectrum of Fe$_{40}$Ni$_{40}$P$_{14}$B$_6$-alloys. *J. Magn. Magn. Mater.* **1977**, *6*, 57. [CrossRef]
37. Mook, H.A.; Nicklow, R.M.; Thompson, E.D.; Wilkinson, M.K. Spin-Wave Spectrum of Nickel Metal. *J. Appl. Phys.* **1969**, *40*, 1450. [CrossRef]
38. Lin, K.W.; Chen, T.-J.; Guo, J.-Y.; Ouyang, H.; Wei, D.-H.; van Lierop, J. Correlating antiferromagnetic spin structures with ion-beam bombardment in exchange-biased NiFe/Mn bilayers. *J. Appl. Phys.* **2009**, *105*, 07D710. [CrossRef]
39. Lin, K.W.; Ouyang, C.H.; van Lierop, J. *Using Ion-Beam-Assisted Deposition and Ion Implantation for the Rational Control of Nanomagnetism in Thin Film and Nanostructured Systems*, 1st ed.; Camley, R.E., Stamps, R.L., Eds.; Solid State Physics; Elsevier Academic Press: London, UK, 2018; Volume 69, pp. 1–45.
40. Yadav, R.; Shepit, M.; Li, X.; Lin, K.-W.; van Lierop, J.; Ruotolo, A. Photo-spin-voltaic effect in PtMn/Y$_3$Fe$_5$O$_{12}$ thin films. *J. Phys. Condens. Matter* **2021**, *33*, 095802. [CrossRef]
41. Cullity, B.D.; Graham, C.D. *Introduction to Magnetic Materials*, 2nd ed.; John Wiley & Sons: Hoboken, NJ, USA, 2009; p. 14.

Article

Microresonators and Microantennas—Tools to Explore Magnetization Dynamics in Single Nanostructures

Hamza Cansever * and Jürgen Lindner *

Helmholtz-Zentrum Dresden-Rossendorf, Institute of Ion Beam Physics and Materials Research, 01328 Dresden, Germany
* Correspondence: h.cansever@hzdr.de (H.C.); j.lindner@hzdr.de (J.L.); Tel.: +49-351-260-3187 (H.C.); +49-351-260-3221 (J.L.)

Abstract: The phenomenon of magnetic resonance and its detection via microwave spectroscopy provide insight into the magnetization dynamics of bulk or thin film materials. This allows for direct access to fundamental properties, such as the effective magnetization, g-factor, magnetic anisotropy, and the various damping (relaxation) channels that govern the decay of magnetic excitations. Cavity-based and broadband ferromagnetic resonance techniques that detect the microwave absorption of spin systems require a minimum magnetic volume to obtain a sufficient signal-to-noise ratio (S/N). Therefore, conventional techniques typically do not offer the sensitivity to detect individual micro- or nanostructures. A solution to this sensitivity problem is the so-called planar microresonator, which is able to detect even the small absorption signals of magnetic nanostructures, including spin-wave or edge resonance modes. As an example, we describe the microresonator-based detection of spin-wave modes within microscopic strips of ferromagnetic A2 $Fe_{60}Al_{40}$ that are imprinted into a paramagnetic B2 $Fe_{60}Al_{40}$-matrix via focused ion-beam irradiation. While microresonators operate at a fixed microwave frequency, a reliable quantification of the key magnetic parameters like the g-factor or spin relaxation times requires investigations within a broad range of frequencies. Furthermore, we introduce and describe the step from microresonators towards a broadband microantenna approach. Broadband magnetic resonance experiments on single nanostructured magnetic objects in a frequency range of 2–18 GHz are demonstrated. The broadband approach has been employed to explore the influence of lateral structuring on the magnetization dynamics of a Permalloy ($Ni_{80}Fe_{20}$) microstrip.

Keywords: ferromagnetic resonance; microantenna; microresonator; magnetic relaxation; thin films; nanostructures

Citation: Cansever, H.; Lindner, J. Microresonators and Microantennas—Tools to Explore Magnetization Dynamics in Single Nanostructures. *Magnetochemistry* **2021**, *7*, 28. https://doi.org/10.3390/magnetochemistry7020028

Academic Editor: David S. Schmool

Received: 25 January 2021
Accepted: 12 February 2021
Published: 19 February 2021

Publisher's Note: MDPI stays neutral with regard to jurisdictional claims in published maps and institutional affiliations.

Copyright: © 2021 by the authors. Licensee MDPI, Basel, Switzerland. This article is an open access article distributed under the terms and conditions of the Creative Commons Attribution (CC BY) license (https://creativecommons.org/licenses/by/4.0/).

1. Introduction

Determining dynamic properties of magnetic materials, i.e., their time-dependent behavior, often provides key insights into understanding of the magnetic response in micro- or nano-sized objects. The understanding of nanomagnetism plays an important role for generating future spintronic applications, such as memory and logic devices based on employing the quanta of magnetic excitations—spin-waves or magnons [1–4]. Here, we review the use of a unique approach to study magnetization dynamics in magnetic samples with small volume via microresonator- and microantenna-based microwave spectroscopy. Microwave spectroscopy allows the investigation of the fundamental (low energy) modes of spin systems. In ferromagnetically coupled spin ensembles, such modes are termed ferromagnetic resonance (FMR) modes.

FMR as a method is one of the main spectroscopic techniques, allowing for an investigation of static properties, such as the effective magnetization that provides the effective internal field acting on the spins (the effective magnetization actually is a magnetic induction with the unit Tesla, although the term magnetization is nonetheless widely used in literature), g-factor, and magnetic anisotropy, as well as dynamical properties such as magnetic relaxation mechanisms [5–7]. Typically, cavity-based (e.g., X-band; ~10 GHz) and broadband spectrometers are commonly used to detect microwave absorption upon exciting FMR modes [8–11]. Due to the minimum number of spins, which are needed to generate measurable signals, conventional cavities (cm-size) are not suited to detect FMR of micro-/nano-sized objects [12]. Therefore, to achieve a significantly better signal-to-noise ratio (S/N), planar microresonators have been introduced for microwave absorption measurements in small specimen—at first for electron spin resonance (ESR) experiments [13,14]. In microresonators, a microcoil produces a homogeneous rf-field inside of the loop into which a magnetic object is placed and homogeneously excited by the rf magnetic induction. A higher S/N ratio is achieved by a tremendous enhancement of the so-called filling factor that describes the concentration of the excitation field to the volume of the sample. As the loop diameter of microresonators can be fabricated down to the 1 μm size, the filling factor is significantly larger than in a conventional cm-sized cavity. The recent decade has seen microresonators become an established tool that has been employed on many different single magnetic objects, such as magnetic nanowires, nanotubes, biological materials, as well as magnetic tunnel junctions [15–19].

In this work, we demonstrate the use of microresonator-FMR on single strip samples made from prototype ferromagnetic materials in form of embedded $Fe_{60}Al_{40}$-stripes. We discuss the fundamental dynamic modes. The sensitivity of single-frequency microresonators (similar to conventional cavity-based systems) is so high that one can detect not only the uniform modes, but also non-uniform ones, such as localized and standing spin-wave modes or uniform edge modes. The dynamics of the strip geometry are compared and explained by simulation results obtained from the mumax^3 code. Besides the microresonator approach, we introduce and describe so-called microantennas, a novel extension towards broadband (i.e., frequency-variable) FMR detection on laterally structured Permalloy ($Ni_{80}Fe_{20}$, hereafter Py) samples. The accessible frequency range of our setup is 2–18 GHz, which is limited only by the frequency range the components of the detection system can operate in. Broadband detection provides a straight-forward insight into magnetic relaxation. In the following, the term μ-FMR is used synonymously with the FMR methodology provided by microresonators and microantennas. The main advantage of a using microresonator/microantenna approach relies on a tremendous increase of the filling factor upon scaling down the resonator volume to the micrometer size, comparable to the one of the nanostructure. This high filling factor allows the increase of the detection sensitivity by orders of magnitude as compared to conventional FMR setups, also based on a measurement of the absorbed microwave power.

2. Materials and Experimental Methods

The FMR measurements on micrometer-sized $Fe_{60}Al_{40}$ and Py strips were performed on a home-built microwave spectrometer. A microwave bridge in combination with field-modulation and lock-in technique is used to improve to signal to noise ratio. Microwave power is divided into two paths. One is the excitation path, where the power level can be adjusted by an attenuator and is launched via the circulator into the resonator; the other arm is the reference arm, which biases the quadrature mixer at the operation frequency (homodyne detection technique). The phase shifter in the reference arm adjusts the phase at the local oscillator (LO) input of the quadrature mixer. Thereby, it allows for detection of absorption as well as dispersion of the FMR signals on the I and Q outputs, respectively (as seen modified sketch in Figure 1 without Mach–Zehnder interferometer). Technical details about the microwave spectrometer can be found in our previous study [17].

For the excitation and detection of the signals, we use planar near field antennas, tuned and matched for operation at a fixed frequency by means of stubs (microresonators), as well as broadband near field antennas with flat frequency response (microantennas), made of a shorted coplanar transmission line. While microresonators offer an increased sensitivity for measurements on micron-sized samples, microantennas allow for broadband measurements, revealing important dynamic magnetic properties like the damping. Microantennas consist of the section of a coplanar stripline, shorted at the end by a narrow strip, which acts as a near field antenna, coupling the microwave power to the precessing magnetic moment of the sample. For even more efficient and uniform excitation perpendicular to the plane, we built a loop into the shorting strip (Figure 1a). The loop size is tailored to be close to the dimensions of the sample. Electromagnetic simulations using the commercial finite element (FEM) simulation software HFSS (ANSYS), confirm the quite homogeneous distribution of the microwave magnetic field inside the loop (Figure 1b). Both the planar microresonator and the microantenna structures are fabricated by optical lithography.

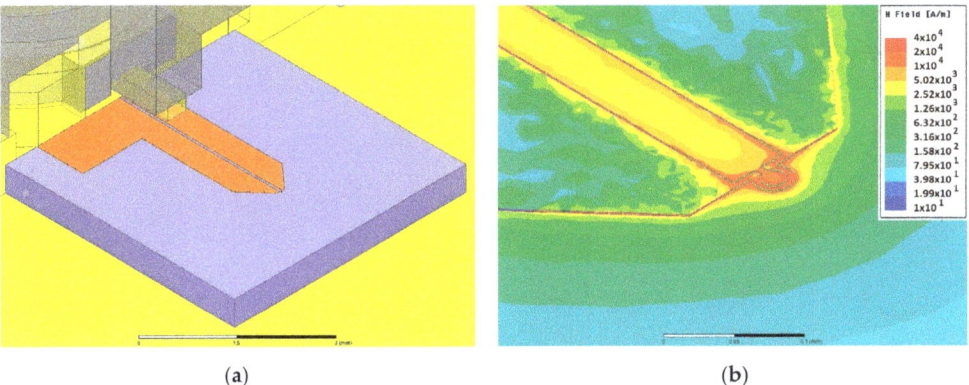

Figure 1. Layout (**a**) and magnetic microwave field (**b**) distribution of the microantenna, obtained by FEM simulation of the structure.

To facilitate the broadband measurements with the microantennas, we added a Mach–Zehnder interferometer to the microwave spectrometer (see Figure 2, [17]): A power divider splits the microwave equally into a fraction used for (i) the resonant excitation of the sample and (ii) for the interferometer's reference arm. For a given operation frequency, the attenuation and phase in the reference arm of the interferometer are adjusted such that the microwave power reflected from the microantenna with the sample is cancelled in the power combiner. This reduces the trace noise level and allows using higher microwave excitation power without the risk of saturating the low-noise amplifier. By sweeping the magnetic field of the electromagnet, we drive the sample into magnetic resonance. At resonance, the impedance of the microantenna is modified by the strong change of the sample's magnetic permeability, and the reflected power reappears at the input of the preamplifier.

FMR experiments were performed on $Fe_{60}Al_{40}$ and Py ($Ni_{80}Fe_{20}$) samples. A 32 nm $Fe_{60}Al_{40}$ thin film was grown on a 270-nm-thick SiO_2/Si substrate by magnetron-sputtering at room temperature. A post-annealing process was applied to the film in order to obtain the pristine (B2-paramagnetic) state [20]. Initially, a 14 µm diameter disc of 32 nm thick B2 $Fe_{60}Al_{40}$ was exposed by using photolithography. After preparation of the $Fe_{60}Al_{40}$ disk, the microresonator with 20 µm loop diameter was prepared around the disk by means of UV lithography and lift-off. The top-side, containing the microstrip lines or coplanar striplines, respectively, was metallized by 5 nm Cr/600 nm Cu/100 nm Au, whereas the backside metallization is serving as a ground. To fabricate the ferromagnetic strip, a focused Ne$^+$ ion beam of 25 keV energy was rastered over a 10 µm × 1 µm region, keeping the fluence fixed at 1×10^{15} ions/cm^2. The region exposed to the incident ions was disordered to form A2 ordered $Fe_{60}Al_{40}$, thereby realizing the embedded ferromagnetic stripe [20]. The frequency is defined by the shape and layout of the microresonator. Here we used a microresonator design with a loop diameter of 20 µm optimized for an eigenfrequency of 14 GHz (empty resonator). As control experiment and to obtain relevant parameters, an extended $Fe_{60}Al_{40}$ film was investigated by VSM and FMR (M_s = 708 kA/m and A = 4 pJ/m [21], not shown here). For the Py structure, a Py film was grown onto a MgO

(001) substrate using electron beam evaporation. A 5 by 2 µm² resist strip was prepared on the film by e-beam lithography, and the unprotected film was etched down to the substrate by Ar ion milling. Similarly to the $Fe_{60}Al_{40}$ strip, the microantenna was fabricated around the Py strip using lithography. However, one should note that the microantenna is designed in a coplanar geometry. It thus requires top side metallization only (5 nm Cr / 600 nm Cu/ 100 nm), comprising the signal as well as the ground lines.

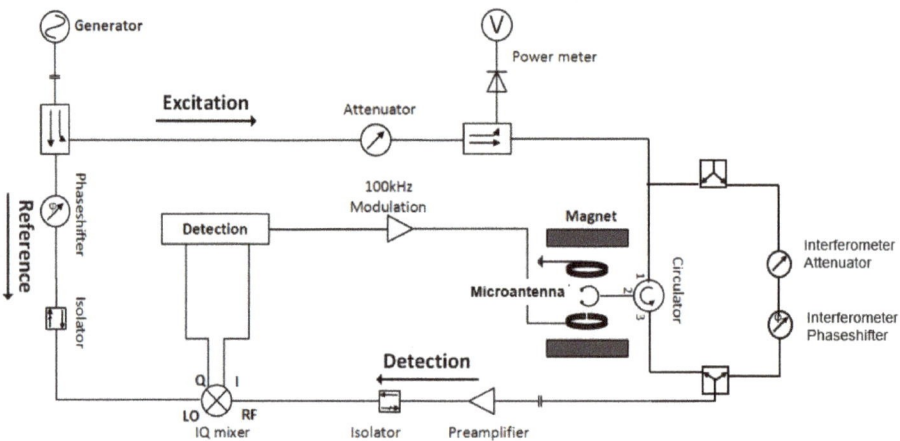

Figure 2. Schematic of the Mach–Zehnder–FMR spectrometer. For broadband measurements, an interferometer arm consisting of two power dividers, variable attenuator, and phase shifter was added parallel to the circulator of the original design [17]. Exchangeable circulators and isolators are used in order to cover a frequency range from 2 to 18 GHz.

3. Experimental Results and Discussion

The microresonator FMR experiments were performed on ferromagnetic 10 µm × 1 µm × 0.032 µm A2-$Fe_{60}Al_{40}$ strips, embedded in a circular paramagnetic B2-$Fe_{60}Al_{40}$ matrix. A sketch of such a sample is shown in the inset of Figure 1a. The details of the preparation are described in Section 2. $Fe_{60}Al_{40}$ exhibits a stable, ordered B2-structure that shows paramagnetic behavior. Irradiation with energetic ions leads to a randomization of the lattice positions of the Fe and Al atoms, forming an A2 structure that is ferromagnetic [20,22–26]. Irradiation induced disorder is a versatile tool for patterning magnetic structures of desired geometries embedded within paramagnetic surroundings. The patterning can be performed using broad-beam irradiation through shadow masks [24], or using a focused ion-beam for direct magnetic writing [22,25]. The magnetic properties of $Fe_{60}Al_{40}$ films under broad-beam irradiation have been reported by Schneider et al. [27]. The effective magnetization ($\mu_0 M_{eff}$) of the films, depending on the degree of disordering, can reach up to 850 mT, which is comparable to that of Py.

Figure 3a shows a measured FMR spectrum with a fixed excitation frequency of 13.72 GHz and a variable external field B_{ext} applied perpendicular to the long axis of the ferromagnetic A2 $Fe_{60}Al_{40}$ stripe, embedded in a B2 $Fe_{60}Al_{40}$ surrounding, produced by direct writing using a focused Ne^+ beam [23,26]. By using highly sensitive microresonator FMR detection, at least nine different resonance modes can be identified in the embedded ferromagnetic structure, as indicated by the numbering in Figure 3a. To visualize the mode character, micromagnetic simulations were performed using the mumax3 code [28]. For the simulations, we chose the following parameters: sample size 10 × 1 µm², thickness 32 nm, saturation magnetization M_s = 708 kA/m (as measured by vibrating sample magnetometry), and an exchange constant A = 4 pJ/m [21] (calculated from (exchange dominated) perpendicular standing spin-wave modes [29] observed in a thin film sample by conventional broadband FMR). To model the FMR experiment, we used a continuous-wave method, described in the literature [30] with an excitation field in z direction (along the thickness of the sample). In Figure 1b, the result of the simulation is shown in terms of the perpendicular dynamic component of the magnetization m_z normalized by M_s. This component is directly related to the experimentally detected FMR signal that is proportional to the high frequency susceptibility. By comparing qualitatively the results of the simulation with the measurement, we find a good agreement between both, as one can identify all nine resonance modes in the simulation as well. The values of the resonance field (for experiment and simulations) are extracted by fitting a complex Lorentzian function [31]. Those values are given in Table 1, proving again the good agreement between experiment and simulation (except the edge mode, No. 9).

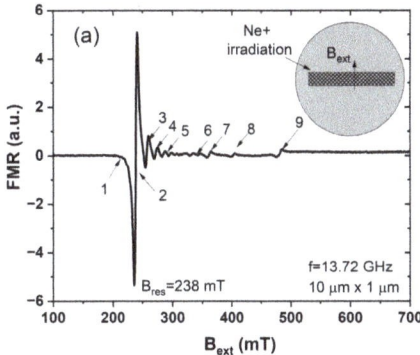 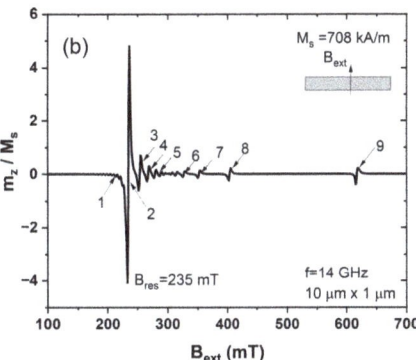

Figure 3. (a) Microresonator FMR experiment on an embedded $Fe_{60}Al_{40}$ strip with the size of $10 \times 1 \times 0.032$ µm (irradiated with Ne^+ with E = 25 keV) performed at 13.72 GHz (b) mumax3 simulation of a free-standing $Fe_{60}Al_{40}$ strip at 14 GHz. FMR signals are labelled from 1 to 9.

Table 1. Comparison of the resonance field values from experiment and simulation. Except for mode (8), the difference between measurement and simulation is larger for modes more confined to the edge region of the sample (i.e., for modes (6), (7), and (9)).

B_{res}, (mT).	(1)	(2)	(3)	(4)	(5)	(6)	(7)	(8)	(9)
Measurement	216	238	257	272	285	344	361	403	481
Simulation	215	235	254	268	279	327	352	403	617

When performing a micromagnetic simulation, it is also possible to create snapshots of the magnetic configuration within the sample system. Those snapshots were always taken at the moment (in time) when the oscillating excitation field (sine-function) crosses the zero line. While a system is in resonance, it has a phase shift of 90° to the excitation field, resulting in a maximum amplitude in the snapshot. The snapshots, corresponding to the resonance mode labeling in Figure 3, are shown in Figure 4. The color contrast corresponds to the local out-of-plane component of the dynamic magnetization, i.e., m_z, which is proportional to the measured FMR signal. The resonance (2) can be identified as the quasi-uniform mode. As seen from the pattern, just the center region of the stripe fulfills the resonance condition, while having a local $m_z = 0$ at the edges of the system. Due to the shape of the sample (demagnetizing field) and boundary conditions at the edges, the expected resonance field in those regions is different, justifying the quasi-uniform mode. The pattern of resonance mode number (1) exhibits periodically varying m_z along the length of the strip. While we are using ferromagnetic resonance as technique, we expect just modes with a standing wave character, as propagating modes would lead to a zero net microwave absorption. Nevertheless, it is possible to assign a wave vector k to the pattern, which is in this case perpendicularly (x-direction) oriented to the static magnetization (y-direction), well-known for a spin wave in Damon-Eshbach geometry [32]. Due to the geometric shape of the sample, it is not possible to excite standing spin waves with arbitrary wavelength, so we can observe only a discrete number of spin waves in Figure 3b. Note that these spin waves with wave vector perpendicular to the static magnetization occur at a smaller external field as compared to the quasi-uniform mode. As known from the dispersion relation of Damon–Eshbach modes [33], those need (for finite wavelength) more energy for excitation than the uniform mode. The reason for this lies in the fact that the dynamic stray fields the magnetic moments produced due to their non-uniform precessional motion are associated with an increased dipolar energy as compared to a uniform excitation for which all spins rotate with the same phase. A smaller resonance field compared to the quasi-uniform mode thus indicates a larger energy of the mode. The pattern maps of the resonances 3–5 are typical for so-called backward volume modes with different wave numbers. In this case, the wave vector is parallel to static magnetization (along the y-direction), while we observe a decreasing wavelength by increasing the applied external field. The resonance modes marked with 6–7–8 are so-called localized modes. As seen from the pattern for those modes, the excited resonant region (blue) is close to the long edge of the strip. In this region of the strip, the demagnetizing field is quite inhomogeneous, which implies even directly neighbored regions to exhibit different resonance conditions. Since the spins in those regions are still coupled to each other via exchange interaction, the excited region (in resonance) sends out propagating spin waves into the neighbored one. In turn, one wave is launched towards the strip center and another one propagates towards the edge of the long axis of the strip. While the wavelength of this propagating wave is given by the size of the excited region, it is small (in the range of a 10th of a nm) compared to the strip width (1 µm). As a result, the propagation length before the wave is damped out is also rather small. Due to this fact, the propagating wave directed to the center of the stripe will never reach the center region. The propagating wave directed to the edge, however, is able to reach it (because the excited location is close to the edge) and will be reflected back. The reflected wave interferes with the primary wave, leading to destructive/constructive interference. Just by having a constructive interference, the ferromagnetic resonance is able to couple to this mode. This explains why the localized modes are appearing also in discrete manner within the FMR spectrum. The mode No. 9 finally is the true edge mode, for which only magnetic moments exactly at the edge of the strip are excited. In contrast to the localized modes discussed before, for the edge mode no interference is occurring. The physical nature of the edge mode is different. It is very much comparable to the quasi-uniform mode, just shifted to higher external field values, due to the demagnetization field at the strip edge being larger than in the center region [34,35]. All uniform and non-uniform modes can be correlated with the simulation results. Only the edge mode was observed at much lower resonance field than expected from the simulation. One has to note that the real edge may differ from the ideal one in terms of its geometrical profile or its magnetic parameters. Moreover, the embedded strip geometry, for which the ferromagnetic spins of the ion-irradiated strip at the edges form an interface to a paramagnetic $Fe_{60}Al_{40}$ surrounding matrix, might magnetically be different as compared to the free-standing strip assumed in the simulation. Note that the edge mode observed at lower magnetic fields implies the edge mode frequency to be larger than those for the edge mode of the simulated free-standing strip.

In the following, we would like to show how broadband µ-FMR can be utilized to determine the magnetization dynamics of a $5 \times 2 \times 0.015$ µm^3 Permalloy (Py) microstrip. While the strip exhibits a mode spectrum similar to the one discussed for the FeAl-strip before, we want to restrict our discussion in the following to the quasi-uniform mode. As discussed above, to increase the amount of insight to the magnetization dynamics, it is advantageous to perform measurements over a broad frequency range. Therefore, a broadband microantenna design was used instead of single-frequency microresonators. The microantenna setup also uses the microwave bridge to achieve high detection sensitivity and, thereby, can detect a spin resonance signal of about 10^6 spins/GHz$^{1/2}$, while conventional spectroscopy techniques require around 10^{10} spins/GHz$^{1/2}$ [36]. In Figure 5a, the FMR spectra of the Py strip are shown, measured at a frequency of 9 GHz for both the easy (B_{ext} parallel to the long strip axis) and hard axis (B_{ext} perpendicular to the long axis). The quasi-uniform mode for both orientations is clearly resolved in the FMR spectra. The main advantage of using a microantenna/microresonator approach is to allow for detecting the FMR response of single structures. Earlier experiments, performed to understand the behavior of magnetic strips, typically have investigated arrays of strips [37,38]. This, however, introduces difficulties in the interpretation of the data, as inter-strip coupling may influence the results. Moreover, modes stemming significantly from the samples' edge are broadened and thus very weak due to the different strips in the array having a distribution of edge properties. The resonance field values of easy and hard directions are found to be close to each other due to a rather small shape anisotropy (as revealed also from the inset a of Figure 5 that shows an optical micrograph of the microantenna loop that is encapsulating the strip, the latter having an aspect ratio of only 2.5). In the inset b of Figure 5, FMR spectra are shown for the lower and upper limit of the frequency range of microantenna (2–18GHz). As seen from FMR spectra, a Lorentzian line shape is obtained.

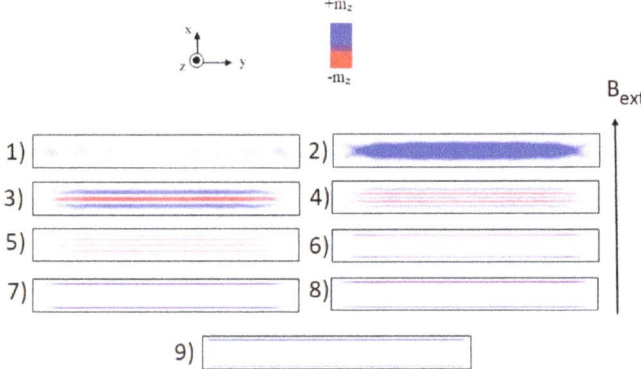

Figure 4. Snapshots of the FMR modes found in the simulated FMR spectra shown in Figure 1b. Blue/white/red colors represent the m_z component.

In Figure 6, the obtained resonance fields are plotted for different microwave frequencies for the Py strip (squares: easy axis, triangles: hard axis). Applying the well-known resonance equations for an extended thin film as given by Equation (1) [31], the effective magnetization M_{eff} and the *g-factor* can be determined as fit parameters.

$$(\omega/\gamma)^2 = \left[H_{res} \cos(\varphi - \varphi_H) + \frac{2K_{2\|}}{M_s} \cos^2(\varphi - \varphi_U) \right] \times \left[H_{res} \cos(\varphi - \varphi_H) + 4\pi M_{eff} + \frac{2K_{2\|}}{M_s} \cos^2(\varphi - \varphi_U) \right] \quad (1)$$

here is $\gamma = g \cdot \mu_B / h$ denotes the gyromagnetic ratio, φ is the in-plane angle of the magnetization M_s, and φ_H is the in-plane angle of the external magnetic field. $K_{2\|}/M_s$ is the uniaxial in-plane anisotropy, which is introduced to mimic the uniaxial symmetry of the strip. The effective magnetization is defined as the difference between the saturation magnetization and the perpendicular uniaxial anisotropy field: $4\pi M_{eff} = 4\pi M_s - 2K_{2\perp}/M_s$. All in-plane angles φ, φ_H, and φ_u are defined with respect to the long dimension of the strip. For definitions of the resonance equation, we refer to ref [31]. In case of easy-axis measurement ($\varphi = \varphi_u = 0$), Equation (1) results in:

$$(\omega/\gamma)^2 = \left[H_{res} \cos(\varphi - \varphi_H) + \frac{2K_{2\|}}{M_s} \right] \times \left[H_{res} \cos(\varphi - \varphi_H) + 4\pi M_{eff} + \frac{2K_{2\|}}{M_s} \right] \quad (2)$$

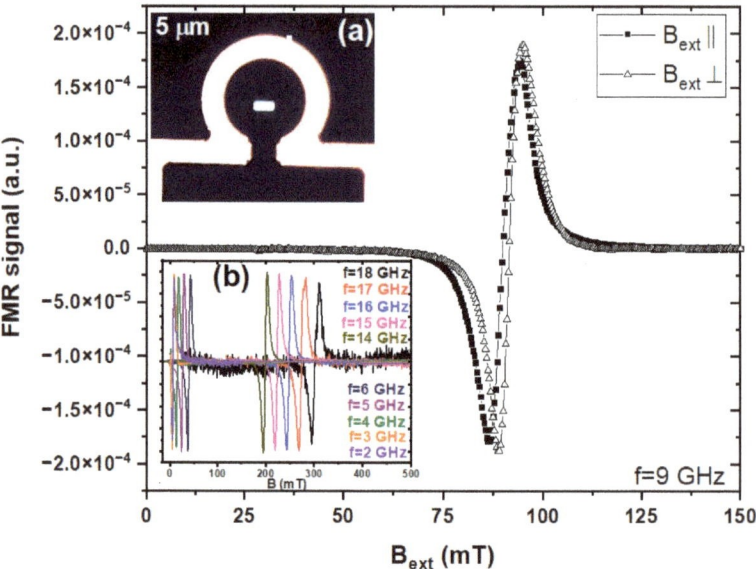

Figure 5. FMR spectra taken at 9 GHz along the hard axis (open triangles) and easy axis (solid squares). (**a**) The inset shows the optical microscopy image of the Py strip inside the microantenna loop. (**b**) FMR spectra measured at the lower and upper limit of the frequency range of the μ-FMR setup.

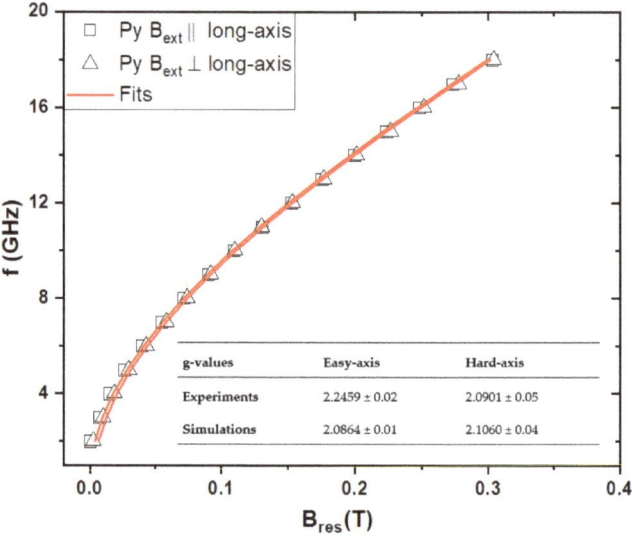

g-values	Easy-axis	Hard-axis
Experiments	2.2459 ± 0.02	2.0901 ± 0.05
Simulations	2.0864 ± 0.01	2.1060 ± 0.04

Figure 6. Field dependences of the resonance frequency of the strip sample with field along the short and long axis, respectively. The inset table shows the experimental (easy and hard axis) g-values as well as the ones that result from fitting the simulated resonance fields to the above mentioned equations.

In case of hard-axis measurements ($\varphi = \varphi_u \pi/2$), Equation (1) yields:

$$(\omega/\gamma)^2 = \left[H_{res} \cos(\varphi - \varphi_H) - \frac{2K_{2\parallel}}{M_s} \right] \times \left[H_{res} \cos(\varphi - \varphi_H) + 4\pi M_{eff} \right] \qquad (3)$$

As given in the inset table, the thin film equations yield anisotropic g-factors, while the rigorous simulation taking into account the true mode pattern (see snapshot 2) in Figure 4 to visualize the pattern of the quasi-uniform mode yields perfect fits for both directions with an isotropic g-factor of 2.12. In contrast, the thin formulas assume all spins to precess in-phase. The example shows that this incorrect scenario results in an erroneous determination of magnetic parameters—here the g-factor. In fact, the g-factor is isotropic, even in the small object, as is clearly revealed by the microantenna measurement together with the micromagnetic simulations. For completeness, we add the values for the effective field, which was found to be 938 mT. As result of the micromagnetic simulation, a comparison of simulation and experimental resonance field values is given in Table 2. For both axes, the resonance field values are in quite good agreement, only slight differences about 1mT between simulation and experimental values occur. Those might result from the shape of the sample being not perfectly rectangular, thereby having impact on the demagnetizing factors, which in fact modify the resonance equations.

Table 2. Comparison of the resonance field values from experiment and simulation of Py strip for both axis at selected frequencies. Resonance field values are given in mT for both axis.

f(GHz)	Bres-Simulation (Easy-Axis)/mT	Bres-Experiment (Easy-Axis)/mT	Bres-Simulation (Hard-Axis)/mT	Bres-Experiment (Hard-Axis)/mT
9	88.5	89.6	92.6	91.8
11	128.6	130.4	132.8	131.3
12	150.6	152.4	154.8	153.4
13	173.6	175.3	177.5	176.8
14	197.6	199.4	201.1	201.1
15	222.4	223.5	225.8	226.7
16	248.0	247.9	251.3	251.4
17	274.3	272.9	277.5	277.6
18	301.1	303.1	304.2	304.4

4. Conclusions

Understanding dynamical properties of nanomagnets plays a crucial role for future spin-based technologies. Our experimental results prove that microresonators are highly sensitive to detecting not only the uniform precession, but also localized spin waves and edge modes in nanometer-sized objects. Besides the microresonator approach, we introduced a "broadband" microantenna design, which adds a variability of the microwave excitation frequency. The method was tested via studying a Py strip sample. The planar (coplanar) structure of the microresonators (microantenna) furthermore provides the advantage of easy access to the material under investigation e.g. in form of light beams. This opens a route to study magnetic resonance in systems that exhibit plasmonic or photonic properties, including the coupling of those fundamental excitations to the magnetic system (e.g., magneto-plasmonics). Moreover, microresonators can be used to study the effects of particle irradiation on the dynamic properties. Recently, the helium ion microscope (HIM) generating a focused ion beam that allows for stepwise "cutting" a sample inside the microresonator loop was used in connection. The process was successfully employed on Fe-filled multi-wall carbon nanotubes (CNT) [19]. The microresonators may further be of use to study magnetism in or of liquids, as they are compatible with liquid environments, e.g., solutions magnetic nanoparticles [18]. In addition, since the magnetic excitation of the resonator loop penetrates into the dielectric resonator substrate by several micrometers, embedded magnetic structures within the dielectric material could be detected. The choice of dielectric material is thereby very flexible, and indeed, prototype resonators based on GaAs have been fabricated, and the method is likely extendable to a variety of other materials.

A disadvantage of the method is that no explicit time-domain measurements are possible, since the external magnetic field is swept quasi-statically. The method thus is a classical frequency domain one that currently in its version of the microantennas provides access to a frequency range of 2–18 GHz, with current efforts being made to achieve up to 35–40 GHz.

As summary, the method which we call "µ-FMR", provides unique insight into the magnetic behavior of a variety of micro/nano-sized magnetic specimens and likely provides a tool for pushing down the detection limit of magnetic resonance experiments to in principle get access to single objects with dimensions below 50 nm.

Author Contributions: Conceptualization: J.L.; methodology: H.C.; formal analysis: H.C.; writing—review and editing: J.L. and H.C.; supervision: J.L. All authors have read and agreed to the published version of the manuscript.

Funding: This study is funded by Institute of Ion Beam Physics and Materials Research at Helmholtz-Zentrum Rossendorf e.V. and the German Research Foundation (DFG)—project number 322462997.

Acknowledgments: We thank S. Stienen for the mumax3 simulations and comments, R. Narkowicz for technical support and comments, K. Lenz and R. Bali for fruitful discussions and comments, and Md. S. Anwar for thin film growth. Additionally, we are thankful to G. Hlawacek for the focused ion beam irradiation. Support by the Nanofabrication Facilities Rossendorf at IBC and the ion beam center of HZDR is gratefully acknowledged.

Conflicts of Interest: The authors declare no conflict of interest.

References

1. Hirohata, A.; Yamada, K.; Nakatani, Y.; Prejbeanu, I.L.; Diény, B.; Pirro, P.; Hillebrands, B. Review on spintronics: Principles and device applications. *J. Magn. Magn. Mater.* **2020**, *509*, 166711. [CrossRef]
2. Barman, A.; Mondal, S.; Sahoo, S.; De, A. Magnetization dynamics of nanoscale magnetic materials: A perspective. *J. Appl. Phys.* **2020**, *128*, 170901. [CrossRef]
3. Wagner, K.; Kákay, A.; Schultheiss, K.; Henschke, A.; Sebastian, T.; Schultheiss, H. Magnetic domain walls as reconfigurable spin-wave nanochannels. *Nat. Nanotechnol.* **2016**, *11*, 432. [CrossRef]
4. Avci, C.A. Picosecond switching in a ferromagnet. *Nat. Electron.* **2020**, *3*, 660. [CrossRef]
5. Wigen, P.E.; Zhang, Z. Ferromagnetic resonance in coupled magnetic multilayer systems. *Braz. J. Phys.* **1992**, *22*, 267.
6. Farle, M. Ferromagnetic resonance of ultrathin metallic layers. *Rep. Prog. Phys.* **1998**, *61*, 755. [CrossRef]
7. Fermin, J.R.; Azevedo, A.; Aguiar, F.M.; Li, B.; Rezende, S.M.J. Ferromagnetic resonance linewidth and anisotropy dispersion in thin Fe films. *Appl. Phys.* **1999**, *85*, 7316. [CrossRef]
8. De Sihues, M.D.; Durante-Rincon, C.A.; Fermin, J.R. A ferromagnetic resonance study of NiFe alloy thin films. *J. Magn. Magn. Mater.* **2007**, *316*, 462. [CrossRef]
9. Lenz, K.; Kosubek, E.; Tolinski, T.; Lindner, J.; Baberschke, K. In situ ferromagnetic resonance in coupled ultrathin trilayers with perpendicularly oriented easy axes. *J. Phys. Condens. Matter* **2003**, *15*, 7175. [CrossRef]
10. Zhang, Z.; Zhou, L.; Wigen, P.E.; Ounadjela, K. Angular dependence of ferromagnetic resonance in exchange-coupled Co/Ru/Co trilayer structures. *Phys. Rev. B* **1994**, *50*, 6094. [CrossRef]
11. Urban, R.; Woltersdorf, G.; Heinrich, B. Gilbert Damping in Single and Multilayer Ultrathin Films: Role of Interfaces in Nonlocal Spin Dynamics. *Phys. Rev. Lett.* **2009**, *87*, 27120. [CrossRef] [PubMed]
12. Poole, C.P., Jr. *Electron Spin Resonance*; Interscience: New York, NY, USA, 1967.
13. Narkowicz, R.; Suter, D.; Stonies, R. Planar microresonators for EPR experiments. *J. Magn. Reson.* **2005**, *175*, 275. [CrossRef]
14. Narkowicz, R.; Suter, D.; Niemeyer, I. Scaling of sensitivity and efficiency in planar microresonators for electron spin resonance. *Rev. Sci. Instrum.* **2008**, *79*, 084702. [CrossRef]
15. Banholzer, A.; Narkowicz, R.; Hassel, C.; Meckenstock, R.; Stienen, S.; Posth, O.; Suter, D.; Farle, M.; Lindner, J. Visualization of spin dynamics in single nanosized magnetic elements. *Nanotechnology* **2011**, *22*, 295713. [CrossRef] [PubMed]
16. Schoeppner, C.; Wagner, K.; Stienen, S.; Meckenstock, R.; Farle, M.; Narkowicz, R.; Suter, D.; Lindner, J. Angular dependent ferromagnetic resonance analysis in a single micron sized cobalt stripe. *J. Appl. Phys.* **2014**, *116*, 033913. [CrossRef]
17. Cansever, H.; Narkowicz, R.; Lenz, K.; Fowley, C.; Ramasubramanian, L.; Yildirim, O.; Niesen, A.; Huebner, T.; Reiss, G.; Lindner, J.; et al. Investigating spin-transfer torques induced by thermal gradients in magnetic tunnel junctions by using micro-cavity ferromagnetic resonance. *J. Phys. D Appl. Phys.* **2018**, *51*, 224009. [CrossRef]
18. Zingsem, B.W.; Feggeler, T.; Terwey, A.; Ghaisari, S.; Spoddig, D.; Faivre, D.; Meckenstock, R.; Farle, M.; Winklhofer, M. Biologically encoded magnonics. *Nat. Commun.* **2019**, *10*, 4345. [CrossRef]
19. Lenz, K.; Narkowicz, R.; Wagner, K.; Reiche, C.F.; Körner, J.; Schneider, T.; Kákay, A.; Schultheiss, H.; Weissker, U.; Wolf, D.; et al. Magnetization Dynamics of an Individual Single-Crystalline Fe-Filled Carbon Nanotube. *Small* **2019**, *15*, 1904315. [CrossRef] [PubMed]
20. Ehrler, J.; Liedke, M.O.; Cizek, J.; Boucher, R.; Butterling, M.; Zhou, S.; Böttger, R.; Hirschmann, E.; Trinh, T.T.; Wagner, A.; et al. The role of open-volume defects in the annihilation of antisites in a B2-ordered alloy. *Acta Mater.* **2019**, *176*, 167. [CrossRef]

21. Tahir, N.; Bali, R.; Gieniusz, R.; Mamica, S.; Gollwitzer, J.; Schneider, T.; Lenz, K.; Potzger, K.; Lindner, J.; Krawczyk, M.; et al. Tailoring dynamic magnetic characteristics of Fe60Al40 films through ion irradiation. *Phys. Rev. B* **2015**, *92*, 144429. [CrossRef]
22. Bali, R.; Wintz, S.; Meutzner, F.; Hubner, R.; Boucher, R.; Unal, S.; Valencia, A.; Neudert, K.; Potzger, J.; Bauch, F.; et al. Fassbender. *Nano Lett.* **2014**, *14*, 435. [CrossRef]
23. La Torre, E.; Smekhova, A.; Schmitz-Antoniak, C.; Ollefs, K.; Eggert, B.; Cöster, B.; Walecki, D.; Wilhelm, F.; Rogalev, A.; Lindner, J.; et al. Local probe of irradiation induced structural changes and orbital magnetism in Fe60Al40 thin films via order-disorder phase transition. *Phys. Rev. B* **2018**, *98*, 024101. [CrossRef]
24. Nord, M.; Semisalova, A.; Kákay, A.; Hlawacek, G.; Maclaren, I.; Liersch, V.; Volkov, O.; Makarov, D.; Paterson, G.W.; Potzger, K.; et al. Strain Anisotropy and Magnetic Domains in Embedded Nanomagnets. *Small* **2019**, *15*, 1904738. [CrossRef]
25. Ehrler, J.; Sanyal, B.; Grenzer, J.; Zhou, S.; Böttger, R.; Wende, H.; Lindner, J.; Faßbender, J.; Leyens, C.; Potzger, K.; et al. Magneto-structural correlations in a systematically disordered B2 lattice. *New J. Phys.* **2020**, *22*, 073004. [CrossRef]
26. Röder, F.; Hlawacek, G.; Wintz, S.; Hübner, R.; Bischoff, L.; Lichte, H.; Potzger, K.; Lindner, J.; Fassbender, J.; Bali, R. Direct Depth- and Lateral- Imaging of Nanoscale Magnets Generated by Ion Impact. *Sci. Rep.* **2015**, *5*, 16786.
27. Schneider, T.; Lenz, K.; Semisalova, A.; Gollwitzer, J.; Heitler-Klevans, J.; Potzger, K.; Fassbender, J.; Lindner, J.; Bali, R. Tuning ferromagnetic resonance via disorder/order interfaces. *J. Appl. Phys.* **2019**, *125*, 195302. [CrossRef]
28. Vansteenkiste, A.; Leliaert, J.; Dvornik, M.; Helsen, M.; Garcia-Sanchez, F.; Van Waeyenberge, B. The design and verification of mumax3. *AIP Adv.* **2014**, *4*, 107133. [CrossRef]
29. Gui, Y.S.; Mecking, N.; Hu, C.M. Quantized spin excitations in a ferromagnetic microstrip from microwave photovoltage measurements. *Phys. Rev. Lett.* **2007**, *98*, 217603. [CrossRef] [PubMed]
30. Wagner, K.; Stienen, S.; Farle, M. Continuous wave approach for simulating Ferromagnetic Resonance in nanosized elements. *arXiv* **2015**, arXiv:1506.05292.
31. Liedke, M.O.; Körner, M.; Lenz, K.; Fritzsche, M.; Ranjan, M.; Keller, A.; Cizmar, E.; Zvyagin, S.A.; Facsko, S.; Potzger, K.; et al. Crossover in the surface anisotropy contributions of ferromagnetic films on rippled Si surfaces. *Phys. Rev. B* **2013**, *87*, 024424. [CrossRef]
32. Möller, M.; Lenz, K.; Lindner, J. Frequency-domain magnetic resonance-alternative detection schemes for samples at the nanoscale. *J. Surf. Interfaces Mater.* **2014**, *2*, 46. [CrossRef]
33. Körner, M.; Lenz, K.; Gallardo, R.A.; Fritzsche, M.; Mücklich, A.; Facsko, S.; Lindner, J.; Landeros, P.; Fassbender, J. Two-magnon scattering in permalloy thin films due to rippled substrates. *Phys. Rev. B* **2013**, *88*, 054405.
34. Trossman, J.; Lim, J.; Bang, W.; Ketterson, J.B.; Tsai, C.C.; Lee, S.J. Effects of an adjacent metal surface on spin wave propagation. *AIP Adv.* **2018**, *8*, 056024. [CrossRef]
35. McMichael, R.D.; Maranville, B.B. Edge saturation fields and dynamic edge modes in ideal and nonideal magnetic film edges. *Phys. Rev. B* **2006**, *74*, 024424. [CrossRef]
36. Boero, G.; Bouterfas, M.; Massin, C.; Vincent, F.; Besse, P.-A.; Popovic, R.S. Electron-spin resonance probe based on a 100 μm planar microcoil. *Rev. Sci. Instrum.* **2003**, *74*, 11. [CrossRef]
37. Chen, X.; Ma, Y.G.; Ong, C.K. Magnetic anisotropy and resonancefrequency of patterned soft magnetic strips. *J. Appl. Phys.* **2008**, *104*, 013921. [CrossRef]
38. Skorohodov, E.V.; Gorev, R.V.; Yakubov, R.R.; Demidov, E.S.; Khivintsev, Y.V.; Filimonov, Y.A.; Mironov, V.L. Ferromagnetic resonance in submicron permalloy stripes. *J. Magn. Magn. Mater.* **2017**, *424*, 118. [CrossRef]

Article

Geometrically Constrained Skyrmions

Swapneel Amit Pathak and Riccardo Hertel *

CNRS, Institut de Physique et Chimie des Matériaux de Strasbourg, Université de Strasbourg, UMR 7504, F-67000 Strasbourg, France; swapneel.pathak@ipcms.unistra.fr
* Correspondence: riccardo.hertel@ipcms.unistra.fr

Abstract: Skyrmions are chiral swirling magnetization structures with nanoscale size. These structures have attracted considerable attention due to their topological stability and promising applicability in nanodevices, since they can be displaced with spin-polarized currents. However, for the comprehensive implementation of skyrmions in devices, it is imperative to also attain control over their geometrical position. Here we show that, through thickness modulations introduced in the host material, it is possible to constrain three-dimensional skyrmions to desired regions. We investigate skyrmion structures in rectangular FeGe platelets with micromagnetic finite element simulations. First, we establish a phase diagram of the minimum-energy magnetic state as a function of the external magnetic field strength and the film thickness. Using this understanding, we generate preferential sites for skyrmions in the material by introducing dot-like "pockets" of reduced film thickness. We show that these pockets can serve as pinning centers for the skyrmions, thus making it possible to obtain a geometric control of the skyrmion position. This control allows for stabilization of skyrmions at positions and in configurations that they would otherwise not attain. Our findings may have implications for technological applications in which skyrmions are used as units of information that are displaced along racetrack-type shift register devices.

Keywords: skyrmions; micromagnetic simulations; geometric pinning; finite-element modelling

Citation: Pathak, S.A.; Hertel, R. Geometrically Constrained Skyrmions. *Magnetochemistry* **2021**, *7*, 26. https://doi.org/10.3390/magnetochemistry7020026

Academic Editor: David S. Schmool

Received: 15 January 2021
Accepted: 4 February 2021
Published: 12 February 2021

Publisher's Note: MDPI stays neutral with regard to jurisdictional claims in published maps and institutional affiliations.

Copyright: © 2021 by the authors. Licensee MDPI, Basel, Switzerland. This article is an open access article distributed under the terms and conditions of the Creative Commons Attribution (CC BY) license (https://creativecommons.org/licenses/by/4.0/).

1. Introduction

Magnetic skyrmions, predicted by theory almost 30 years ago, have advanced to a central topic of research [1–3] in nanoscale magnetism over the last decade following their experimental observation [4,5]. Their particular topological properties [6], which impart them high stability and particle-like behavior [7–9], combined with their room-temperature availability [10,11], reduced dimensions [12], and their unique dynamic properties [13], render these magnetic structures promising candidates for future spintronic applications [14]. Skyrmions are formed in non-centrosymmetric magnetic materials exhibiting a sufficiently strong Dzyaloshinsky–Moriya Interaction (DMI) [4,5,15], that is, an antisymmetric energy term that favors the arrangement of the magnetization in helical spin structures with a specific handedness and spiral period. In extended thin films, in addition to the DMI, the formation and stability of skyrmions depends sensitively on various parameters, such as the strength of an externally applied magnetic field, the film thickness, temperature, and the magnetic history of the sample. Phase diagrams have been reported in the literature [10,16–18], displaying the parameter ranges within which skyrmions are stable and where they may take different forms. Skyrmions may typically either develop individually or in the form of a hexagonal skyrmion lattice. While the occurrence of individual skyrmions makes them attractive candidates for units of information that can be displaced in a controlled way by spin-polarized electric currents, their spontaneous arrangement in the form of a periodic lattice could be interesting for magnonic applications [19], where these point-like magnetic structures could play the role of scattering centers of planar spin waves. One drawback of possible applications of skyrmions is the difficulty of controlling their position. For instance, if skyrmions are to be used as units of information in racetrack-type shift-register devices, it is not only necessary to be able to displace them in a controlled way, but also to make sure that they are shifted between well-defined positions along the track. In domain-wall-based concepts for race-track memory devices [20], which preceded the skyrmion-based variants, this control of the position was typically achieved by inserting indentations ("notches") into the strips [21,22]. It was shown that such notches represent preferential sites for domain walls, making it possible to trap domain walls at these specific positions, from which they could only be detached after overcoming a certain depinning energy [23]. Although the possibility to capture skyrmions at specific sites has been addressed in the case of ultrathin films, geometric control analogous to the pinning of domain walls at notches does not yet seem to be firmly established for skyrmions. In a recent study, Suess and coworkers reported that skyrmions could be pinned in a racetrack-type geometry by introducing semicircular notches at the lateral boundaries [24]. However, the authors also found that skyrmions have a tendency to lose their topological stability and to dissolve when they interact with these notches. In two-dimensional systems, strategies for the pinning of skyrmions include the insertion of point-like defects [25,26] or atomic-scale vacancies [27]. Remarkably, randomly distributed point defects in ultrathin films have also been reported to have little effect on the current-driven skyrmion dynamics [7]. Motivated to further the discussion on this topic by addressing the three-dimensional case of "bulk" DMI, we use finite-element micromagnetic simulations to study the extent to which geometric control of the skyrmion position in a thin-film element can be achieved by introducing a patterning in the form of local variations of the film thickness. Compared to holes or lateral notches, these geometric features have the advantage of preserving the topological stability of skyrmions interacting with them. Our simulations show that, by locally lowering the film thickness in sub-micron-sized, dot-shaped regions, skyrmions can in fact be "captured" at these geometrically defined sites. We find that, by using geometrical constrains of this type, skyrmions can be stabilized at positions that they would otherwise not adopt. For instance, these geometric manipulations make it possible to generate regular, square lattices of skyrmions which, apart from exceptional situations [28], are not observed naturally in non-centrosymmetric ferromagnets. It is argued that this control of skyrmion positions in magnetic thin films can open up new possibilities for skyrmionic devices, as well as for concepts of magnonic metamaterials.

2. Results

Before addressing the question of how preferential sites for skyrmions can be generated through nanopatterning, we first investigate, as a preliminary study, the field- and thickness dependence of skyrmionic structures forming in rectangular FeGe platelets.

2.1. Chiral Magnetization States in a Helimagnetic Rectangular Platelet

We consider rectangular thin-film elements with a lateral size of 180 nm × 310 nm and thicknesses ranging between 5 nm and 75 nm, and simulate the magnetic structures forming in the presence of a perpendicular external magnetic field with a flux density varying between 0 mT and 900 mT. The simulations yield a large variety of possible magnetization states in this thickness and field range, which can be classified into six non-trivial types, summarized in Figure 1. The three main types are the helical state shown in panel (a), which is characterized by the presence of regular spin spirals extending over large parts of the sample, the bimeron state (c), which can be interpreted either as a particular type of skyrmion structure that is stretched along one axis or, alternatively, as a helical state in which the extension of the helices is limited, and finally, the skyrmion lattice state (e), which is characterized by a regular, hexagonal arrangement of skyrmions.

In addition to these three fundamental states, there are also hybrid states in which two different types of structures coexist [29], such as the helical-bimeron state shown in Figure 1b and the bimeron-skyrmion state shown in Figure 1d. These mixed states can be considered as transitional configurations between one fundamental state and another, which appear with changes in the external field value or in the film thickness.

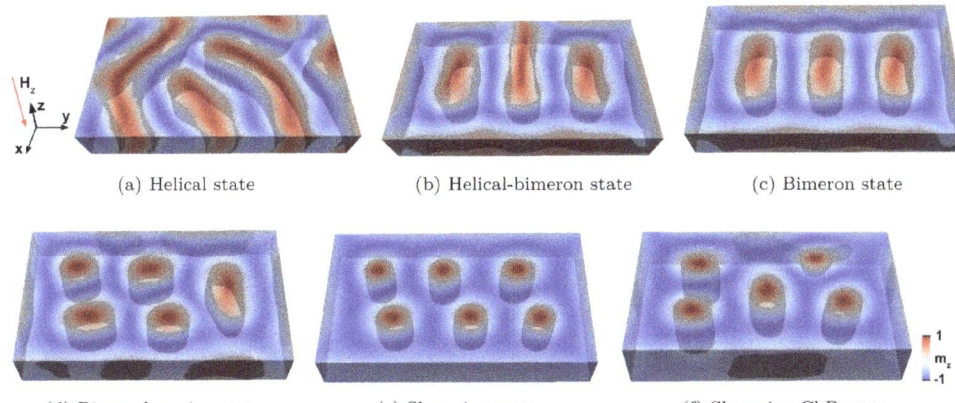

Figure 1. Non-trivial magnetization states forming in a rectangular FeGe platelet (310 nm × 180 nm) of varying thickness (between 5 nm and 60 nm) at different external field values. The color code describes the out-of-plane component m_z of the normalized magnetization, and the isosurfaces indicate the regions where m_z is equal to zero. Structures of this type appear at different film thicknesses as the external magnetic field is applied along the negative z direction and is varied between 0 mT and 900 mT. The arrangement of these configurations in the image corresponds, roughly, to the order in which the preferential configurations appear upon increasing the field strength.

At sufficiently large field values, the platelet can also sustain individual skyrmions which are not arranged in the form of a lattice. Figure 2a shows an example of a magnetic structure containing a single skyrmion, located at the center of a 60 nm thick platelet in a 650 mT field. At this film thickness, the single-skyrmion state does not represent the minimum energy configuration. Nevertheless, the skyrmion is stable and possesses the usual properties of topological protection. In particular, the skyrmion could be manipulated and displaced, such as by means of spin-polarized electrical currents, as is done in racetrack-type devices. We will show later that it is possible to influence the position of such freely moving skyrmions by introducing geometric variations in the platelet, and thereby generate effective pinning sites for skyrmions. In order to obtain more information on the size and the profile of the skyrmion, we display the magnetization components along a line scan through the center, as shown in Figure 2b. The graphs show that the skyrmion is of Bloch type, with vanishing radial magnetization component along the central line. The diameter of the skyrmion core, defined as the distance between two diametrically opposed zero-crossings of the z-component of the magnetization, is almost exactly 30 nm. We found that the skyrmion diameter does not display noticeable variations if the film thickness changes, such as from 60 nm to 30 nm.

At elevated field values and larger film thicknesses, a quasi-homogeneous state is formed (not shown), where the magnetization is largely aligned along the external field direction. At fields below saturation, chiral bobber (ChB) [30,31] structures are also observed. These complex configurations of the magnetization can be considered as variants of skyrmions which do not traverse the entire thickness of the sample. Instead, they have a skyrmion-like structure only on one surface, which evolves into a quasi-saturated configuration on the opposite surface on a path along the film thickness. The apex of the ChB contains a Bloch point at which the magnetic structure changes in a discontinuous way. ChB structures have interesting micromagnetic properties, and have recently been discussed as magnetic structures that could be attractive in the context of spintronic devices [31], but they are not of primary interest for our study. We display an example of a ChB structure only for completeness in the upper right of Figure 1f, where it coexists alongside four ordinary skyrmions. The magnetic structures shown in Figure 1 were obtained by starting from a random initial configuration and by a subsequent energy minimization. For more details, see Section 4.

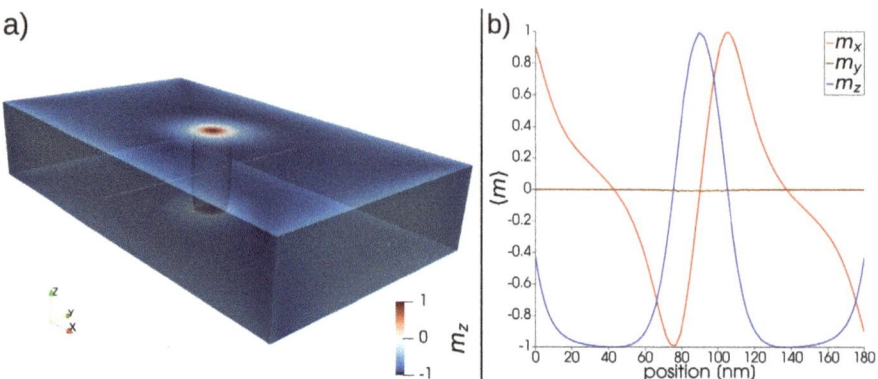

Figure 2. (a) A single magnetic skyrmion in a 60 nm thick platelet, stabilized by a 650 mT field, can form as a metastable state. The skyrmion is located precisely at the center of the thin-film element. The cylindrical shape in the middle is the $m_z = 0$ isosurface, which represents the core region of the skyrmion. (b) The normalized magnetization components along a central cutline—oriented parallel to the y direction and shown as a grey line in panel (a)—display the profile of the skyrmion. From the distance between two consecutive zero values of m_z, we obtain the skyrmion core diameter to be 30 nm. The Bloch character of the skyrmion is evidenced by the antisymmetric shape of the x (azimuthal) component and the vanishing y (radial) component of the magnetization.

2.2. Phase Diagram of the Magnetization States

The various magnetic states described in the previous section are possible equilibrium configurations of the magnetization forming in the FeGe platelets at different values of the external field and the film thickness. It is important to note that these magnetic structures are not uniquely determined by the film thickness and the field strength. Because of this, in order to avoid possible misunderstandings, we did not specify the values of the thickness and the field strength at which the states shown in Figure 1 occur. In fact, several metastable states that can be significantly different from each other are often possible under identical conditions, depending only on the magnetic history of the sample or, in a numerical experiment, on the initial conditions of the simulation. While it is generally not possible to identify a unique magnetization state that develops in the thin-film element, micromagnetic simulations can be used to determine the type of magnetic structure that has the lowest energy. The results of these calculations are summarized in the phase diagram shown in Figure 3a.

Although the magnetic structure at a specific thickness and field value is generally not unique, the phase diagram helps identifying the most preferable structure as far as the total energy is concerned. While at lower field values (below about 400 mT) the phase diagram is rather complex, evidencing a multitude of possible magnetic structures showing neither any clearly dominating state nor a significant thickness dependence, the situation becomes simpler at larger field strengths (above about 600 mT). Two main states emerge in these ranges of larger field values—the skyrmion configuration and the quasi-saturated states. Moreover, these states are separated by a clearly defined boundary in the phase diagram, showing a distinct impact of the film thickness. Specifically, if a field of 650 mT is applied, the formation of skyrmion structures will be energetically favorable if the film thickness is below 50 nm, while a quasi-saturated state will be the lowest-energy configuration at larger thickness values, as shown in Figure 3b. This observation represents the fundamental of the concept of geometrically constrained skyrmions that we present in this study. The idea is the following. If the film thickness is *locally* modulated within a small dot-shaped region such that, at a given field, the skyrmion structure is favorable in that thinner part while in the rest of the sample, the thickness is large enough to favor a quasi-homogeneous state, these thickness modulations can be designed to capture skyrmions. As we will show,

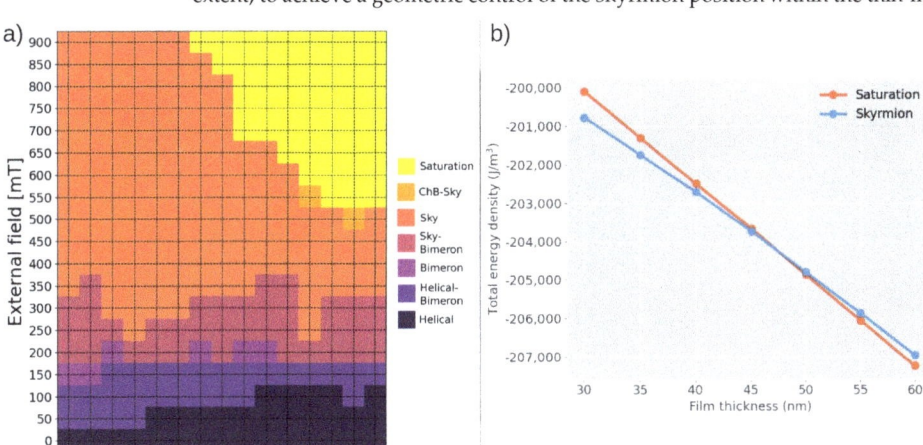

Figure 3. (**a**) Phase diagram displaying the lowest-energy magnetic configuration in the FeGe platelet as a function of the film thickness and the external field strength. At high fields and large film thickness, the quasi-saturated state is the ground state. By lowering the film thickness, the formation of skyrmion structures tends to become energetically favorable. (**b**) Energy density as a function of the film thickness in the case of the skyrmion state (blue line) and the quasi-saturated state (red line) in an external field of 650 mT.

2.3. Geometrically Constrained Skyrmions

We now consider magnetic structures forming in an FeGe platelet of 60 nm thickness containing dot-like cylindrical cavities within which the thickness is locally reduced to 30 nm. The phase diagram displayed in Figure 3 suggests that, at external field values of about 650 mT, the insertion of these cavities results in a geometry with specific regions favoring the stability of skyrmion structures in a thin-film element which would otherwise favor a quasi-homogeneous magnetic configuration. This can lead to the formation, or the trapping, of skyrmions that are geometrically constrained to the regions in which the pockets have been introduced. Figure 4 shows such a geometrically constrained skyrmion in a 60 nm thick platelet. The skyrmion remains confined to the small region in which the thickness is reduced by 50 % through two cylindrical pockets with a depth of 15 nm and radius of $r = 20$ nm, inserted symmetrically on both the top and bottom surfaces. In order to accommodate a single skyrmion, the pocket radius is chosen to be slightly larger than the radius of the skyrmion core (15 nm), obtained by a line-scan of the magnetization components of an isolated skyrmion, as shown in Figure 2.

The geometrically constrained skyrmion, shown in Figure 4, is stabilized by the geometry for two reasons. Firstly, as discussed before, in this field range the skyrmion state is generally favored because of the reduced film thickness. Secondly, the vortex-like magnetic configuration forming on the interior cylinder surfaces of the cavity helps in pinning the position of the skyrmion to the center of the pocket. This cylindrical flux-closure structure thereby provides boundary conditions, albeit not in a mathematical sense, which constrain the skyrmion to this dot-like geometry. By forming such a cylindrical vortex structure, the magnetization finds a nearly optimal way to adapt to competing micromagnetic interactions. It thereby satisfies both the tendency of the DMI to introduce chiral, swirling patterns, as well as the tendency imposed by the magnetostatic interaction to form flux-closure structures with the magnetization aligned along the surfaces. The simulations show that a symmetric insertion of these pockets on both the top and bottom surfaces is necessary to obtain the desired stability and localization of skyrmions. If the thickness variation is introduced only on one of the surfaces, the pinning of skyrmions appears to be much less effective. This result suggests that the previously mentioned swirling of the magnetization at the interior of the cylindrical pockets contributes significantly to the stabilization of the skyrmion position, and that sufficiently strong pinning can only be achieved if these swirling boundary conditions are imposed on both sides of the film.

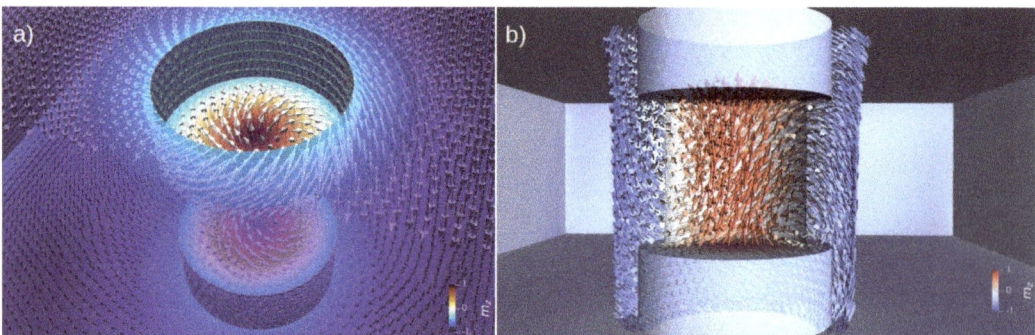

Figure 4. (**a**) A skyrmion is formed at the base of the cylindrical pocket. At the inner cylinder surface of the cavities, the magnetization circulates on closed loops, thereby facilitating the formation of the skyrmion in the center. The semitransparent representation of the surfaces shows the formation of the skyrmion in both pockets, on the top and bottom surfaces. The magnetic structure is displayed by arrows on the sample surfaces. Some of the arrows have been removed in order to improve the visibility of the structure. (**b**) View on the simulated skyrmion structure from inside the film. The skyrmion core connects the bases of the cylindrical pockets in the positive z direction, while the surrounding volume is magnetized in the negative z direction. The core of the skyrmion is delimited by a cylindrical isosurface $m_z = 0$, shown here as a weak, transparent contrast in order to preserve the view on the central magnetic structure. Only a small subset of the calculated local magnetization vectors is displayed.

If geometric modifications of the sample surface, as described above, can stabilize a skyrmion, the question arises whether this effect can be used to place skyrmions at specific positions where they might be generated or removed in a controlled way through external manipulation. This could be of interest, such as for device concepts in which skyrmions are utilized as binary units of information, in a context similar to that of dot-patterned magnetic media for high-density data storage [32]. In this case, the skyrmion pockets would take the role of the magnetic nanodots in bit-patterned media. While it is beyond the scope of this study to discuss the technical feasibility of such storage media or to explore the ability to write and delete individual skyrmion patterns into the pockets, we can show that, indeed, it is possible to stabilize skyrmions in various geometrically predefined locations that could be addressed individually.

Figure 5a–e shows several examples of simulations in which the position of skyrmions in a thin-film element can be predetermined by introducing several pockets of the type discussed before. As shown in Figure 5e, our simulations predict the possibility to stabilize six skyrmions at well-defined positions, placed on a regular grid, in our sub-micron FeGe platelet. Although the results shown in Figure 5 may suggest a nearly optimal geometric control of the skyrmion positions, it is important to note that the pockets discussed here merely provide preferential sites for skyrmions. The latter may or may not form or remain pinned at those sites. In particular, it is not sufficient to thin-out a part of the sample to ensure the appearance of geometrically constrained skyrmions. The purpose of such pockets could rather be to capture existing skyrmions and to fix them at well-defined positions, similar to the domain-wall pinning role that is played by notches in conventional racetrack-memory devices [20,33]. It should also be noted that the geometric trapping of skyrmions with such pockets does not always work, in particular when the pockets are too closely packed. As a rule of thumb, the material must observe a characteristic minimal distance between the skyrmions that is given by the material-dependent, long-range helical period l_D, which in the case of FeGe, is about 70 nm (see Section 4).

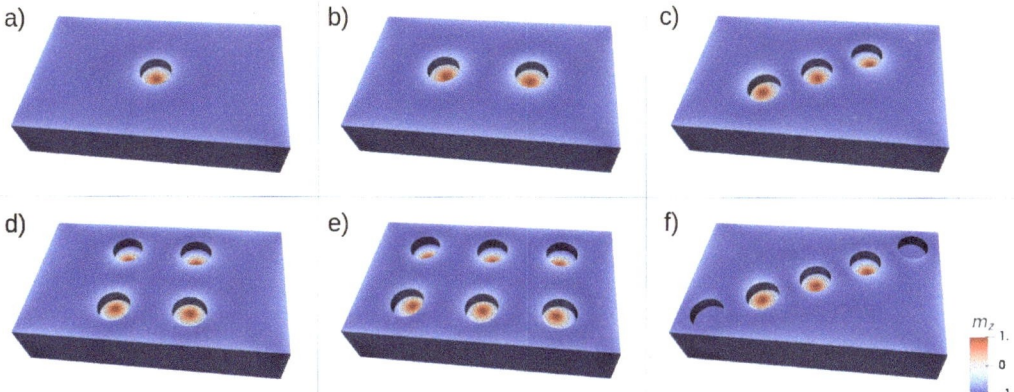

Figure 5. Geometrically constrained skyrmions in FeGe platelets. By introducing circular pockets at specific positions, skyrmions can be artificially stabilized at positions that they would otherwise not attain. Panels (**a**–**e**) show examples in which each pocket contains a skyrmion. The geometric control, however, is not unlimited. Attempts to pack skyrmions too closely or to place them too close to the sample boundary can fail. This is shown in panel (**f**), where skyrmions are stabilized only in the three central pockets, while the two outermost pockets remain empty.

If two skyrmions are constrained in adjacent pockets, the magnetization rotates smoothly by 360° along a line connecting the cores of these skyrmions. Such a continuous rotation of the magnetization direction involves the formation of a spin spiral that must be compatible with the properties of the material. In particular, two skyrmions cannot be constrained geometrically at distances that would be too small to accommodate spin spirals with a periodicity that is much smaller than l_D. We emphasize that, in this context, l_D only serves as an estimate for the *minimal* distance between skyrmions, and that inter-skyrmion distances may be larger than l_D, in particular in the case of stronger external fields [34]. Beyond the simple analytic estimate of the minimal skyrmion spacing based on l_D, detailed studies have established inter-skyrmion repulsion as a general effect [35–37], which ensures that a minimum distance between neighboring skyrmions is preserved. As an example of a dense array of constrained skyrmions approaching this limit, the nearest-neighbor spacing in the array (measured as the distance between the centers of the pockets) of constrained skyrmions shown in Figure 5a is 90 nm. This spacing is compatible with the analytically estimated minimum distance of 70 nm given by the material's helical long-range period, l_D. In this geometry, adding more pockets would reduce the minimal distance below this value, and thereby destabilize the pinning effect. We also found that skyrmions cannot be stabilized at positions too close to the lateral sample boundaries. This observation is consistent with the skyrmion-edge repulsion effect [8,35,37–39], which leads to an increase in energy as a skyrmion approaches the edges of a thin-film element. An example of such a failed attempt to stabilize skyrmions close to the lateral boundaries is shown in Figure 5f. In spite of these limitations, the ability to geometrically constrain skyrmions provides an attractive way to obtain control over the skyrmion position in thin-film elements, which could have important technological implications.

3. Discussion

By means of micromagnetic finite-element simulations, we have presented a possibility to control the position of magnetic skyrmions at predefined positions within a thin-film element by introducing cylindrical nano-pockets graved into the surface. Our concept for geometrically constraining skyrmions *via* such dot-like thickness variations is, in many ways, analogous to the idea of geometrically constrained domain walls [40] in cylindrical nanowires, or to studies in which indentations have been introduced in rectangular strips in order to capture head-to-head domain walls in racetrack-type memory devices [22]. In those cases, too, the desired effect of the geometric constraint is to define preferential sites for specific micromagnetic structures, such that the magnetic structures constrained at those artificial pinning sites require a certain activation energy in order to detach from them. The pockets described in this work could effectively play this role in the case of skyrmions driven along magnetic strips by means of spin-polarized electrical currents. Such geometric control of their position would allow for shifting skyrmions between well-defined points on the track. With the perspective of a possible implementation of this concept in skyrmion-based racetrack devices, future research could address the precise pinning strength that would result from those pockets and the current density that would be required to depin skyrmions captured in such pockets. If the skyrmion pinning effect resulting from pockets, as described in this study, should turn out to be too strong for application purposes, the pinning potential could be reduced in a gradual and straightforward way by modifying the geometric parameters of the pockets. For instance, a weaker pinning effect could be achieved by reducing the depth of the pockets, or by smoothing the edges of the cylinder, such as to yield rounded or cone-shaped pockets.

While racetrack-type skyrmion devices are probably the most straightforward application in which our idea to capture skyrmions at geometrically defined sites could be implemented, the concept of constrained skyrmions could also be useful for other purposes. As mentioned before, the trapping of skyrmions at dot-like sites could serve as a principle for skyrmion-based data storage devices, without necessarily involving any displacement or depinning processes. If skyrmions can be selectively generated and dissolved at such preferential sites, such as by means of the field of a magnetized nano-tip or through a localized spin-polarized current traversing the film thickness, the geometrically constrained skyrmions could represent units of information that could be written and erased. Perhaps such skyrmionic dot material could even be stacked in three dimensions for ultra high-density storage purposes. To address such possibilities, future research directions could explore ways to reversibly insert skyrmions in these geometrically defined regions. Another potentially interesting use of our concept concerns magnonic applications [19,41]. Since skyrmions can act as point-like scattering centers for spin waves, the ability to arrange them at regular lattice sites, as described in this study, could open up new perspectives, as this could result in a new type of magnonic metamaterial in the form of artificial magnon Bragg lattices consisting of skyrmions. Such artificial structures could be tailored to yield specific scattering and interference properties for spin waves that could not be obtained otherwise.

4. Materials and Methods

The material modelled in this study is FeGe. Due to its well-known helimagnetic properties, this B20-type, non-centrosymmetric material serves as a prototype for materials hosting chiral magnetic structures that develop due to the "bulk" DMI effect, as opposed to certain systems of ultra-thin magnetic films and substrates that can generate an "interfacial" DMI [1]. The micromagnetic parameters of FeGe are [18,42] $A = 8.78 \times 10^{-12}$ J m^{-1}, $M_s = 384$ kA m^{-1}, and $D = 1.58 \times 10^{-3}$ J m^{-2}, where A is the ferromagnetic exchange constant, M_s the saturation magnetization, and D the DMI constant. We neglect any magnetocrystalline anisotropy of the material, setting the uniaxial anisotropy to zero, $K_u = 0$ J m^{-3}. A characteristic length scale of this material is the long-range helical period $l_d = 4\pi A/|D| \simeq 70$ nm [43]. This length scale describes the typical period length of magnetic spirals forming as a result of the competing interactions of the ferromagnetic exchange on one hand, and the DMI on the other. The ordering temperature of FeGe is 278.7 K [43]. Therefore, skyrmion devices based on this material are not expected to be operational at room temperature. Chiral structures in FeGe have been observed experimentally, such as at 100 K [37], but recent studies have evidenced that in this material system, skyrmions can be stable also near room-temperature [10,44]. These developments suggest that, although thermal stability is a topic of central importance in skyrmion research [3], temperature limits do not represent a significant obstacle in the case of FeGe.

With the material parameters defined above, the total energy E_{tot} of the system is given by the sum of the Zeeman term, the ferromagnetic exchange, the DMI interaction, and the magnetostatic energy:

$$E_{\text{tot}} = \int_V \left(\mu_0 \boldsymbol{H}_{\text{ext}} \cdot \boldsymbol{M} + A \cdot \sum_{i=x,y,z} (\boldsymbol{\nabla} m_i)^2 + D\boldsymbol{m} \cdot (\boldsymbol{\nabla} \times \boldsymbol{m}) - \frac{\mu_0}{2} \boldsymbol{M} \cdot \boldsymbol{\nabla} u \right) \mathrm{d}V \quad (1)$$

Here, V is the sample volume, $\boldsymbol{H}_{\text{ext}}$ is the externally applied magnetic field, $\mu_0 = 4\pi \times 10^{-7}\,\mathrm{V\,s\,A^{-1}\,m^{-1}}$ is the vacuum permeability, $\boldsymbol{m} = \boldsymbol{M}/M_s$ is the reduced (normalized) magnetization, and u is the magnetostatic scalar potential. The magnetostatic (demagnetizing) field $\boldsymbol{H}_d = -\boldsymbol{\nabla} u$ is the gradient field of the magnetostatic potential. We calculate the magnetostatic potential u, which accounts for the long-range dipolar interaction, by using the hybrid finite-element method/boundary element method (FEM/BEM) introduced by Fredkin and Koehler [45,46]. The dense matrix occurring in the boundary integral part of this formalism is represented using $\mathcal{H}^2$-type hierarchical matrices [47]. This data-sparse representation effectively overcomes size limitations arising from the boundary element method, as it yields a linear scaling of the computational resources required for the calculation of the magnetostatic term, which would otherwise grow quadratically with the number of degrees of freedom on the surface.

For each energy term, an effective field $\boldsymbol{H}_{\text{eff}}$ is defined as the variational derivative of the corresponding partial energy E,

$$\boldsymbol{H}_{\text{eff}}(\boldsymbol{r},t) = -\frac{\delta E[\boldsymbol{M}(\boldsymbol{r},t)]}{\mu_0 \delta \boldsymbol{M}}. \quad (2)$$

Specifically, the effective field of the ferromagnetic exchange is

$$\boldsymbol{H}_{\text{eff}}^{(\text{xc})}(\boldsymbol{r},t) = \frac{2A}{\mu_0 M_s} \Delta \boldsymbol{m}, \quad (3)$$

and the effective field of the DMI is

$$\boldsymbol{H}_{\text{eff}}^{(\text{DMI})}(\boldsymbol{r},t) = -\frac{2D}{\mu_0 M_s}(\nabla \times \boldsymbol{m}). \quad (4)$$

Together with the magnetostatic field and the external (Zeeman) field, these effective fields enter the Landau-Lifshitz-Gilbert (LLG) equation [48], which describes the evolution of the magnetization field $\boldsymbol{M}(\boldsymbol{r},t)$ in time,

$$\frac{\mathrm{d}\boldsymbol{M}}{\mathrm{d}t} = -\gamma(\boldsymbol{M} \times \boldsymbol{H}_{\text{eff}}) + \frac{\alpha}{M_s}\left(\boldsymbol{M} \times \frac{\mathrm{d}\boldsymbol{M}}{\mathrm{d}t}\right), \quad (5)$$

where γ is the gyromagnetic ratio and α is a phenomenological, dimensionless damping constant. We use the LLG equation to calculate equilibrium structures $\boldsymbol{M}(\boldsymbol{r})$ of the magnetization, by integrating in time until convergence is reached. In the numerical simulations, convergence is achieved when either the total energy ceases to change over a long period, or when the torque (magnitude of the right hand side of the LLG equation) drops below a user-defined threshold. The skyrmions stabilized in the pockets, as shown in Figure 5, result from a relaxation process starting from an out-of-plane saturated state of the film. As is common practice in micromagnetic simulations, we consider thermal effects only implicitly via the material parameters. Hence, temperature does not enter directly as a parameter in the simulations.

The geometry of the samples is designed with FreeCAD [49] and the discretization into linear tetrahedral elements is performed with Netgen [50]. The visualization of the

FEM data was done with ParaView [51]. The finite-element cell size does not exceed 2.5 nm, which is well below the exchange length $l_{ex} = \sqrt{2A/\mu_0 M_s^2} \simeq 9.7$ nm, in order to avoid discretization errors. The finite element meshes in this study contain typically about one million finite elements. The micromagnetic simulations are done with our proprietary GPU-accelerated finite-element software [47].

The discretized representation of the vector field of the magnetization is given by a value of M_i defined at each node (vertex) i of the finite-element mesh. The magnetostatic field, as well as the effective fields of the ferromagnetic exchange and the DMI, are calculated within each tetrahedral element. The element-based data of these fields are then mapped onto the nodes of the mesh, in order to calculate the effective field acting on the magnetization, and thus to calculate the evolution of the magnetization in time at each node according to the LLG equation. More details on the calculation of the converged magnetization states are given in Appendix A.

Author Contributions: Conceptualization, S.A.P.; methodology, R.H. and S.A.P.; software, R.H.; writing—original draft preparation, R.H. and S.A.P.; writing—review and editing, R.H. and S.A.P.; visualization, R.H. and S.A.P.; supervision, R.H.; project administration, R.H.; funding acquisition, R.H. All authors have read and agreed to the published version of the manuscript.

Funding: This work has benefited from support by the initiative of excellence IDEX-Unistra (ANR-10-IDEX-0002-02) through the French National Research Agency (ANR) as part of the "Investment for the Future" program.

Institutional Review Board Statement: Not applicable.

Informed Consent Statement: Not applicable.

Data Availability Statement: The simulation data are available from the authors upon reasonable request.

Acknowledgments: The authors acknowledge the High Performance Computing center of the University of Strasbourg for supporting this work by providing access to computing resources. Part of the computing resources were funded by the Equipex Equip@Meso project (Programme Investissements d'Avenir) and the CPER Alsacalcul/Big Data.

Conflicts of Interest: The authors declare no conflict of interest. The funders had no role in the design of the study; in the collection, analyses, or interpretation of data; in the writing of the manuscript, or in the decision to publish the results.

Abbreviations

The following abbreviations are used in this manuscript:

DMI Dzyaloshinksii-Moryia interaction
LLG Landau-Lifshitz-Gilbert equation
FEM Finite Element Method
BEM Boundary Element Method
GPU Graphical Processing Unit
3D   three-dimensional
ChB chiral bobber

Appendix A. Energy Minimization

Because in this particular study we are not interested in the dynamic evolution of the magnetization but only in static, converged magnetic structures, the integration of the LLG equation in the code fulfils the practical role of guiding the system along a path of energy-minimization in an iterative way. Since the dynamics of the magnetization during the transition from the initial to the converged state is irrelevant for this work, we are free to choose a conveniently large damping parameter $\alpha = 0.5$ in order to accelerate the energy minimization. Furthermore, we remove the precession term by setting $\gamma = 0$ in Equation (5), thereby effectively using a a direct energy minimization scheme instead of following the path of the magnetization dynamics described by the LLG equation.

The numerical integration is done with a Dormand-Prince algorithm [52], and the effective field values are refreshed several times during each time step. The choice of a large value of the damping allows us to use time steps of up to 1 ps, which is about ten times larger than the step size that we would usually employ in dynamic simulations with low damping. With these parameters, and owing to the GPU acceleration of our code, it takes only a short time (between several minutes and a few hours) to simulate the magnetic structures discussed in this work. To calculate the skyrmion states, we either start from a random configuration or saturate the magnetization along the positive z direction and subsequently let the system relax in the presence of an external magnetic field aligned along the negative z direction. The z axis is oriented parallel to the surface normal, as shown in Figure 1.

References

1. Finocchio, G.; Büttner, F.; Tomasello, R.; Carpentieri, M.; Kläui, M. Magnetic skyrmions: From fundamental to applications. *J. Phys. D Appl. Phys.* **2016**, *49*, 423001. [CrossRef]
2. Everschor-Sitte, K.; Masell, J.; Reeve, R.M.; Kläui, M. Perspective: Magnetic skyrmions—Overview of recent progress in an active research field. *J. Appl. Phys.* **2018**, *124*, 240901. [CrossRef]
3. Back, C.; Cros, V.; Ebert, H.; Everschor-Sitte, K.; Fert, A.; Garst, M.; Ma, T.; Mankovsky, S.; Monchesky, T.L.; Mostovoy, M.; et al. The 2020 skyrmionics roadmap. *J. Phys. D Appl. Phys.* **2020**, *53*, 363001. [CrossRef]
4. Muhlbauer, S.; Binz, B.; Jonietz, F.; Pfleiderer, C.; Rosch, A.; Neubauer, A.; Georgii, R.; Boni, P. Skyrmion Lattice in a Chiral Magnet. *Science* **2009**, *323*, 915–919. [CrossRef]
5. Yu, X.; Onose, Y.; Kanazawa, N.; Park, J.; Han, J.; Matsui, Y.; Nagaosa, N.; Tokura, Y. Real-space observation of a two-dimensional skyrmion crystal. *Nature* **2010**, *465*, 901–904. [CrossRef] [PubMed]
6. Oike, H.; Kikkawa, A.; Kanazawa, N.; Taguchi, Y.; Kawasaki, M.; Tokura, Y.; Kagawa, F. Interplay between topological and thermodynamic stability in a metastable magnetic skyrmion lattice. *Nat. Phys.* **2016**, *12*, 62–66. [CrossRef]
7. Iwasaki, J.; Mochizuki, M.; Nagaosa, N. Universal current-velocity relation of skyrmion motion in chiral magnets. *Nat. Commun.* **2013**, *4*, 1463. [CrossRef]
8. Iwasaki, J.; Mochizuki, M.; Nagaosa, N. Current-induced skyrmion dynamics in constricted geometries. *Nat. Nanotechnol.* **2013**, *8*, 742–747. [CrossRef]
9. Xuan, S.; Liu, Y. Nonuniform gyrotropic oscillation of skyrmion in a nanodisk. *AIP Adv.* **2018**, *8*, 045312. [CrossRef]
10. Yu, X.Z.; Kanazawa, N.; Onose, Y.; Kimoto, K.; Zhang, W.Z.; Ishiwata, S.; Matsui, Y.; Tokura, Y. Near room-temperature formation of a skyrmion crystal in thin-films of the helimagnet FeGe. *Nat. Mater.* **2011**, *10*, 106–109. [CrossRef]
11. Boulle, O.; Vogel, J.; Yang, H.; Pizzini, S.; de Souza Chaves, D.; Locatelli, A.; Menteş, T.O.; Sala, A.; Buda-Prejbeanu, L.D.; Klein, O.; et al. Room-temperature chiral magnetic skyrmions in ultrathin magnetic nanostructures. *Nat. Nanotechnol.* **2016**, *11*, 449. [CrossRef] [PubMed]
12. Heinze, S.; Von Bergmann, K.; Menzel, M.; Brede, J.; Kubetzka, A.; Wiesendanger, R.; Bihlmayer, G.; Blügel, S. Spontaneous atomic-scale magnetic skyrmion lattice in two dimensions. *Nat. Phys.* **2011**, *7*, 713–718. [CrossRef]
13. Yu, X.; Kanazawa, N.; Zhang, W.; Nagai, T.; Hara, T.; Kimoto, K.; Matsui, Y.; Onose, Y.; Tokura, Y. Skyrmion flow near room temperature in an ultralow current density. *Nat. Commun.* **2012**, *3*, 988. [CrossRef] [PubMed]
14. Fert, A.; Cros, V.; Sampaio, J. Skyrmions on the track. *Nat. Nanotechnol.* **2013**, *8*, 152–156. [CrossRef]
15. Seki, S.; Yu, X.; Ishiwata, S.; Tokura, Y. Observation of skyrmions in a multiferroic material. *Science* **2012**, *336*, 198–201. [CrossRef]
16. Rybakov, F.N.; Borisov, A.B.; Bogdanov, A.N. Three-dimensional skyrmion states in thin films of cubic helimagnets. *Phys. Rev. B* **2013**, *87*, 094424. [CrossRef]
17. Rybakov, F.N.; Borisov, A.B.; Blügel, S.; Kiselev, N.S. New spiral state and skyrmion lattice in 3D model of chiral magnets. *New J. Phys.* **2016**, *18*, 045002. [CrossRef]
18. Beg, M.; Carey, R.; Wang, W.; Cortés-Ortuño, D.; Vousden, M.; Bisotti, M.A.; Albert, M.; Chernyshenko, D.; Hovorka, O.; Stamps, R.L.; et al. Ground state search, hysteretic behaviour, and reversal mechanism of skyrmionic textures in confined helimagnetic nanostructures. *Sci. Rep.* **2015**, *5*, 17137. [CrossRef]
19. Ma, F.; Zhou, Y.; Braun, H.B.; Lew, W.S. Skyrmion-Based Dynamic Magnonic Crystal. *Nano Lett.* **2015**, *15*, 4029–4036. [CrossRef]
20. Parkin, S.S.P.; Hayashi, M.; Thomas, L. Magnetic Domain-Wall Racetrack Memory. *Science* **2008**, *320*, 190–194. [CrossRef] [PubMed]
21. Bedau, D.; Kläui, M.; Rüdiger, U.; Vaz, C.A.F.; Bland, J.A.C.; Faini, G.; Vila, L.; Wernsdorfer, W. Angular dependence of the depinning field for head-to-head domain walls at constrictions. *J. Appl. Phys.* **2007**, *101*, 09F509. [CrossRef]
22. Bogart, L.K.; Eastwood, D.S.; Atkinson, D. The effect of geometrical confinement and chirality on domain wall pinning behavior in planar nanowires. *J. Appl. Phys.* **2008**, *104*, 033904. [CrossRef]
23. Garcia-Sanchez, F.; Kákay, A.; Hertel, R.; Asselin, P. Depinning of Transverse Domain Walls from Notches in Magnetostatically Coupled Nanostrips. *Appl. Phys. Express* **2011**, *4*, 033001. [CrossRef]
24. Suess, D.; Vogler, C.; Bruckner, F.; Heistracher, P.; Slanovc, F.; Abert, C. Spin Torque Efficiency and Analytic Error Rate Estimates of Skyrmion Racetrack Memory. *Sci. Rep.* **2019**, *9*, 4827. [CrossRef]

25. Liu, Y.H.; Li, Y.Q. A mechanism to pin skyrmions in chiral magnets. *J. Phys. Condens. Matter* **2013**, *25*, 076005. [CrossRef]
26. Hanneken, C.; Kubetzka, A.; Bergmann, K.V.; Wiesendanger, R. Pinning and movement of individual nanoscale magnetic skyrmions via defects. *New J. Phys.* **2016**, *18*, 055009. [CrossRef]
27. Müller, J.; Rosch, A. Capturing of a magnetic skyrmion with a hole. *Phys. Rev. B* **2015**, *91*, 054410. [CrossRef]
28. Karube, K.; White, J.S.; Reynolds, N.; Gavilano, J.L.; Oike, H.; Kikkawa, A.; Kagawa, F.; Tokunaga, Y.; Rønnow, H.M.; Tokura, Y.; et al. Robust metastable skyrmions and their triangular–square lattice structural transition in a high-temperature chiral magnet. *Nat. Mater.* **2016**, *15*, 1237–1242. [CrossRef] [PubMed]
29. Mandru, A.O.; Yıldırım, O.; Tomasello, R.; Heistracher, P.; Penedo, M.; Giordano, A.; Suess, D.; Finocchio, G.; Hug, H.J. Coexistence of distinct skyrmion phases observed in hybrid ferromagnetic/ferrimagnetic multilayers. *Nat. Commun.* **2020**, *11*, 6365. [CrossRef] [PubMed]
30. Rybakov, F.N.; Borisov, A.B.; Blügel, S.; Kiselev, N.S. New Type of Stable Particlelike States in Chiral Magnets. *Phys. Rev. Lett.* **2015**, *115*, 117201. [CrossRef] [PubMed]
31. Zheng, F.; Rybakov, F.N.; Borisov, A.B.; Song, D.; Wang, S.; Li, Z.A.; Du, H.; Kiselev, N.S.; Caron, J.; Kovács, A.; et al. Experimental observation of chiral magnetic bobbers in B20-type FeGe. *Nat. Nanotechnol.* **2018**, *13*, 451–455. [CrossRef] [PubMed]
32. Ross, C. Patterned Magnetic Recording Media. *Annu. Rev. Mater. Res.* **2001**, *31*, 203–235. [CrossRef]
33. Hayashi, M.; Thomas, L.; Rettner, C.; Moriya, R.; Jiang, X.; Parkin, S.S.P. Dependence of Current and Field Driven Depinning of Domain Walls on Their Structure and Chirality in Permalloy Nanowires. *Phys. Rev. Lett.* **2006**, *97*, 207205. [CrossRef]
34. Wilson, M.N.; Butenko, A.B.; Bogdanov, A.N.; Monchesky, T.L. Chiral skyrmions in cubic helimagnet films: The role of uniaxial anisotropy. *Phys. Rev. B* **2014**, *89*, 094411. [CrossRef]
35. Brearton, R.; van der Laan, G.; Hesjedal, T. Magnetic skyrmion interactions in the micromagnetic framework. *Phys. Rev. B* **2020**, *101*, 134422. [CrossRef]
36. Lin, S.Z.; Reichhardt, C.; Batista, C.D.; Saxena, A. Particle model for skyrmions in metallic chiral magnets: Dynamics, pinning, and creep. *Phys. Rev. B* **2013**, *87*, 214419. [CrossRef]
37. Zhang, X.; Zhao, G.P.; Fangohr, H.; Liu, J.P.; Xia, W.X.; Xia, J.; Morvan, F.J. Skyrmion-skyrmion and skyrmion-edge repulsions in skyrmion-based racetrack memory. *Sci. Rep.* **2015**, *5*, 7643. [CrossRef] [PubMed]
38. Sampaio, J.; Cros, V.; Rohart, S.; Thiaville, A.; Fert, A. Nucleation, stability and current-induced motion of isolated magnetic skyrmions in nanostructures. *Nat. Nanotechnol.* **2013**, *8*, 839. [CrossRef]
39. Duine, R. Skyrmions singled out. *Nat. Nanotechnol.* **2013**, *8*, 800–802. [CrossRef]
40. Bruno, P. Geometrically Constrained Magnetic Wall. *Phys. Rev. Lett.* **1999**, *83*, 2425–2428. [CrossRef]
41. Garst, M.; Waizner, J.; Grundler, D. Collective spin excitations of helices and magnetic skyrmions: Review and perspectives of magnonics in non-centrosymmetric magnets. *J. Phys. D Appl. Phys.* **2017**, *50*, 293002. [CrossRef]
42. Cortés-Ortuño, D.I.; Beg, M.; Nehruji, V.; Breth, L.; Pepper, R.; Kluyver, T.; Downing, G.; Hesjedal, T.; Hatton, P.; Lancaster, T.; et al. Proposal for a micromagnetic standard problem for materials with Dzyaloshinskii-Moriya interaction. *New J. Phys.* **2018**. [CrossRef]
43. Lebech, B.; Bernhard, J.; Freltoft, T. Magnetic structures of cubic FeGe studied by small-angle neutron scattering. *J. Phys. Condens. Matter* **1989**, *1*, 6105–6122. [CrossRef]
44. Zhao, X.; Jin, C.; Wang, C.; Du, H.; Zang, J.; Tian, M.; Che, R.; Zhang, Y. Direct imaging of magnetic field-driven transitions of skyrmion cluster states in FeGe nanodisks. *Proc. Natl. Acad. Sci. USA* **2016**, *113*, 4918–4923. [CrossRef]
45. Fredkin, D.; Koehler, T. Hybrid method for computing demagnetizing fields. *IEEE Trans. Magn.* **1990**, *26*, 415–417. [CrossRef]
46. Koehler, T.; Fredkin, D. Finite element methods for micromagnetics. *IEEE Trans. Magn.* **1992**, *28*, 1239–1244. [CrossRef]
47. Hertel, R.; Christophersen, S.; Börm, S. Large-scale magnetostatic field calculation in finite element micromagnetics with H2-matrices. *J. Magn. Magn. Mater.* **2019**, *477*, 118–123. [CrossRef]
48. Gilbert, T.L. A phenomenological theory of damping in ferromagnetic materials. *IEEE Trans. Magn.* **2004**, *40*, 3443–3449. [CrossRef]
49. Riegel, J.; Mayer, W.; van Havre, Y. FreeCAD (0.18). Available online: https://www.freecadweb.org/ (accessed on 12 December 2020).
50. Schöberl, J. NETGEN An advancing front 2D/3D-mesh generator based on abstract rules. *Comput. Vis. Sci.* **1997**, *1*, 41–52. [CrossRef]
51. Ayachit, U. *The ParaView Guide: A Parallel Visualization Application*; Kitware: Clifton Park, NY, USA, 2015.
52. Ahnert, K.; Mulansky, M. Odeint—Solving Ordinary Differential Equations in C++. *AIP Conf. Proc.* **2011**, *1389*, 1586–1589. [CrossRef]

Article

Novel Magnetic Nanohybrids: From Iron Oxide to Iron Carbide Nanoparticles Grown on Nanodiamonds

Panagiotis Ziogas [1], Athanasios B. Bourlinos [1], Jiri Tucek [2], Ondrej Malina [3] and Alexios P. Douvalis [1,4,*]

[1] Physics Department, University of Ioannina, 45110 Ioannina, Greece; p.ziogas@oui.gr (P.Z.); bourlino@uoi.gr (A.B.B.)
[2] Department of Mathematics and Physics, Faculty of Electrical Engineering and Informatics, University of Pardubice, Náměstí Čs. legií 565, 530 02 Pardubice, Czech Republic; jiri.tucek@upce.cz
[3] Regional Centre of Advanced Technologies and Materials, Palacky University Olomouc, 17. Listopadu 1192/12, 771 46 Olomouc, Czech Republic; ondrej.malina@upol.cz
[4] Institute of Materials Science and Computing, University Research Center of Ioannina (URCI), 45110 Ioannina, Greece
* Correspondence: adouval@uoi.gr

Received: 7 November 2020; Accepted: 17 December 2020; Published: 21 December 2020

Abstract: The synthesis and characterization of a new line of magnetic hybrid nanostructured materials composed of spinel-type iron oxide to iron carbide nanoparticles grown on nanodiamond nanotemplates is reported in this study. The realization of these nanohybrid structures is achieved through thermal processing under vacuum at different annealing temperatures of a chemical precursor, in which very fine maghemite (γ-Fe_2O_3) nanoparticles seeds were developed on the surface of the nanodiamond nanotemplates. It is seen that low annealing temperatures induce the growth of the maghemite nanoparticle seeds to fine dispersed spinel-type non-stoichiometric ~5 nm magnetite ($Fe_{3-x}O_4$) nanoparticles, while intermediate annealing temperatures lead to the formation of single phase ~10 nm cementite (Fe_3C) iron carbide nanoparticles. Higher annealing temperatures produce a mixture of larger Fe_3C and Fe_5C_2 iron carbides, triggering simultaneously the growth of large-sized carbon nanotubes partially filled with these carbides. The magnetic features of the synthesized hybrid nanomaterials reveal the properties of their bearing magnetic phases, which span from superparamagnetic to soft and hard ferromagnetic and reflect the intrinsic magnetic properties of the containing phases, as well as their size and interconnection, dictated by the morphology and nature of the nanodiamond nanotemplates. These nanohybrids are proposed as potential candidates for important technological applications in nano-biomedicine and catalysis, while their synthetic route could be further tuned for development of new magnetic nanohybrid materials.

Keywords: magnetic nanohybrid materials; nanodiamonds; nanoparticles; iron carbides; Fe_3C; spinel-type iron oxide; Mössbauer spectroscopy

---

1. Introduction

Iron carbides (ICs) are among the oldest synthetic materials that are known to, and produced by, humans, arising historically even before the discovery of pure iron [1,2]. They are well known for their prominent structural and mechanical properties and have been used as adjuvant agents in concretes and metal alloys [3]. The presence of the most known member of the family of ICs, cementite (θ-Fe_3C), in pearlitic steels, is the main parameter for the development of the exceptional mechanical properties (high strength and ductility) these technologically and economically important materials possess relative to soft iron [3–9]. ICs have also been known to possess important catalytic properties, used as relative agents in the Fisher-Tropsch synthetic fuel production process [10–12] and carbon nanotube (CNT) synthesis [13–15].

Nowadays, novel interest has been raised again over the ICs in the form of nanostructures, due to their accessional magnetic properties [16]. In particular, ICs' ferromagnetic properties demonstrating high T_C and saturation magnetization (M_S) [2], adjoined to their chemical corrosion resistance and inertness and combining the fact that their main elemental content, iron, is rather sustainable and relatively nontoxic, have launched new efforts for development and investigation of these materials in the nanoscale [1,17]. ICs present better chemical and thermal stability over metallic iron, as well as higher M_S than some types of iron oxides (IOs) [18,19], which can also be used in magnetic applications. Recently, more types of magnetic nanoparticles (NPs) than the traditional metallic alloys have been recruited technologically on a prospect to facilitate or even to make a breakthrough in many scientific fields like data storage, ferrofluids and biomedicine. IC NPs could indeed be suitable for a diversity of applications, from biomedicine [20,21], to electronics [22,23] and the design of novel catalysts exploiting the magnetically induced heating effect [24–26].

ICs thermodynamically stable and metastable phases can exist in many Fe:C stoichiometries, forming several compounds which can be classified in octahedral, tetrahedral and trigonal prismatic structures according to the sites occupied by the carbon atoms [16,27–30]. In general, due to the large number of available Fe:C stoichiometries, their corresponding phase interconnection and ease of formation, the practical synthesis of pure IC samples of certain defined composition usually suffers from the presence of other related IC phase impurities, especially when the quest is focused in the preparation of nanostructured materials, which is essential for most contemporary applications [26,31]. In the frame of this scope, several strategies have been applied following physical and chemical routes to realize pure ICs either as stand-alone NPs or in some supported medium [1,17,32,33]. Carbon-type supports of IC NPs could be favorable over other types of supports because of the ease of reducibility of iron on carbon relative to other elements or compounds. Therefore, the use of carbon-type materials that will carry other materials as the supporting template, either in nanoscale or in bulk sizes, would induce high scientific and technological interest and potential for future dynamic applications. Moreover, the nature and physical and chemical characteristics of the NPs' support medium can be used to develop factors that will determine, through their interaction, the NPs' morphology and interconnection, affecting thus their overall properties [34,35].

On the other hand, it is widely known that diamonds are used in a variety of technological applications due to their unique structural, morphological, mechanical, electrical and thermal properties [36]. Moreover, in recent years great interest has been emerged for diamonds in the nanoscale, the nanodiamonds (NDs), due to their excellent biocompatibility and their ability to form clustered aggregations developing tight nanotemplates, which can operate as support matrices for the further development of other nanomaterials [37–42].

Following the trend of our group's recent development of hybrid $L1_0$ FePt NPs/NDs nanostructures [43], we report here the synthesis, characterization and study of the morphological, structural and magnetic properties of a new line of hybrid nanostructured system, that combines a set of different types of magnetic NPs and nanostructures, from IOs to ICs NPs and carbon nanotubes (CNTs), developed on NDs nanotemplates (IO-IC NPs/NDs). In our current study we have taken the path of producing a chemical precursor (CP) via wet chemical methods, which was subsequently thermally treated (annealed) under controlled conditions in a range of temperatures. The samples were characterized by X-ray diffraction (XRD), transmission electron microscopy (TEM), magnetization measurements and ^{57}Fe Mössbauer spectroscopy. The results reveal that the annealing temperature determines to a large extend the type and nature of the nanophases produced on the surface of the NDs nanotemplates nanohybrids (NHDs). Relatively low annealing temperatures favor the production of IOs, high annealing temperatures the production of a mixture of different IC phases and large CNTs, while for intermediate annealing temperatures, high quality single phase Fe_3C NPs/NDs NHDs with uniform size distribution and nice dispersion of the cementite NPs over the NDs nanotemplates assemblies are produced. This NHDs system presents magnetic properties that hold potential for proposed applications as agents for contrast enhancement in magnetic resonance imaging (MRI) [44,45] and/or magnetic particle imaging (MPI) [46,47], as well as for magnetic hyperthermia [48] and magnetically induced heating heterogeneous catalysis [24,49].

2. Experimental

2.1. Materials Synthesis

The hybrid nanostructured materials were synthesized by a two stage procedure: in the first stage, a CP was produced following the wet chemistry impregnation method [50,51], in which the NDs nanotemplates were functionalized with the appropriate IO NPs development seeds. In particular, 300 mg Fe(NO$_3$)$_3$·9H$_2$O (99.999%, Aldrich 529303) were diluted in 3 mL of deionized water and the solution was mixed with 540 mg of NDs powder (98%, Aldrich 636428). The mixture was blended and homogenized well in the form of a moist paste on an agate mortar and left to dry at 100 °C for 24 h. After dehydration and re-homogenization into fine powder, the material was calcined at 400 °C for 1 h in order to release the nitrates and produce ferric IO NPs seeds on the surfaces of the NDs nanotemplates (Figure 1).

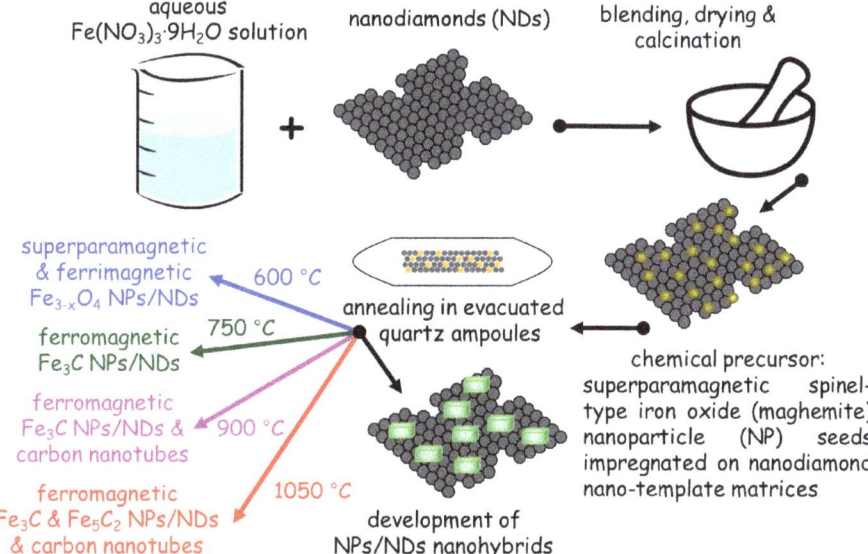

Figure 1. Schematic representation of the synthesis stages followed and the resulting nanohybrid samples produced in this work.

The initial Fe(NO$_3$)$_3$·9H$_2$O/NDs mass ratio was calculated to produce the CP containing a nominal average 10 wt% ferric IO loading relative to the NDs nanotemplates, with the oxide chemical formula composition estimated as Fe$_2$O$_3$. In the second stage, the CP was sealed in quartz ampoules under vacuum (10^{-3} Torr) and annealed at annealing temperatures of 1050 °C (NHDs-1050), 900 °C (NHDs-900), 750 °C (NHDs-750) and 600 °C (NHDs-600) for 4 h. Depending on the magnitude of the annealing temperature, a range of different nanophases were developed on the surfaces of the NDs nanotemplates (Figure 1).

2.2. Materials Characterization

XRD of the powder CP and NHD samples were collected on a Bruker Advance D8 diffractometer using a Cu K_α radiation in order to examine the structural properties of the phases present in them and their average particle sizes. The samples' particle morphology, size and stoichiometry were investigated by TEM using a JEOL JEM2010 microscope operated at 200 kV with a point-to-point resolution of 1.9 Å and element-mapping capability by means of high-angle annular dark field (HAADF) microscopy. Before TEM measurements, the samples were dispersed in ethanol, and the suspension was treated in ultrasound for 10 min. A drop of very dilute suspension was placed on a carbon coated grid and allowed to dry by evaporation at ambient temperature. A superconducting quantum interference device (SQUID) magnetometer (Quantum Design MPMS XL-7) was used to investigate the magnetic properties of the samples by means of magnetization (M) and mass magnetic susceptibility (χ_g) measurements. M versus (vs) external applied magnetic field (H) hysteresis loops were collected at temperatures of 5 and 300 K in fields up to 50 kOe. The zero-field-cooled (ZFC) and field-cooled (FC) χ_g vs. temperature curves were recorded on warming the samples in the temperature range from 5 to 300 K under H = 1000 Oe, after cooling them in zero magnetic field and on cooling, immediately after the warming procedure under the above magnetic field, respectively. ^{57}Fe Mössbauer spectra (MS) of the CP and the synthesized NHDs were collected in transmission geometry at 300, 77 and 11 K using constant-acceleration spectrometers, equipped with ^{57}Co(Rh) sources kept at room temperature (RT), in combination with a liquid N_2 bath (Oxford Instruments Variox 760) and a gas He closed loop (ARS DMX-20) Mössbauer cryostats. Velocity calibration of the spectrometers was carried out using metallic α-Fe at 300 K and all isomer shift (IS) values are given relative to this standard. The experimentally recorded MS were fitted and analyzed using the IMSG code [52].

3. Results and Discussion

3.1. XRD

The XRD patterns of the CP and the annealed NHD samples are shown in Figure 2.

Two broad diffraction peaks characteristic of the cubic NDs structure at 43.9 (111) and 75.3 (220) degrees 2θ dominate the XRD diagram of the CP sample, where two additional very broad peak regions spanning from around 30 to 40 and 55 to 65 degrees 2θ are compatible with contributions from the respective angular positions of the main diffraction peaks of a spinel-type γ-Fe_2O_3 (maghemite) IO structure at 30 (220), 35 (311), 57 (511) and 63 (440) degrees 2θ [53]. The very broad diffraction peaks of this phase, overcoming the angular widths of single peaks by being expanded in widths including several single peaks (e.g., ~25–40 degrees 2θ), constitute identifying evidence of its extremely small NPs sizes and low crystallinity in the CP.

It is evident from Figure 2b that annealing the CP at 1050 °C has immediate effect on the formation of crystalline phases. In particular, apart from the presence of the characteristic NDs diffraction peaks, a major contribution from the (002) planes of a graphitic-type structure is evident by a very strong peak at 25.6 degrees 2θ. The exact nature and morphology of this phase cannot be resolved from the XRD results alone, and further analysis with TEM will reveal its features (vide infra). A combination of several diffraction peaks characteristic of the orthorhombic Fe_3C structure dominate the part of this XRD diagram between 35 and 90 degrees 2θ, while a careful inspection of the area between 40 and 50 degrees 2θ reveals the presence of the major diffraction peaks of the monoclinic Fe_5C_2 structure. The XRD diagram of the NHDs-900 sample in Figure 2c is quite similar to that of the NHDs-1050 sample; however, the intensity of the diffraction peak of the graphitic-type planes is reduced and contributions of the diffraction peaks of the monoclinic Fe_5C_2 structure are absent. In the XRD diagram of the NHDs-750 sample in Figure 2d, the diffraction peak of the graphitic-type planes is completely absent, while there is also no evidence of the presence of diffraction peaks for the Fe_5C_2 phase. The characteristic diffraction peaks of the NDs and the Fe_3C phase are the only contributions to this diagram, in which a further broadening of the diffraction peaks of this IC phase is clearly shown, indicating a further reduction in its average particle size, relative to the sharper peaks appearing at the XRD diagrams of the higher annealing temperatures samples. Figure 2e reveals an XRD diagram of the NHDs-600 sample exempt from the appearance of any graphitic-type or ICs contributions, while the presence of the NDs diffraction peaks is accompanied only by the occurrence of the characteristic diffraction peaks of a spinel-type magnetite/maghemite (Fe_3O_4/γ-Fe_2O_3) structure.

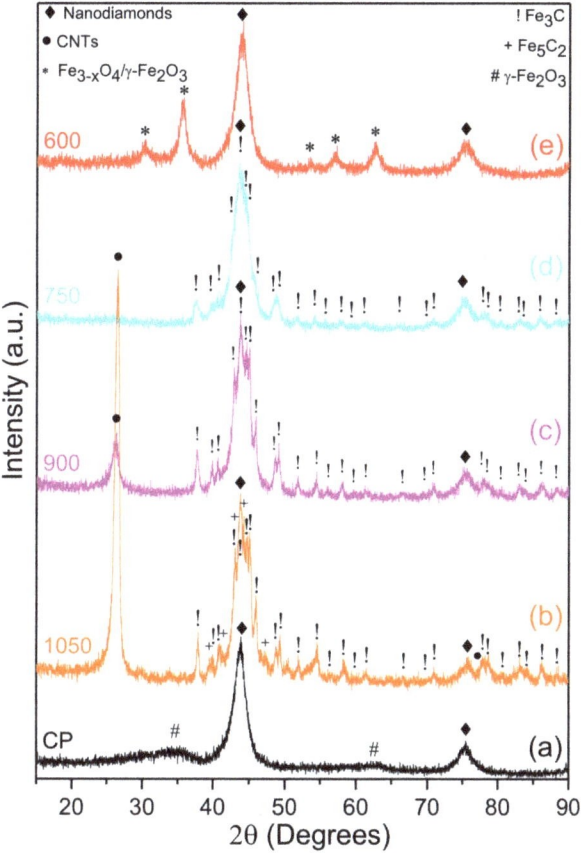

Figure 2. XRD patterns of the CP (**a**) and the NHDs samples resulting by annealing the CP at different temperatures indicated (in °C): 1050 (**b**), 900 (**c**), 750 (**d**) and 600 (**e**). The presence of the different crystalline phases in the samples is denoted by the relative symbols on their diffraction peaks.

The XRD diagrams of all samples present relative broad diffraction peaks, which constitute the striking feature of the nanostructured nature of the phases appearing in them. An estimation of the average NPs crystalline domain size <D> for each phase, in the cases where this is resolvable and possible to be derived from the width of the diffraction peaks using the Scherrer formula [54], was attempted, and the results are listed in Table 1.

Table 1. Average NPs crystalline domain size <D> values, in nm, of the crystalline phases detected in the XRD diagrams of the samples as resulting using the Scherrer formula. The figures in parentheses denote the uncertainty attributed to the relevant last digit.

Sample	NDs	Fe$_3$C	Fe$_5$C$_2$	Spinel-Type Iron Oxide	C-Graphitic
CP	4 (1)	-	-	non-resolvable	-
NHD-1050	7 (1)	20 (1)	16 (1)	-	11 (1)
NHD-900	5 (1)	16 (1)	-	-	8 (1)
NHD-750	5 (1)	12 (1)	-	-	-
NHD-600	4 (1)	-	-	9 (1)	-

As evident from these values, the average size of the NDs NPs is essentially unaffected by the heat treatments up to 900 °C and only a slight increase is observed at the highest annealing temperature in this work. This is important and reflects the thermal, chemical and structural stability of the chosen nanotemplate base within a wide range of applied annealing temperatures. However, the annealing temperature seems to play an important role for the NPs size in the case of Fe$_3$C, as the <D> value for this phase scales with the annealing temperature value, exhibiting a positive slope of about 2.7 nm/100 °C. The estimated <D> values for the graphitic-type phases in NHD-1050 and NHD-900 samples is based on the Scherrer model, assuming a mosaic of rectangular or round-type NPs [54]. As the true nature of the morphology of this phase will be revealed by following TEM measurements, this result from XRD analysis is thus only indicative, and might reveal only one part of the nanostructural nature of the relative phases.

3.2. TEM

The morphology, arrangement and interconnection of the nanophases present in the samples are revealed by TEM measurements. Representative characteristic images of the CP and the NHD samples are displayed in Figure 3. Additional images revealing similar features of the samples can be found in the Supplementary Material (SM) (Figures S1–S5).

Figure 3a–c reveal a system of closed packed ND NPs forming roughly round, as well as irregular shape nanotemplates dispersed in a range of sizes from ~50 to ~300 nm. It is not so easy to distinguish between the CP's IO (maghemite) NPs from the dominant presence of the ND NPs in these nanotemplates, due to the quite small sizes of the former kind and their low crystallinity, as evidenced by the XRD measurements. However, Figure 3b,c reveal several NPs with rather darker contrast in comparison to their adjacent NPs, resulting from the higher, compared to the NDs, density of the oxide phase, which might include also more than one oxide NPs clustered in groups, as the XRD results suggest. All ND NPs seem to be uniform in size, at about 4–5 nm, in perfect agreement with the XRD measurements.

Figure 3d shows that the morphology of the NHD-1050 sample combines the presence of large CNTs and assemblies of NDs nanotemplates. The CNTs diameter and length reaches from tens to a few hundred nm and from a few to several µm, respectively. In addition, some of the CNTs have partially filled ends or interiors with denser elongated sections of ICs phases, while smaller IC NPs seem to be caught within their walls, most probably during their growth procedure. This is an indication that the formation of the ICs phases triggers catalytically the growth of these large CNTs, due to the increased annealing temperature [55]. By taking closer looks to the regions at and around the NDs nanotemplates, we can disclose assemblies of dense IC NPs regions of several tens of nm encapsulated in CNTs in Figure 3e, as well as some quite smaller (of the order of few nm) IC NPs dispersed on the surface of the nanotemplates in Figure 3f. These results agree well with the XRD findings, where sharp and intense CNTs and ICs peaks are detected, suggesting relatively high crystallinity and sizes of the corresponding phases. The morphologies of the nanophases in the NHD-900 sample depicted in Figure 3g–i seem to be quite similar to those of the NHD-1050 sample (see also SM Figures S4 and S5). However, relative decreased number of CNTs and increased abundance of small IC

NPs in the ND nanotemplates are observed, combined with regions of larger CNTs-encapsulated IC particles of increased sizes that reach several tens of nm, confirming the XRD results. The TEM images of the NHD-750 sample shown in Figure 3j–l reveal a system of homogeneously dispersed ND nanotemplates of quite smaller sizes compared to those found in the samples synthesized at higher annealing temperature. Another striking difference of this sample compared to the formers is the complete absence of CNTs. The ND nanotemplates in Figure 3k,l contain what, according also to the XRD results, appear to be small Fe_3C NPs, of the order of 5–10 nm, which are also quite homogeneously dispersed on the surface of the nanotemplates with no agglomeration tendency. In addition, these nanotemplates appear also to be relieved from the presence of neighboring large CNTs-encapsulated ICs NPs. The overall morphology of the nanotemplates in Figure 3m–o for sample NHD-600 seem to resemble that of sample NHD-750, with wide size dispersion and no presence of CNTs. The nanotemplates are surface-decorated with evenly dispersed NPs of greater density than the NDs and sizes ranging between 5 and 10 nm, which, as the XRD diagram of this sample has indicated, adopt the spinel-type IO structure.

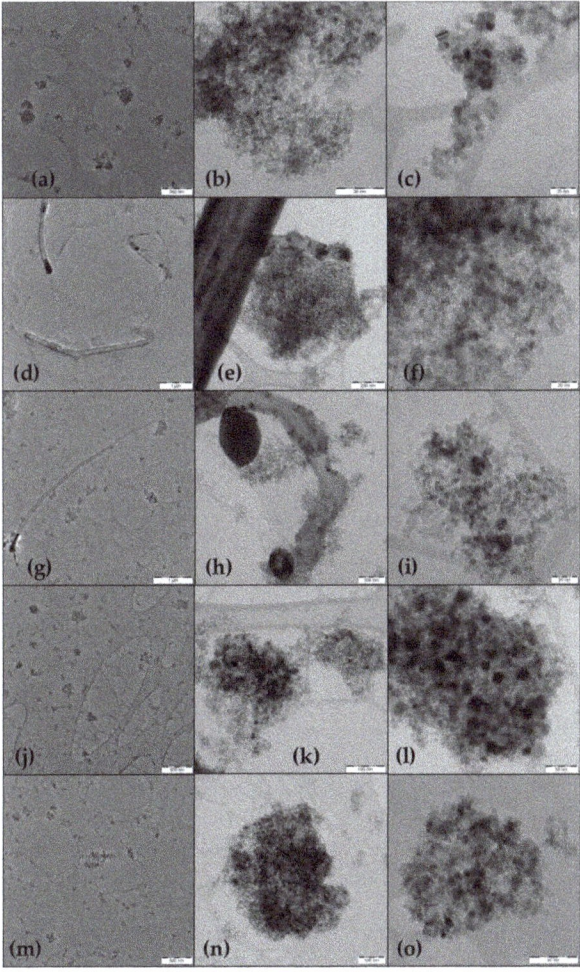

Figure 3. TEM images of the CP (**a–c**), NHD-1050 (**d–f**), NHD-900 (**g–i**), NHD-750 (**j–l**) and NHD-600 (**m–o**) samples at different magnifications.

From the TEM images displayed in Figure 3 and the preceding description, it is evident that NHD-750 is the sample with the highest homogeneity and purity of containing phases. In order to shed more light in the morphology of the nanotemplates, verify the presence and investigate the dispersion of the IC phase in this sample, additional HAADF microscopy images of parts of this sample were collected and specific elemental mapping was performed on them. A characteristic example of these analyses is shown in Figure 4, while additional images can be found in SM (Figure S6). Some HAADF microscopy images of the NHD-900 sample are also demonstrated there (Figures S7–S9) for comparison.

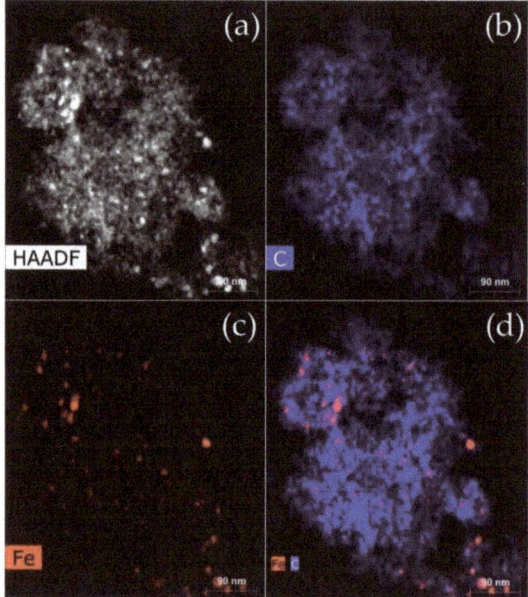

Figure 4. HAADF microscopy image from a certain nanotemplate cluster of the NHD-750 sample (**a**) with specific elemental mapping of C (**b**); Fe (**c**) and Fe & C (**d**).

The presence of Fe in this Figure reveals that the Fe_3C phase is related to the NPs situated on the points of the highest contrast, corresponding to the NPs with higher density (darker NPs in the normal contrast images in Figure 3 or lighter NPs in the reverse contrast image in Figure 4). These NPs are also evenly and homogeneously disseminated on the surface of the nanotemplate, as indeed the regular TEM images of Figure 3 already indicated. In the case of the C atoms, it is difficult to distinguish their presence on the Fe_3C NPs from the total assembly of C atoms in the NDs, which constitute the background in this nanotemplate. Nonetheless, C atoms of the NDs make a fine spreading and enclose in all cases the Fe atoms. This remark validates further the hybrid nature of the sample.

An important outcome of the characterization of all NHD samples with TEM is that no areas of isolated unsupported stand-alone IC or IO NPs assemblies separated from the NDs nanotemplates are detected, without taking into consideration the larger particles encapsulated in CNTs for the cases of the higher annealing temperature samples. This confirms the high quality of the hybrid nature of the NDs nanotemplates in all samples and especially the NHD-750 and NHD-600 samples.

3.3. Magnetization and Magnetic Susceptibility

The magnetic properties of the CP and the NHD samples are, to a large extent, exposed through the behavior of their M vs. H under constant temperature (T), as well as their χ_g vs. T under constant H measurements, which are exhibited for all samples in Figures 5 and 6, respectively. The isothermal

M vs. H loops were collected at RT (300 K) and 5 K, while the χ_g vs. T scans were performed in ZFC and FC modes under H = 1000 Oe.

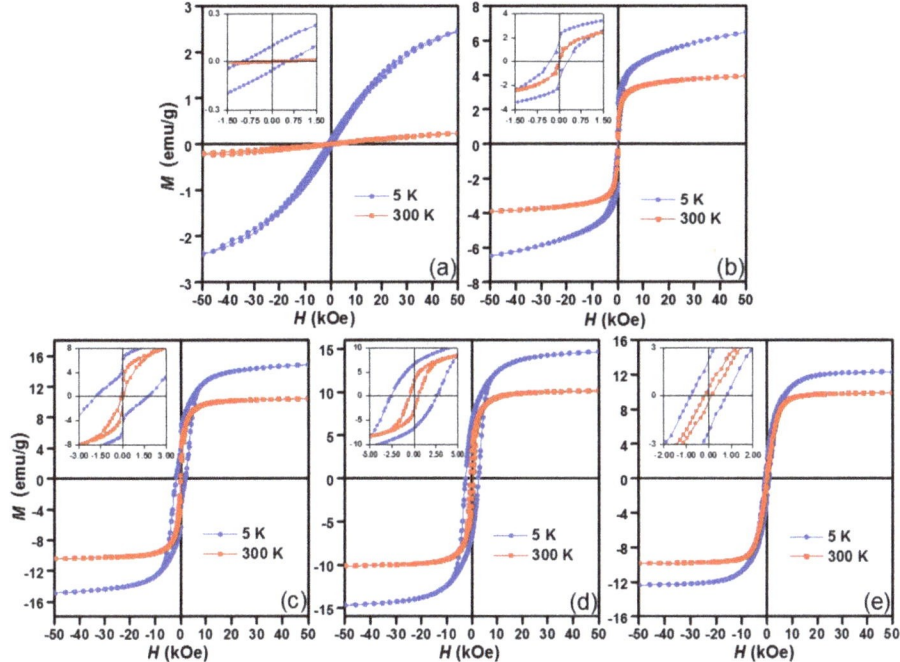

Figure 5. Isothermal M vs. H loops of the CP (**a**); NHD-600 (**b**); NHD-750 (**c**); NHD-900 (**d**) and NHD-1050 (**e**) samples collected at RT (red squares) and 5 K (blue circles). The insets show the detailed features of the loops around H = 0.

Starting the description from the CP sample, the M vs. H loop at RT in Figure 5a shows linear paramagnetic-like behavior, while a ferromagnetic/ferrimagnetic sigmoidal-type curve with non-saturated M values and non-vanishing and asymmetric coercive fields (H_Cs) is developed at 5 K. The maximum M values at 50 kOe (M_{max}), along with all other characteristics of the loops for all samples, are listed in Table 2. The corresponding χ_g vs. T ZFC curve begins with a maximum at 5 K and continues with a local maximum at ~25 K, followed by a monotonic decrease for higher T values, while the FC curve exhibits a monotonic increase throughout the whole T range with an asymptotic behavior at low T. The bifurcation of the two curves occurs at the irreversibility temperature of T_{irr} ~60 K. The previously described characteristics are indicative of an assembly of ferromagnetic/ferrimagnetic-type NPs that are completely superparamagnetic (SPM) at RT and partially magnetically blocked at low T [56]. The existence of two χ_g maxima at blocking temperatures of T_B ~5 K and T_B ~25 K for the ZFC curve, along with the T_{irr}-T_B difference of about 35 K, indicate a dispersion of NP sizes, which however, due to the low T_B values, seem to be quite small in magnitude, while the asymmetry in H_C at 5 K denotes the presence of exchange-bias interactions between different types of magnetic ordered phases, that might result, e.g., due to possible variations in stoichiometry or/and a core-shell NPs structure [56]. Due to their extremely small sizes, the smaller NPs could take a more drastic shift in their spinel-type ferric oxide (maghemite) stoichiometry, mainly affecting their surface atomic layers, as well as a reduction in their crystallinity towards a more amorphous structure. These structural characteristics, accompanied by the magnetic interactions between interconnected NPs, could justify their observed magnetic properties that resemble spin-glass-like behavior at low temperatures [57–60], and explain the asymmetry found in the coercivity values of the hysteresis loop of this sample at 5 K. Moreover, the asymptotic behavior of the FC curve at low T reveals that these NPs are magnetically non- or very weakly-interacting, reflecting their spatial isolation on the surface of the corresponding NDs nanotemplates [51,61,62].

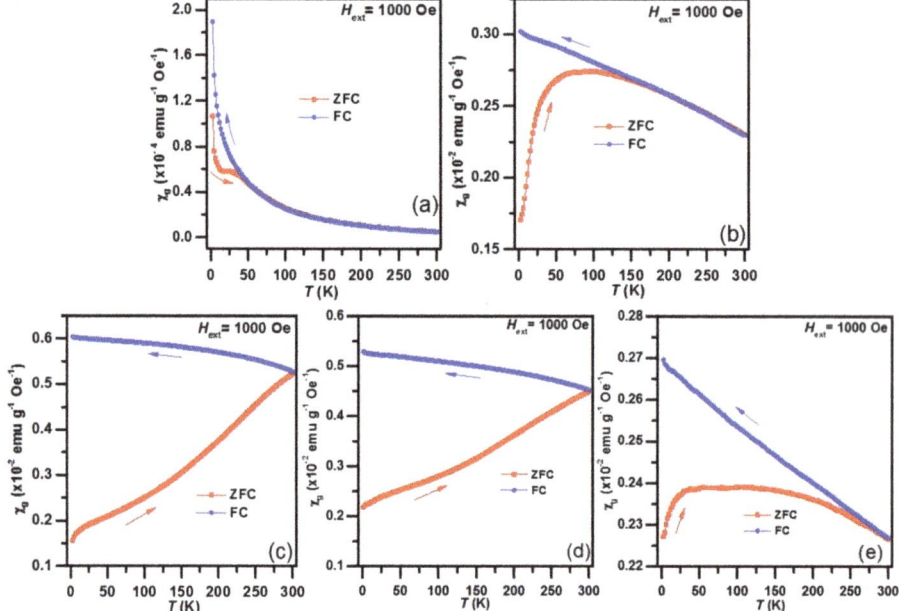

Figure 6. χ_g vs. T measurements of the CP (**a**); NHD-600 (**b**); NHD-750 (**c**); NHD-900 (**d**) and NHD-1050 (**e**) samples collected under H = 1000 Oe following ZFC (red squares) and FC (blue circles) modes.

Table 2. Isothermal hysteresis loops magnetic characteristics of the samples.

Sample	T (K)	M_{max+} (emu/g)	M_{max-} (emu/g)	M_{R+} (emu/g)	M_{R-} (emu/g)	H_{c+} (kOe)	H_{c-} (kOe)
CP	300	0.23	−0.22	0.00	0.00	0.00	0.00
	5	2.46	−2.40	0.10	−0.06	0.54	−0.99
NHD-600	300	3.91	−3.91	0.00	0.00	0.00	0.00
	5	6.47	−6.48	1.88	−1.51	0.28	−0.32
NHD-750	300	10.41	−10.39	2.15	−1.63	0.09	−0.12
	5	14.82	−14.86	5.43	−5.20	1.78	−1.85
NHD-900	300	10.11	−10.12	3.33	−2.90	0.53	−0.46
	5	14.65	−14.64	6.68	−6.50	2.55	−2.53
NHD-1050	300	9.84	−9.84	0.51	−0.35	0.14	−0.16
	5	12.27	−12.30	2.26	−2.25	0.80	−0.80

A T_B of ~100K and a T_{irr} of ~190 K are observed from the χ_g vs. T ZFC and FC curves of the NHD-600 sample. The higher T_B and T_{irr}-T_B ≈ 90 K difference values, compared to the CP sample case, indicate a system of ferromagnetic/ferrimagnetic-type NPs with relatively larger average sizes and wider size dispersion compared to those in the CP. Indeed, the increased NP size of the NHD-600 sample affords clear ferromagnetic characteristics in the M vs. H loops; however, the non-vanishing dM/dH slope at high fields and the increased H_C values at 5 K relative to those observed at 300 K, declare the presence of a part of the NP assembly that retains SPM characteristics. On the other side, the corresponding χ_g values in the FC curve is almost linearly related to the decrease in T, and do not follow an asymptotic behavior at low temperatures, which suggests that magnetic interparticle interactions, most probably of dipolar or exchange nature [61,63,64], must be present, a result that should be expected from the respective size growth of the corresponding IO NPs in the CP.

Ferromagnetic characteristics are observed also in the M vs. H loops of the NHD-750 sample; however, there is a slight tendency for lack of saturation in the of M values at high fields. Further, the inset in Figure 5c reveals that the variation of M around $H = 0$ is not smooth but rather complex, and seems to be composed of two contributions: one with magnetically harder characteristics that lends non-vanishing H_C values to the loops and one with magnetically softer characteristics that are responsible for the sadden drop of the M values at $H = 0$. The χ_g values of the ZFC curve for this sample show a continuous increase with increasing T with no local extrema up to 300 K, while the FC curve is also continuous and smoother over a quite narrower χ_g values range. These results are indicative of a system of ferromagnetic NPs with combined hard and soft magnetic characteristics that could result from size dispersion or/and magnetic interparticle interactions strength variation. Moreover, the behavior of the system seems to be dominated from the larger in size or/and strongly magnetically interacting NPs, which are magnetically blocked even at RT. On the other hand, the smaller in size or/and weakly magnetically interacting NPs reveal their presence through their softer magnetic characteristics and their non-saturation M values tendency. Thus, as Fe_3C NPs with both multi-domain or single-domain characteristics can exist simultaneously in the sample, they can contribute different properties to the magnetic measurements, i.e., both strong (multi-domain) and soft (single-domain) ferromagnetic features, decisively influencing the magnetic characteristics of the system [43,56,65].

For the NHD-900 sample, very similar characteristics to the χ_g vs. T curves of the NHD-750 sample are observed, while its M vs. H loops are more saturated at high H and quite smooth around $H = 0$, with clear symmetric hystereses that reach H_C values of the order of ~0.5 kOe at 300 K and 2.5 kOe at 5 K (see Table 2 and inset of Figure 5d). These results show that here, the system of ferromagnetic NPs seems to acquire on average larger sizes or/and experience stronger magnetic interparticle interactions. The NPs size and morphology in this sample involving the presence of larger elongated cementite NPs entering the interior or filling the ends of the CNTs and/or caught on their walls, should indeed induce an effect on the increased H_C values. Similar behavior of high H_C values has been found for elongated cementite NPs encapsulated by CNTs [66,67], where also the NPs size dispersion has been proposed to be a crucial factor for the appearance of this characteristic.

The M vs. H loops of the NHD-1050 sample are completely saturated at high H and symmetric around $H = 0$, showing hystereses with reduced H_C values relative to those found for the NHD-900 sample (see Table 2). The χ_g values of the ZFC curve increase up to ~30 K and stay almost constant in a wide T range up to ~150 K, before dropping further smoothly up to 300 K, while for the FC branch χ_g increases almost linearly with the decrease in T. These characteristics reflect a system of ferromagnetic NPs with wide size dispersion and possible compositional variations, in which, however, the larger in size NPs are shaping the system's magnetic behavior.

3.4. ^{57}Fe Mössbauer Spectroscopy

The iron-containing phases present in the samples, their crystal structure, particle size and morphology, as well as their magnetic properties are further investigated by means of the atomic-level-probing technique of ^{57}Fe Mössbauer spectroscopy. ^{57}Fe MS of the studied samples recorded at RT (300 K) and 77 K appear in Figure 7. Some corresponding MS collected at lower temperature (11 K) are shown in SM (Figures S10 and S11).

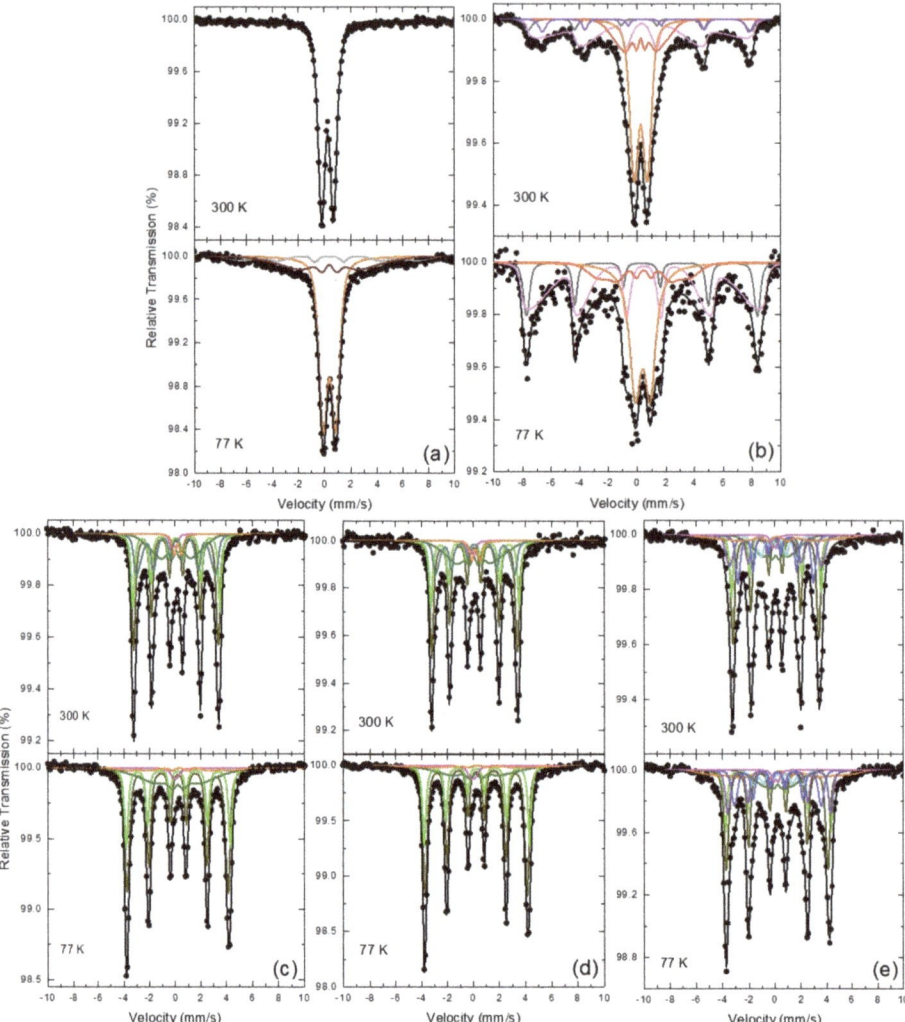

Figure 7. ^{57}Fe Mössbauer spectra of the CP (**a**); NHD-600 (**b**); NHD-750 (**c**); NHD-900 (**d**) and NHD-1050 (**e**) samples collected at 300 and 77 K.

The 300 K spectrum of the CP sample in Figure 7a exhibits only a central quadrupole split contribution, while development of partial magnetic splitting appears at the spectrum of this sample at 77 K in the form of broad magnetically split contributions, in addition to the main quadrupole split contribution that still dominates this spectrum. In order to fit these MS adequately, we used a single quadrupole split doublet with Lorentzian line-shapes for the RT spectrum and a combination of a quadrupole split doublet and two magnetically split components, for which a Gaussian-type spreading of their hyperfine magnetic field (B_{hf}) values (ΔB_{hf}) [52] was allowed to model their broadening. The resulting Mössbauer parameters values for the RT spectra of all samples are listed in Table 3, while, for the lower temperature MS, the corresponding parameters are listed in SM (Tables S2 and S3). The IS, quadrupole splitting (QS), quadrupole shift (2ε) and B_{hf} values of all components of the CP sample correspond to Fe^{3+} ions in magnetically ordered γ-Fe_2O_3 NPs, which, due to their reduced size and influence of thermal agitation to their magnetization, undergo fast SPM relaxation, confirming the XRD, TEM and magnetization measurements [43,51,68–70].

Table 3. Mössbauer hyperfine parameters resulting from the best fits of the corresponding spectra of the samples recorded at 300 K. IS is the isomer shift (given relative to α-Fe at 300 K), Γ/2 is the half line-width, QS is the quadrupole splitting, 2ε is the quadrupole shift, B_{hf} is the central value of the hyperfine magnetic field, ΔB_{hf} is the spreading of B_{hf}, and AA is the relative spectral absorption area of each component used to fit the spectra. Typical errors are ± 0.02 mm/s for IS, Γ/2, 2ε and QS, ± 3 kOe for B_{hf} and ± 5% for AA. * denotes the cases where asymmetric ΔB_{hf} spreading was allowed for lower/higher values relative to B_{hf}. Component colors (CL): B = black, BU = blue, C = cyan, DC = dark cyan, DY = dark yellow, G = gray, GR = green, LM = light magenta, M = magenta, O = orange, OL = olive, R = red, V = violet.

Sample	Component Assignment	IS (mm/s)	Γ/2 (mm/s)	QS or 2ε (mm/s)	B_{hf} (kOe)	ΔB_{hf} (kOe)	AA (%)	CL
CP	SPM γ-Fe_2O_3	0.35	0.24	0.90	0	0	100	B
NHD-600	$Fe_{3-x}O_4$ (Fe^{3+})	0.25	0.15	−0.02	495	11/0 *	7	G
	$Fe_{3-x}O_4$ ($Fe^{2.5+}$)	0.68	0.15	0.05	447	5/0 *	5	V
	SPM γ-Fe_2O_3	0.36	0.18	0.89	0	0	36	O
	MCOL γ-Fe_2O_3/$Fe_{3-x}O_4$	0.37	0.12	0.02	102	38	17	R
	MRES $Fe_{3-x}O_4$	0.41	0.15	0.00	489	78/0 *	35	LM
NHD-750	Fe_3C (1)	0.19	0.14	0.01	209	3/0 *	36	DY
	Fe_3C (2)	0.21	0.14	0.05	212	0	20	GR
	MCOL Fe_3C	0.20	0.14	0.03	110	45	17	OL
	MRES Fe_3C	0.20	0.14	0.03	202	12/0 *	22	DC
	SPM metallic Fe	−0.02	0.15	0.38	0	0	2	M
	SPM Fe^{3+} (IO)	0.32	0.16	0.58	0	0	3	O
NHD-900	Fe_3C (1)	0.19	0.14	0.01	209	3/0 *	39	DY
	Fe_3C (2)	0.21	0.14	0.05	212	0	21	GR
	MCOL Fe_3C	0.20	0.14	0.07	119	53	19	OL
	MRES Fe_3C	0.20	0.14	0.07	198	9/0 *	16	DC
	SPM metallic Fe	−0.02	0.15	0.42	0	0	2	M
	SPM Fe^{3+} (IO)	0.32	0.16	0.63	0	0	3	O
NHD-1050	Fe_3C (1)	0.19	0.14	0.01	209	3/0 *	27	DY
	Fe_3C (2)	0.21	0.14	0.05	214	0	15	GR
	MCOL Fe_3C	0.20	0.14	0.02	91	47	13	OL
	Fe_5C_2 (1)	0.14	0.14	0.09	220	12	14	V
	Fe_5C_2 (2)	0.15	0.14	0.07	181	9	14	BU
	Fe_5C_2 (3)	0.10	0.14	0.12	103	5	9	C
	SPM IC	0.07	0.15	0.31	0	0	1	M
	MCOL Fe^{3+} (IO)	0.36	0.14	0.01	273	93	7	O

The characteristic SPM relaxation time, τ, depends on the structural, morphological and magnetic characteristics of these NPs, through the magnetic anisotropy constant K, the size (or volume V) of the NPs, the presence and the strength of magnetic inter-particle interactions and the temperature [43,56,64,71,72]. Thanks to their very small size and good dispersion on the surfaces of the NDs nanotemplates, the IO NPs of the CP are relatively isolated, with loose inter-attachment or inter-connection to each other and experience no, or weak, inter-particle magnetic interactions, so they are not magnetically blocked at 300 K. For all these NPs represented by the SPM doublet at RT, the SPM relaxation is very fast, meaning that under these conditions (increased T), τ falls far below the characteristic ^{57}Fe Mössbauer spectroscopy measuring time $\tau_{MS\text{-}exp}$ (τ < $\tau_{MS\text{-}exp}$), which is of the order of $\tau_{MS\text{-}exp}$ ~10^{-8} s [73,74]. As a consequence, for these IO NPs the B_{hf} values at RT average to zero (they collapse completely).

By lowering the temperature to 77 K, the appearance of a minority, in absorption area (AA), set of broad magnetically split contributions indicates that a small part of the assembly of these IO NPs develops non-zero B_{hf} values. The existence of two different magnetically split components, one that acquires magnetically collapsing (MCOL) B_{hf} characteristics (Figure 7a 77 K wine color, SM Table S1 MCOL γ-Fe$_2$O$_3$ component) and another that presents broad lines but magnetically resolved (MRES) characteristics (Figure 7a 77 K light gray color, SM Table S1 MRES γ-Fe$_2$O$_3$ component), suggests that the assembly of these IO NPs in the CP sample can be described by the different aspects of the SPM relaxation. These aspects refer to the size of the NPs and their interactions through their inter-connection, which both influence τ as T is reduced from 300 to 77 K.

The assembly of the IO NPs of the CP can be viewed to be composed of three groups: The IO NPs, which are larger in size or/and better inter-connected to each other (or assembled together), have increased V or/and are experiencing stronger inter-particle magnetic interactions, acquire $\tau > \tau_{MS-exp}$ at 77 K and are represented by the MRES Fe^{3+} component. The IO NPs, which are intermediate in size or/and less inter-connected, have relatively decreased V or/and are experiencing weaker inter-particle magnetic interactions, acquire $\tau \sim \tau_{MS-exp}$ at 77 K and are represented by the MCOL Fe^{3+} component. However, still at 77 K the majority of the IO NPs are completely SPM as they acquire $\tau < \tau_{MS-exp}$ and are represented by the SPM doublet (Figure 7a 77 K orange color, SM Table S1 SPM γ-Fe$_2$O$_3$ component). This further confirms the picture drawn from all characterization methods used here for the CP, that presents an assembly of very small maghemite NPs relatively isolated on the surfaces of the NDs nanotemplates, which shows fast SPM relaxation at RT, but which is partially getting slower at lower temperatures.

The MS of the NHD-600 sample presents a combination of quadrupole and magnetically split contributions both at RT and 77 K, with the magnetically split part increasing its AA as the temperature decreases. For the RT spectrum, we used a set of one quadrupole and four magnetically split components and their resulting Mössbauer parameters are listed in Table 3. The doublet presents very similar parameters to the corresponding doublet of the CP, while there are two well resolved magnetically split components, one of which presents Fe^{3+} and the other Fe$^{2.5+}$ valence state characteristics, which lie quite close to those of the corresponding ions of magnetite (Fe$_3$O$_4$) [75]. However, the ratio of their relative AA values, AA(Fe^{3+})/AA(Fe$^{2.5+}$) = 1.4 is quite different from the nominal 0.5 expected for Fe$_3$O$_4$, indicating that the corresponding stoichiometry is shifted to non-stoichiometric Fe$_{3-x}$O$_4$ (0 < x < 0.33). For the other two magnetically split components, one presents broad and asymmetric lines, high B_{hf} value, increased IS relative to that of the SPM doublet and closer to the average of the Fe^{3+} and Fe$^{2.5+}$ components, and the other broad and symmetric lines, low B_{hf} value and similar IS relative to that of the SPM doublet. Combining these results with the XRD, TEM and magnetization measurements and analyses, it is evident that this sample contains an assembly of spinel-type IO NPs dispersed on the surfaces of the NDs nanotemplates. The stoichiometry of these spinel-type IO NPs varies, most probably according to their sizes. The larger NPs have Fe$_{3-x}$O$_4$ stoichiometries (intermediate between maghemite x = 0.33 and magnetite x = 0), while the smaller NPs are of the maghemite type. A similar set of components is used to fit the 77 K spectrum of this sample, with the magnetic components increasing their AAs in total relative to those at RT at the expense of the AA of the SPM doublet. However, the presence of the Fe$^{2.5+}$ component is not detected directly at 77 K, due to its low contribution, as evidenced from the RT spectrum, which is additionally screened by the major contribution of the broad asymmetric magnetically resolved component (see also SM).

The spectra of the NHD-750 sample appearing in Figure 7c show a clear dominant six-line pattern contribution with relative narrow resonant lines, in superposition to a central broad magnetically split part. This central broad part is more intense at RT and less at 77 K. In addition, an asymmetry (referring to the shape difference between the lower and higher absolute velocity sides) of the resonant lines for the clear magnetically resolved part is observed at RT, which is, however, reduced substantially at 77 K. In order to describe these characteristics, we used a set of six components to fit the RT spectrum. Four of them (colored with green tints) describe the cementite Fe$_3$C phase, one minor component (colored magenta) acquires IS value corresponding to SPM metallic iron, and one quadrupole split component (colored orange) to an SPM IO phase of Fe^{3+} character. Of the four components describing the Fe_3C phase, two of them have Mössbauer parameters values that are quite close to those of the bulk Fe_3C phase [16,27]. The other two acquire IS and 2ε values that fall on the average of the two "bulk-like" components, while their B_{hf} values are reduced compared to the "bulk-like" components, slightly for one of them, which retains clear magnetically resolved characteristics (MRES Fe_3C), and substantially for the other, which receives B_{hf} collapsing characteristics (MCOL Fe_3C). These featuress reveal a system of Fe_3C NPs that experience different types of SPM relaxation effects, similar to the case of the NHD-600 sample: the larger in size and more inter-connected Fe_3C NPs acquire "bulk-like" characteristics with slow SPM relaxation, while the smaller and more isolated ones experience faster SPM relaxation at RT. However, in the case of the Fe_3C phase there is no complete collapse of the B_{hf} value, which is attributed both to the larger size of the NPs and to the increased K value of Fe_3C compared to those of the spinel-type IO NPs of the NHD-600 sample [67,76]. The thermal development of the shape of the MS from RT to 77 and 11 K is the expected one for an assembly of NPs which undergo SPM relaxation phenomena: the MRES component is absent at low temperatures, being merged with the "bulk-like" components, while the AA values of the MCOL component are constant at about 20%. This means that a fraction of the Fe_3C NPs is still under the influence of SPM relaxation at temperatures as low as 11 K.

Taking into account the nature of the other two remaining minor components which were used to fit the MS of this sample and the fact that there are no additional diffraction peaks detected at the corresponding XRD diagram apart from those of the Fe_3C and NDs phases, it is revealed that these components are related to iron-containing phases with SPM characteristics and very small particle sizes. The SPM component with the IS corresponding to a metallic iron phase, acquires zero B_{hf} values at all temperatures, but non-zero QS values as well. According to our fitting model, this component is attributed to a very small amount of metallic iron, which forms very fine NPs, most probably below ~5 nm. In such small sizes, these fine iron NPs have been found to lose their crystallinity and adopt amorphous structure characteristics, which is reflected as shifts in their hyperfine Mössbauer parameters values [77,78]. Moreover, the most probable presence of C atoms that might have diffused in the structure of these NPs could heighten further these shifts. The SPM IO doublet with the Fe^{3+} characteristics at the RT spectrum develops magnetic splitting with broad resonant lines at lower temperatures. This phase could be related to a minority of IO NPs developed during the annealing procedure, or to surface oxide layers related to the metallic iron NPs. The contributions of these two components sum up to AA levels of the order of ~5%.

Very similar MS to the NHD-750 sample are found also for the NHD-900 sample, which are shown in Figure 7d. The evolution of these spectra with respect to the decrease in temperature is also very similar to that found for the NHD-750 sample. Consequently, we have applied a fitting model which includes the same set of components that we used to fit the MS of the NHD-750 sample in order to fit the MS of the NHD-900 sample, and the resulting Mössbauer parameters for the later sample are almost identical to those resulting for the former (see Table 3 and SM Tables S2 and S3). The main difference between the two cases appears for the AA values of the "bulk-like" and MCOL Fe_3C components at low temperatures. The AA values of the MCOL Fe_3C component are reduced for the NHD-900 sample relative to the NHD-750 sample and the gain from this reduction for the NHD-900 sample is directed towards its "bulk-like" components, suggesting an increase in the relative population for the larger in size Fe_3C NPs of the corresponding assembly. These results come in perfect agreement with the XRD, TEM and SQUID measurements of both samples.

The MS of the NHD-1050 sample synthesized at the highest annealing temperature, appearing in Figure 7e, resemble those of the samples annealed at 900 and 750 °C, but an additional contribution at the inner (lower absolute velocity sides) parts of the magnetically split pattern persists both at 300 and 77 K. Combining this feature with the evidence for the presence of the Fe_5C_2 phase confirmed by XRD, led us to include a sub-set of three additional components (colored with blue tints) to the fitting model we used to fit the MS of the NHD-750 and NHD-900 samples, in order to fit the MS of this sample. These components correspond to the Fe_5C_2 IC phase. The resulting Mössbauer parameters for these components are very close to those reported for the bulk Fe_5C_2 phase in the literature [27,79,80]. The presence of a central magnetically collapsing component is related to the Fe_3C NPs assembly, as evidenced by its Mössbauer parameters values. Another broad magnetically split contribution of Fe^{3+} character and collapsing B_{hf} characteristics is attributed to an IO phase with SPM features. A B_{hf}-collapsed SPM component with small AA is also included in the fitting model, as in the cases of the NHD-750 and NHD-900 samples. However, here the IS of this component is shifted to values characteristic of the IC phases rather than metallic iron. Again, these results come in perfect agreement with the XRD, TEM and SQUID measurements for this sample.

4. Discussion

Summarizing the experimental data from all characterization methods used to study the NHD samples presented here, we can describe the evolution of the development of the different phases, as well as their properties in these NHDs, as a function of the syntheses conditions.

The CP itself constitutes a hybrid nanomaterial, composed of very fine γ-Fe_2O_3 NPs dispersed evenly on the surfaces of the ND nanotemplates, providing it with SPM characteristics. The effect of annealing these pristine NHDs under vacuum at relatively low temperatures (600 °C) is to increase the particle size of the maghemite NPs, and simultaneously, to partially reduce some of the Fe^{3+} ions to Fe^{2+}. Wherever this valence reduction occurs, it alters the local environment of the iron ions, shifting the spinel-type structure and composition from maghemite (γ-Fe_2O_3 = $Fe_{8/3}O_4$ = $Fe_{2.67}O_4$) towards non-stoichiometric magnetite ($Fe_{3-x}O_4$, $0 < x < 0.33$), as the heating under vacuum conditions represents a soft-reduction agent. The resulting material acquires ferrimagnetic characteristics due to the development of the spinel-type ferrimagnetic IO phases.

Increasing the annealing temperature to 750 °C triggers the involvement of a harder reduction agent present in the pristine NHDs to the synthesis mechanism of the final product. This agent is no other than the C atoms of the surface layers of the NDs nanotemplates assemblies, which are also known to exist partially in the form of graphitic-type coatings [38,81,82]. These C atoms not only provide the conditions for the full reduction of the CP's Fe^{3+} ions to Fe^0 character, but are able to enter the structure of the resulting NPs in the material, forming thus the cementite Fe_3C phase. It seems that the synthesis procedure of the Fe_3C phase under these conditions is almost complete, as the majority of the γ-Fe_2O_3 NPs of the CP are transformed to cementite, following the original pattern established by their presence as ancestors in the CP. However, a very small minority of them remains as γ-Fe_2O_3 NPs, or as surface layers of a small part in the sample comprised of metallic iron NPs which were reduced from the γ-Fe_2O_3 NPs without adopting the C atoms in their structure, or at least not to the level of forming the complete carbide phase. Due to the presence of the Fe_3C phase, the resulting NHD material acquires ferromagnetic features, combining hard and soft magnetic phases which are attributed to the dispersion of size of the individual cementite NPs, as well as the different interconnection characteristics of their assemblies.

By altering further the annealing temperature to 900 °C, the effect of the annealing conditions, apart from the formation of the cementite NPs phase in the resulting NHDs, is to lead some part of the C atoms of the CP to become involved in the growth of large-sized CNTs. The presence of the cementite phase itself at this annealing temperature plays the most important role in this CNTs growth procedure: it acts as the catalyst that is activated due to the increased temperature of 900 °C, compared to the lower annealing temperature of 750 °C where the production of CNTs could not be triggered [83]. The Fe_3C NPs acquire, as expected, on average larger sizes than those developed at the lower annealing temperature of 750 °C. On the other hand, the cementite phase that is involved in the CNTs growth seems to enter partially their interior, forming larger elongated sections covering their ends, or being caught as smaller NPs within their walls. The increased sizes, as well as the elongated schemes of these Fe_3C NPs, provide hard ferromagnetic characteristics to the resulting NHD material, with H_C values reaching ~2.5 kOe at 5 K.

Impelling the CP system to more elevated annealing temperatures of the 1050 °C level, stimulates further the size increase in the Fe$_3$C NPs, the production of the additional IC Fe$_5$C$_2$ phase, as well as the further growth of CNTs, both in concentration and in size. The IC phases are not only involved in the growth of CNTs, but are frequently included as moieties in their interiors or are encapsulated by them. Simultaneously, some IC NPs retain the dispersion form provided by their γ-Fe$_2$O$_3$ NPs ancestors in the CP and remain at the surfaces of the NDs nanotemplates. The magnetic properties of the resulting NHD material is influenced by the wider dispersion of NPs sizes, morphology and stoichiometry, but is governed by the larger IC NPs that provide hard ferromagnetic characteristics, albeit with reduced H$_C$ values relative to the sample annealed at 900 °C, most probably due to the multi-domain character of the NPs induced by their size growth.

5. Conclusions

In the present work, a versatile synthesis technique of magnetic nanostructured hybrid materials focused on iron carbides is deployed. A chemical precursor composed of fine maghemite nanoparticles dispersed on the surfaces of nanodiamond nanotemplates was used as the starting material. We have proven that by treating the chemical precursor in evacuated quartz ampules under different annealing conditions we can control and tailor the production of a variety of different nanostructured phases present in the nanohybrids, from spinel-type iron oxides, to iron carbides of Fe$_3$C and Fe$_5$C$_2$ stoichiometries, as well as large-size carbon nanotubes. The magnetic properties of the resulting hybrid nanomaterials reflect the characteristics of their bearing magnetic phases, which span from superparamagnetic to soft and hard ferromagnetic. It is demonstrated that a hybrid nanomaterial composed of single phase ~10 nm Fe$_3$C nanoparticles dispersed evenly on the surface of nanodiamond nanotemplates can be produced, which could be suitable for important technological applications in the fields of nano-biomedicine and catalysis.

Further development and adjustment of the present proposed synthetic route provides a good prospect for the development of a new category of magnetic nanohybrid materials based on nanodiamonds.

Supplementary Materials: The following are available online at http://www.mdpi.com/2312-7481/6/4/73/s1, Figure S1. TEM images of the CP sample. Figure S2. TEM images of the NHD-600 sample. Figure S3. TEM images of the NHD-750 sample. Figure S4. TEM images of the NHD-900 sample. Figure S5. TEM images of the NHD-1050 sample. Figure S6. HAADF image from a certain nanotemplate cluster of the NHD-750 sample with specific elemental mapping. Figure S7. HAADF image from a certain nanotemplate cluster of the NHD-900 sample with specific elemental mapping. Figure S8. HAADF image from a certain portion of the NHD-900 sample including NDs nanotemplates and CNTs with specific elemental mapping. Figure S9. HAADF image from a certain portion of the NHD-900 sample including NDs nanotemplates and CNTs with specific elemental mapping. Figure S10. Mössbauer spectrum of the NHD-750 sample recorded at 11K. Figure S11. Mössbauer spectrum of the NHD-900 sample recorded at 11 K. Table S1. Mössbauer Parameters as resulting from the best fits of the MS of all samples recorded at 77 K. Table S2. Mössbauer Parameters as resulting from the best fits of the MS of the NHD-750 and NHD-900 samples recorded at 11 K.

Author Contributions: Conceptualization, A.P.D.; Data curation, P.Z., A.B.B., J.T., O.M. and A.P.D.; Formal analysis, P.Z., A.B.B., J.T., O.M. and A.P.D.; Investigation, P.Z., A.B.B., J.T., O.M. and A.P.D.; Methodology, P.Z., A.B.B. and A.P.D.; Software, P.Z. and A.P.D.; Supervision, A.P.D.; Writing—original draft, P.Z. and A.P.D.; Writing—review and editing, P.Z., A.B.B. and A.P.D. All authors have read and agreed to the published version of the manuscript.

Funding: This research received no external funding.

Acknowledgments: A.P.D. acknowledges the partial support of this work by the project MIS 5002772, implemented under the Action "Reinforcement of the Research and Innovation Infrastructure", funded by the Operational Programme "Competitiveness, Entrepreneurship and Innovation" (NSRF 2014–2020) and co-financed by Greece and the European Union (European Regional Development Fund). O.M. acknowledges the financial support from the ERDF/ESF "Nano4Future" grant (No. CZ.02.1.01/0.0/0.0/16_019/0000754).

Conflicts of Interest: The authors declare no conflict of interest.

Abbreviations/Acronyms

2ε	quadrupole shift
B_{hf}	hyperfine magnetic field
CNT(s)	carbon nanotube (s)
CP	chemical precursor
FC	field-cooled
H	applied magnetic field
HAADF	high-angle annular dark field
H_C(s)	coercive field (s)
IC(s)	iron carbide (s)
IO(s)	iron oxide (s)
IS	isomer shift
K	magnetic anisotropy constant
M	magnetization
MCOL	magnetically collapsing
M_{max}	maximum M value at 50 kOe
MPI	magnetic particle imaging
M_R	remnant magnetization
MRES	magnetically resolved
MRI	magnetic resonance imaging
M_S	saturation magnetization
MS	Mössbauer spectra
ND(s)	Nanodiamond (s)
NP(s)	nanoparticle(s)
QS	quadrupole splitting
RT	room temperature
SM	Supplementary Material
SPM	superparamagnetic
SQUID	superconducting quantum interference device
T	temperature
TEM	transmission electron microscopy
V	volume
vs	versus
XRD	X-ray diffraction
ZFC	zero-field-cooled
ΔB_{hf}	spreading of hyperfine magnetic field
$\tau_{MS\text{-}exp}$	characteristic ^{57}Fe Mössbauer spectroscopy measuring time
τ	relaxation time
χ_g	mass magnetic susceptibility

References

1. Giordano, C.; Kraupner, A.; Wimbush, S.C.; Antonietti, M. Iron carbide: An ancient advanced material. *Small* **2010**, *6*, 1859–1862. [CrossRef] [PubMed]
2. Ye, Z.; Zhang, P.; Lei, X.; Wang, X.; Zhao, N.; Yang, H. Iron Carbides and Nitrides: Ancient Materials with Novel Prospects. *Chem. A Eur. J.* **2018**, *24*, 8922–8940. [CrossRef] [PubMed]
3. Bhadeshia, H.K.D.H. Cementite. *Int. Mater. Rev.* **2020**, *65*, 1–27. [CrossRef]
4. Weng, Y.; Dong, H.; Yong, G. *Advanced Steels*; Weng, Y., Dong, H., Yong, G., Eds.; Springer: Berlin/Heidelberg, Germany; Dordrecht, The Netherlands; London, UK; New York, NY, USA, 2011. [CrossRef]
5. Hosford, W.F. *Iron and Steel*; Cambridge University Press: Cambridge, UK, 2012.
6. Han, K.; Edmonds, D.V.; Smith, G.D.W. Optimization of mechanical properties of high-carbon pearlitic steels with Si and V additions. *Metall. Mater. Trans. A* **2001**, *32*, 1313–1324. [CrossRef]
7. Han, K.; Chen, J.P. Achievable Strength of Nanostructured Composites with Co-Deformable Components. *Mater. Sci. Forum* **2011**, *683*, 243–247. [CrossRef]

8. Li, L.; Virta, J. Ultrahigh strength steel wires processed by severe plastic deformation for ultrafine grained microstructure. *Mater. Sci. Technol.* **2011**, *27*, 845–862. [CrossRef]
9. Elwazri, A.M.; Wanjara, P.; Yue, S. The effect of microstructural characteristics of pearlite on the mechanical properties of hypereutectoid steel. *Mater. Sci. Eng. A* **2005**, *404*, 91–98. [CrossRef]
10. De Smit, E.; Cinquini, F.; Beale, A.M.; Safonova, O.V.; van Beek, W.; Sautet, P.; Weckhuysen, B.M. Stability and Reactivity of ε–χ–θ Iron Carbide Catalyst Phases in Fischer–Tropsch Synthesis: Controlling μC. *J. Am. Chem. Soc.* **2010**, *132*, 14928–14941. [CrossRef]
11. Xu, K.; Sun, B.; Lin, J.; Wen, W.; Pei, Y.; Yan, S.; Qiao, M.; Zhang, X.; Zong, B. ε-Iron carbide as a low-temperature Fischer–Tropsch synthesis catalyst. *Nature Commun.* **2014**, *5*, 5783. [CrossRef]
12. Niemantsverdriet, J.W.; van der Kraan, A.M.; van Dijk, W.L.; van der Baan, H.S. Behavior of metallic iron catalysts during Fischer-Tropsch synthesis studied with Mössbauer spectroscopy, x-ray diffraction, carbon content determination, and reaction kinetic measurements. *J. Phys. Chem.* **1980**, *84*, 3363–3370. [CrossRef]
13. Yoshida, H.; Takeda, S.; Uchiyama, T.; Kohno, H.; Homma, Y. Atomic-Scale In-situ Observation of Carbon Nanotube Growth from Solid State Iron Carbide Nanoparticles. *Nano Lett.* **2008**, *8*, 2082–2086. [CrossRef] [PubMed]
14. Schaper, A.K.; Hou, H.; Greiner, A.; Phillipp, F. The role of iron carbide in multiwalled carbon nanotube growth. *J. Catal.* **2004**, *222*, 250–254. [CrossRef]
15. Pérez-Cabero, M.; Taboada, J.B.; Guerrero-Ruiz, A.; Overweg, A.R.; Rodríguez-Ramos, I. The role of alpha-iron and cementite phases in the growing mechanism of carbon nanotubes: A 57Fe Mössbauer spectroscopy study. *Phys. Chem. Chem. Phys.* **2006**, *8*, 1230–1235. [CrossRef] [PubMed]
16. Le Caer, G.; Dubois, J.M.; Pijolat, M.; Perrichon, V.; Bussiere, P. Characterization by Moessbauer spectroscopy of iron carbides formed by Fischer-Tropsch synthesis. *J. Phys. Chem.* **1982**, *86*, 4799–4808. [CrossRef]
17. Abel, F.M.; Pourmiri, S.; Basina, G.; Tzitzios, V.; Devlin, E.; Hadjipanayis, G.C. Iron carbide nanoplatelets: Colloidal synthesis and characterization. *Nanoscale Adv.* **2019**, *1*, 4476–4480. [CrossRef]
18. Lin, J.-F.; Struzhkin, V.V.; Mao, H.-k.; Hemley, R.J.; Chow, P.; Hu, M.Y.; Li, J. Magnetic transition in compressed Fe_3C from X-ray emission spectroscopy. *Phys. Rev. B* **2004**, *70*, 212405. [CrossRef]
19. Zhao, X.Q.; Liang, Y.; Hu, Z.Q.; Liu, B.X. Oxidation characteristics and magnetic properties of iron carbide and iron ultrafine particles. *J. Appl. Phys.* **1996**, *80*, 5857–5860. [CrossRef]
20. Schnepp, Z.; Wimbush, S.C.; Antonietti, M.; Giordano, C. Synthesis of Highly Magnetic Iron Carbide Nanoparticles via a Biopolymer Route. *Chem. Mater.* **2010**, *22*, 5340–5344. [CrossRef]
21. Huang, G.; Hu, J.; Zhang, H.; Zhou, Z.; Chi, X.; Gao, J. Highly magnetic iron carbide nanoparticles as effective T2 contrast agents. *Nanoscale* **2014**, *6*, 726–730. [CrossRef]
22. Liang, Y.; Liu, P.; Xiao, J.; Li, H.; Wang, C.; Yang, G. A microfibre assembly of an iron-carbon composite with giant magnetisation. *Sci. Rep.* **2013**, *3*, 3051. [CrossRef]
23. Gao, S.; Yang, S.-H.; Wang, H.-Y.; Wang, G.-S.; Yin, P.-G. Excellent electromagnetic wave absorbing properties of two-dimensional carbon-based nanocomposite supported by transition metal carbides Fe_3C. *Carbon* **2020**, *162*, 438–444. [CrossRef]
24. Bordet, A.; Lacroix, L.-M.; Fazzini, P.-F.; Carrey, J.; Soulantica, K.; Chaudret, B. Magnetically Induced Continuous CO_2 Hydrogenation Using Composite Iron Carbide Nanoparticles of Exceptionally High Heating Power. *Angew. Chem. Int. Ed.* **2016**, *55*, 15894–15898. [CrossRef] [PubMed]
25. Kale, S.S.; Asensio, J.M.; Estrader, M.; Werner, M.; Bordet, A.; Yi, D.; Marbaix, J.; Fazzini, P.-F.; Soulantica, K.; Chaudret, B. Iron carbide or iron carbide/cobalt nanoparticles for magnetically-induced CO2 hydrogenation over Ni/SiRAlOx catalysts. *Catal. Sci. Technol.* **2019**, *9*, 2601–2607. [CrossRef]
26. Meffre, A.; Mehdaoui, B.; Kelsen, V.; Fazzini, P.F.; Carrey, J.; Lachaize, S.; Respaud, M.; Chaudret, B. A Simple Chemical Route toward Monodisperse Iron Carbide Nanoparticles Displaying Tunable Magnetic and Unprecedented Hyperthermia Properties. *Nano Lett.* **2012**, *12*, 4722–4728. [CrossRef] [PubMed]
27. Liu, X.-W.; Zhao, S.; Meng, Y.; Peng, Q.; Dearden, A.K.; Huo, C.-F.; Yang, Y.; Li, Y.-W.; Wen, X.-D. Mössbauer Spectroscopy of Iron Carbides: From Prediction to Experimental Confirmation. *Sci. Rep.* **2016**, *6*, 26184. [CrossRef]
28. Fang, C.M.; van Huis, M.A.; Zandbergen, H.W. Structure and stability of Fe2C phases from density-functional theory calculations. *Scr. Mater.* **2010**, *63*, 418–421. [CrossRef]
29. Elsukov, E.P.; Dorofeev, G.A.; Ul'yanov, A.L.; Vytovtov, D.A. On the problem of the cementite structure. *Phys. Metals Metallogr.* **2006**, *102*, 76–82. [CrossRef]

30. Ron, M.; Mathalone, Z. Hyperfine Interactions of ^{57}Fe in Fe$_3$C. *Phys. Rev. B* **1971**, *4*, 774–777. [CrossRef]
31. Li, S.; Yang, J.; Song, C.; Zhu, Q.; Xiao, D.; Ma, D. Iron Carbides: Control Synthesis and Catalytic Applications in COx Hydrogenation and Electrochemical HER. *Adv. Mater.* **2019**, *31*, 1901796. [CrossRef]
32. Sajitha, E.P.; Prasad, V.; Subramanyam, S.V.; Mishra, A.K.; Sarkar, S.; Bansal, C. Size-dependent magnetic properties of iron carbide nanoparticles embedded in a carbon matrix. *J. Phys. Condens. Matter* **2007**, *19*, 046214. [CrossRef]
33. Schneeweiss, O.; Zbořil, R.; David, B.; Heřmánek, M.; Mashlan, M. *Solid-State Synthesis of α-Fe and Iron Carbide Nanoparticles by Thermal Treatment of Amorphous Fe$_2$O$_3$*; Springer: Berlin/Heidelberg, Germany, 2009; pp. 167–173.
34. Lin, S.C.; Phillips, J. Study of relaxation effects in the 57Fe Mössbauer spectra of carbon-supported iron carbide particles. *J. Appl. Phys.* **1985**, *58*, 1943–1949. [CrossRef]
35. Lipert, K.; Kazmierczak, J.; Pelech, I.; Narkiewicz, U.; Slawska-Waniewska, A.; Lachowicz, H.K. Magnetic properties of cementite (Fe$_3$C) nanoparticle agglomerates in a carbon matrix. *Mater. Sci. Pol.* **2007**, *25*, 2.
36. Pierson, H.O. *Handbook of Carbon, Graphite, Diamond And Fullerenes: Properties, Processing and Applications*; Noyes Publications: Park Ridge, NJ, USA, 1993.
37. Shenderova, O.A.; Gruen, D.M. *Ultrananocrystalline Diamond: Synthesis, Properties and Applications*, 2nd ed.; Elsevier: Oxford, UK, 2012; pp. 1–558.
38. Vul', A.; Shenderova, O. *Detonation Nanodiamonds: Science and Applications*; CRC Press: Boca Raton, FL, USA, 2013.
39. Mochalin, V.N.; Shenderova, O.; Ho, D.; Gogotsi, Y. The properties and applications of nanodiamonds. *Nat. Nanotechnol.* **2011**, *7*, 11–23. [CrossRef] [PubMed]
40. Bourlinos, A.B.; Zbořil, R.; Kubala, M.; Stathi, P.; Deligiannakis, Y.; Karakassides, M.A.; Steriotis, T.A.; Stubos, A.K. Fabrication of fluorescent nanodiamond@C core-shell hybrids via mild carbonization of sodium cholate-nanodiamond complexes. *J. Mater. Sci.* **2011**, *46*, 7912–7916. [CrossRef]
41. Ho, D. *Nanodiamonds: Applications in Biology and Nanoscale Medicine*; Springer: New York, NY, USA, 2010.
42. Chen, M.; Pierstorff, E.D.; Lam, R.; Li, S.Y.; Huang, H.; Osawa, E.; Ho, D. Nanodiamond-mediated delivery of water-insoluble therapeutics. *ACS Nano* **2009**, *3*, 2016–2022. [CrossRef]
43. Douvalis, A.P.; Bourlinos, A.B.; Tucek, J.; Čépe, K.; Bakas, T.; Zboril, R. Development of novel FePt/nanodiamond hybrid nanostructures: L10 phase size-growth suppression and magnetic properties. *J. Nanopart. Res.* **2016**, *18*, 115. [CrossRef]
44. Laurent, S.; Henoumont, C.; Stanicki, D.; Boutry, S.; Lipani, E.; Belaid, S.; Muller, R.N.; Vander Elst, R.N. *MRI Contrast Agents: From Molecules to Particles*; Springer: Berlin/Heidelberg, Germany, 2017. [CrossRef]
45. Pierre, V.C.; Allen, M.J. *Contrast Agents for MRI: Experimental Methods*; The Royal Society of Chemistry: London, UK, 2018.
46. Knopp, T.; Buzug, T.M. *Magnetic Particle Imaging: An Introduction to Imaging Principles and Scanner Instrumentation*; Springer: Berlin/Heidelberg, Germany, 2012.
47. Erbe, M. *Field Free Line Magnetic Particle Imaging*; Springer: Berlin/Heidelberg, Germany, 2014.
48. Deatsch, A.E.; Evans, B.A. Heating efficiency in magnetic nanoparticle hyperthermia. *J. Magn. Magn. Mater.* **2014**, *354*, 163–172. [CrossRef]
49. Wang, W.; Tuci, G.; Duong-Viet, C.; Liu, Y.; Rossin, A.; Luconi, L.; Nhut, J.-M.; Nguyen-Dinh, L.; Pham-Huu, C.; Giambastiani, G. Induction Heating: An Enabling Technology for the Heat Management in Catalytic Processes. *ACS Catal.* **2019**, *9*, 7921–7935. [CrossRef]
50. Bourlinos, A.; Simopoulos, A.; Petridis, D.; Okumura, H.; Hadjipanayis, G. Silica-Maghemite Nanocomposites. *Adv. Mater.* **2001**, *13*, 289–291. [CrossRef]
51. Tsoufis, T.; Douvalis, A.P.; Lekka, C.E.; Trikalitis, P.N.; Bakas, T.; Gournis, D. Controlled preparation of carbon nanotube–iron oxide nanoparticle hybrid materials by a modified wet impregnation method. *J. Nanopart. Res.* **2013**, *15*, 1924–1927. [CrossRef]
52. Douvalis, A.P.; Polymeros, A.; Bakas, T. IMSG09: A 57Fe-119Sn Mössbauer spectra computer fitting program with novel interactive user interface. *J. Phys. Conf. Ser.* **2010**, *217*, 012014. [CrossRef]
53. Cornell, R.M.; Schwertmann, U. *The Iron Oxides: Structure, Properties, Reactions, Occurrences and Uses*; Wiley-VCH: Weinheim, Germany, 2003.
54. Cullity, B.D.; Stock, S.R. *Elements of X-Ray Diffraction*, 3rd ed.; Pearson Education Limited: London, UK, 2014.
55. Gournis, D.; Karakassides, M.A.; Bakas, T.; Boukos, N.; Petridis, D. Catalytic synthesis of carbon nanotubes on clay minerals. *Carbon* **2002**, *40*, 2641–2646. [CrossRef]

56. Cullity, B.D.; Graham, C.D. *Introduction to Magnetic Materials*; John Wiley & Sons: Hoboken, NJ, USA, 2009.
57. Khurshid, H.; Lampen-Kelley, P.; Iglesias, Ò.; Alonso, J.; Phan, M.-H.; Sun, C.-J.; Saboungi, M.-L.; Srikanth, H. Spin-glass-like freezing of inner and outer surface layers in hollow γ-Fe_2O_3 nanoparticles. *Sci. Rep.* **2015**, *5*, 15054. [CrossRef] [PubMed]
58. Cabreira-Gomes, R.; Silva, F.G.; Aquino, R.; Bonville, P.; Tourinho, F.A.; Perzynski, R.; Depeyrot, J. Exchange bias of $MnFe_2O_4@\gamma Fe_2O_3$ and $CoFe_2O_4@\gamma Fe_2O_3$ core/shell nanoparticles. *J. Magn. Magn. Mater.* **2014**, *368*, 409–414. [CrossRef]
59. Zhu, C.; Tian, Z.; Wang, L.; Yuan, S. Exchange bias effect in spin glass $CoCr2O4$ nanoparticles. *J. Magn. Magn. Mater.* **2015**, *393*, 116–120. [CrossRef]
60. Giri, S.K.; Poddar, A.; Nath, T.K. Evidence of exchange bias effect and surface spin glass ordering in electron doped $Sm0.09Ca0.91MnO3$ nanomanganites. *J. Appl. Phys.* **2012**, *112*, 113903. [CrossRef]
61. Fiorani, D. *Surface Effects in Magnetic Nanoparticles*; Springer: New York, NY, USA, 2005.
62. Gubin, S.P. *Magnetic Nanoparticles*; Wiley-VCH: Weinheim, Germany, 2009.
63. Kostopoulou, A.; Brintakis, K.; Vasilakaki, M.; Trohidou, K.N.; Douvalis, A.P.; Lascialfari, A.; Manna, L.; Lappas, A. Assembly-mediated interplay of dipolar interactions and surface spin disorder in colloidal maghemite nanoclusters. *Nanoscale* **2014**, *6*, 3764–3776. [CrossRef]
64. Mørup, S.; Hansen, M. Superparamagnetic Particles. In *Handbook of Magnetism and Advanced Magnetic Materials*; Kronmüller, H., Parkin, S., Eds.; Novel Materials; John Wiley & Sons: Hoboken, NJ, USA, 2007; Volume 4.
65. Li, Q.; Kartikowati, C.W.; Horie, S.; Ogi, T.; Iwaki, T.; Okuyama, K. Correlation between particle size/domain structure and magnetic properties of highly crystalline Fe_3O_4 nanoparticles. *Sci. Rep.* **2017**, *7*, 9894. [CrossRef]
66. Morelos-Gómez, A.; López-Urías, F.; Muñoz-Sandoval, E.; Dennis, C.L.; Shull, R.D.; Terrones, H.; Terrones, M. Controlling high coercivities of ferromagnetic nanowires encapsulated in carbon nanotubes. *J. Mater. Chem.* **2010**, *20*, 5906–5914. [CrossRef]
67. Liu, D.; Zhu, J.; Ivaturi, S.; He, Y.; Wang, S.; Wang, J.; Zhang, S.; Willis, M.A.C.; Boi, F.S. Giant magnetic coercivity in Fe3C-filled carbon nanotubes. *RSC Adv.* **2018**, *8*, 13820–13825. [CrossRef]
68. Corr, S.A.; Gun'ko, Y.K.; Douvalis, A.P.; Venkatesan, M.; Gunning, R.D.; Nellist, P.D. From Nanocrystals to Nanorods: New Iron Oxide-Silica Nanocomposites from Metallorganic Precursors. *J. Phys. Chem. C* **2008**, *112*, 1008. [CrossRef]
69. Biddlecombe, G.B.; Gun'ko, Y.K.; Kelly, J.M.; Pillai, S.C.; Coey, J.M.D.; Venkatesan, M.; Douvalis, A.P. Preparation of magnetic nanoparticles and their assemblies using a new Fe(ii) alkoxide precursor. *J. Mater. Chem.* **2001**, *11*, 2937–2939. [CrossRef]
70. Tsoufis, T.; Tomou, A.; Gournis, D.; Douvalis, A.P.; Panagiotopoulos, I.; Kooi, B.; Georgakilas, V.; Arfaoui, I.; Bakas, T. Novel nanohybrids derived from the attachment of FePt nanoparticles on carbon nanotubes. *J. Nanosci. Nanotechnol.* **2008**, *8*, 5942–5951. [CrossRef] [PubMed]
71. Mørup, S. Magnetic Hyperfine Splitting in Mössbauer Spectra of Microcrystals. *J. Magn. Magn. Mater.* **1983**, *37*, 39. [CrossRef]
72. Mørup, S. Mössbauer Effect in Small Particles. *Hyperfine Interact.* **1990**, *60*, 959. [CrossRef]
73. Greenwood, N.N.; Gibb, T.C. *Mössbauer Spectroscopy*; Chapman and Hall Ltd.: London, UK, 1971.
74. Gutlich, P.; Bill, E.; Trautwein, A.X. *Mössbauer Spectroscopy and Transition Metal Chemistry: Fundamentals and Applications*; Springer: Berlin/Heidelberg, Germany, 2011. [CrossRef]
75. Vandenberghe, R.E.; de Grave, E. Mossbauer Effect Studies of Oxidic Spinels. In *Mössbauer Spectroscopy Applied to Inorganic Chemistry*; Long, G.J., Grandjean, J., Eds.; Springer Science & Business Media, LLC: New York, NY, USA, 1989; Volume 3.
76. Fardis, M.; Douvalis, A.P.; Tsitrouli, D.; Rabias, I.; Stamopoulos, D.; Kehagias, T.; Karakosta, E.; Diamantopoulos, G.; Bakas, T.; Papavassiliou, G. Structural, static and dynamic magnetic properties of dextran coated γ-Fe_2O_3 nanoparticles studied by 57Fe NMR, Mössbauer, TEM and magnetization measurements. *J. Phys. Condens. Matter* **2012**, *24*, 156001. [CrossRef]
77. Long, G.J.; Hautot, D.; Pankhurst, Q.A.; Vandormael, D.; Grandjean, F.; Gaspard, J.P.; Briois, V.; Hyeon, T.; Suslick, K.S. M\"ossbauer-effect and x-ray-absorption spectral study of sonochemically prepared amorphous iron. *Phys. Rev. B* **1998**, *57*, 10716–10722. [CrossRef]

78. Carroll, K.J.; Pitts, J.A.; Zhang, K.; Pradhan, A.K.; Carpenter, E.E. Nonclassical crystallization of amorphous iron nanoparticles by radio frequency methods. *J. Appl. Phys.* **2010**, *107*, 09A302. [CrossRef]
79. Le Caer, G.; Dubois, J.M.; Senateur, J.P. Etude par spectrométrie Mössbauer des carbures de Fer Fe_3C et Fe_5C_2. *J. Solid State Chem.* **1976**, *19*, 19–28. [CrossRef]
80. Gatte, R.R.; Phillips, J. The influence of particle size and structure on the Mössbauer spectra of iron carbides formed during Fischer-Tropsch synthesis. *J. Catal.* **1987**, *104*, 365–374. [CrossRef]
81. Williams, O.A. Nanocrystalline diamond. *Diam. Relat. Mater.* **2011**, *20*, 621–640. [CrossRef]
82. Williams, O. *Nanodiamond*; Royal Society of Chemistry: Cambridge, UK, 2014.
83. Mykhaylyk, O.O.; Solonin, Y.M.; Batchelder, D.N.; Brydson, R. Transformation of nanodiamond into carbon onions: A comparative study by high-resolution transmission electron microscopy, electron energy-loss spectroscopy, x-ray diffraction, small-angle x-ray scattering, and ultraviolet Raman spectroscopy. *J. Appl. Phys.* **2005**, *97*, 074302. [CrossRef]

Publisher's Note: MDPI stays neutral with regard to jurisdictional claims in published maps and institutional affiliations.

© 2020 by the authors. Licensee MDPI, Basel, Switzerland. This article is an open access article distributed under the terms and conditions of the Creative Commons Attribution (CC BY) license (http://creativecommons.org/licenses/by/4.0/).

MDPI
St. Alban-Anlage 66
4052 Basel
Switzerland
Tel. +41 61 683 77 34
Fax +41 61 302 89 18
www.mdpi.com

Magnetochemistry Editorial Office
E-mail: magnetochemistry@mdpi.com
www.mdpi.com/journal/magnetochemistry

www.ingramcontent.com/pod-product-compliance
Lightning Source LLC
LaVergne TN
LVHW070042120526
838202LV00101B/387